ESSAYS
ON THE EXTERNAL POLICY OF INDIA

ESSAYS
ON THE EXTERNAL POLICY OF INDIA.

BY THE LATE **J. W. S. WYLLIE,**
M.A., C.S.I.

EDITOR: W. W. HUNTER, B.A., LL.D.

GYAN

Published by

Gyan Publishing House
5, Ansari Road
Daryaganj, New Delhi-110002
Phone: 011-47034999, 9811692060
E-mail: books@gyanbooks.com

Distribution Network
gyanbooks.com
India, USA, Canada, UK, Australia

ISBN: 978-93-6208-279-4 (PB)
First Published, 1875

2nd Impression 2024

Printed at: Gyan Press, Delhi.

ESSAYS ON THE EXTERNAL POLICY OF INDIA
Author: J. W. S. WYLLIE

THE EXTERNAL POLICY OF INDIA.

ESSAYS

ON THE EXTERNAL POLICY OF INDIA.

BY THE LATE J. W. S. WYLLIE, M.A., C.S.I.

H.M. INDIA CIVIL SERVICE ; SOMETIME ACTING FOREIGN SECRETARY TO THE GOVERNMENT OF INDIA

EDITED, WITH A BRIEF LIFE, BY

W. W. HUNTER, B.A., LL.D.

H.M. INDIA CIVIL SERVICE.

LONDON :

SMITH, ELDER, & CO., 15 WATERLOO PLACE.

1875.

TO HIS PARENTS

THIS VOLUME OF JOHN WYLLIE'S ESSAYS

IS INSCRIBED.

INTRODUCTORY MEMOIR.

OF a life which was not destined to complete itself, a brief narrative is best. The writer of these essays lived long enough to do good work for the State, to be recognised as the literary exponent of one of the great lines of Indian policy, and to win the lasting love and honour of many men. He died at the age of thirty-four, with the plans of usefulness which he had laid out for his future unfulfilled, and with the chill of a grievous disappointment lying heavy on his heart. He left behind him a memory brilliant, yet singularly tender, the memory of one who at each stage of his career was felt by his fellows to be their foremost man, but whose winning gentleness disarmed jealousy, and inflicted no wound on self-love. He had the art of being distinguished without being envied. Mr. Wyllie came to India as one of the earliest members of a new service, of a service grafted on a stem rich in a most honourable past, but which had its own traditions to form. The bright vigour of his mind and pen helped to influence in a noble sense the body of men to whom he belonged. If the old traditions of unwatched fidelity which they inherited from those who had gone before, have been quickened by aspirations after a more sustained intellectual life amid the discouragements of an Indian career, they owe it in some measure to the example of him whose work I now record.

John William Shaw Wyllie, eldest son of General Sir William Wyllie, K.C.B., was born at Púná, in the Bombay Presidency, on October 6, 1835. His mother was a daughter of the late Richard Hutt, Esq., of Appley, in the Isle of Wight, and a sister of the present Right Honourable Sir William Hutt. His father entered the Bombay army in 1819, commanded a field detachment in the Deccan in 1822, and another in Gujarát in 1823. He was thanked in General Orders for his gallantry on the heights of Jerun, and served with the Field Force in Cutch in 1824 and the following years. In 1838–39 he was brigade-major with the Bombay column of the Army of the Indus under Lord Keane, and was present at the storming of Ghazní, and during the occupation of Kábul. He next served as Assistant Adjutant-General to the Force under Sir Thomas Willshire, and accompanied the storming party at the capture of Kilát (Khelat). He held the same post on the staff of Sir Richard England in Sind and Beluchistán in 1841-42, being present at both attacks on the heights of Hykulzye, the forcing of the Kojack Pass to and from Kandahar, and other operations. He was again Assistant Adjutant-General to the Forces in Sind and Afghánistán under Sir Charles Napier, and was dangerously wounded at the battle of Meání. In 1844–45 he commanded the troops on the sea coast of the Southern Konkan in the Marhattá rebellion. General Wyllie is now Colonel of Her Majesty's 103rd Regiment of Foot.

The father being absent on a campaign, the mother brought home John with her other two children to England in 1841.[1] His mother's letters of those days give one the impression of her eldest son as an amiable and intelligent child, who entertained the rather original idea that in receiving his lessons from

[1] Francis Robert Shaw Wyllie, now of the Bombay Civil Service; and Emily, married to the Right Hon. William P. Adam, of Blair Adam, M.P. To the former I owe the materials for this sketch, and valuable assistance in editing the Essays.

her he was the obliging, and not the obliged party. After some time with a private tutor, he was sent to the Edinburgh Academy. Here he met boys destined in after life to distinguish themselves in the service to which he himself eventually belonged; among them Mr. A. M. Monteath, now Director-General of the Indian Post Office, and Mr. J. D. Gordon, C.S.I., Judicial Commissioner in Mysore. On his father's return to India after furlough, John Wyllie was placed with his brother Frank at Cheltenham College. The head master at that time was the Rev. William Dobson, under whose able administration the school rose from comparative obscurity to a high rank among the educational establishments of the kingdom. As a proof of Mr. Dobson's careful training of his head form, I may mention that at this period in three successive years, boys direct from Cheltenham obtained the Balliol scholarship, while Wyllie himself got a scholarship first at Lincoln, then at Trinity. Wyllie early won a position for himself in the school. Although shortsighted, and debarred in consequence from cricket, he worked his way up into the football 'twenty' before he left, and was one of the founders of the athletic sports which now form an annual feature of the college. As regards scholastic distinctions, each year brought him some success, and to quote a paper in the College Magazine, the 'school records show him to have gained the prize in almost every class where it was possible to do so.' His pleasing and amiable manners made him a popular boy, and a schoolfellow records that 'at the yearly meeting for speeches and distributing the prizes, John Wyllie's name was always sure to be received with a loud clapping of hands.'

His father had intended him for the India Civil Service, and hoped to obtain a nomination for him through his brother-in-law, Sir William Hutt,[1] then an active Liberal member of the

[1] Vice-President of the Board of Trade, 1860–1865.

House of Commons. The head master, however, begged his parents to send Wyllie to the University, and predicted for him a distinguished academical career. The following letter to his mother discloses the feelings with which John received the news of the change in his destination (æt. 17).

'I for my part do not know whether to be sorry or glad at what has happened. At first I was cruelly disappointed; for though I had often wished to go to college, I had so thoroughly made up my mind that my future fate was to be in the India Civil Service, that I felt almost frightened at first at the ground being completely cut from under my feet. But still with exertion (and nothing can be done in any line without exertion), I think I should stand a little (Dobson says a *very good*) chance of success at the University. And if that were certain, I should infinitely prefer going to Oxford or the Bar to taking the writership. But to go to college I must obtain some scholarship to defray part of the expenses; and if working hard will gain me a scholarship, a scholarship I will get. But still I labour under peculiar disadvantages in going up for any scholarship, in consequence of having been born in India, for the majority of the Oxford scholarships (and it is to Oxford I should prefer to go) are restricted to the natives of some particular county in England. So the only scholarships I could enter for would be the open ones, which are on that very account the most hotly contested, and this it is which gives such *éclat* to the scholars of Balliol and Trinity Colleges. However, I am still quite young, have moderate abilities, and can and *will* work hard. Dobson had a long and very kind palaver with me to-day, in which he was profuse of praise and encouragement, the sum and substance of which was that I must take to Greek, cut Hindustani, and in the course of a couple of years go up for an open scholarship at Oxford.'[1]

[1] February 27, 1852.

He did work hard, and in June 1853 went up to Oxford to compete for an open scholarship at Lincoln College, which he promptly won. He remained at school, however, until the end of December, and commenced his University career at the beginning of 1854, æt. 18. It had been the ambition of his school days, if ever he went to Oxford, to compete for a Balliol scholarship. The Rector of Lincoln very judiciously pointed out, however, that he could not now be permitted to compete for a Balliol scholarship unless he threw up that which he already held. So during six months Wyllie hesitated to give up a certainty for the chance of carrying out his own private ambition. In June 1854, however, he decided to run this risk by competing for one of the open scholarships at Trinity. This he gained (æt. 19), and thenceforward resided at that college while at the University.

The brief records of his Oxford career are precisely those which a well-nurtured youth would like to leave behind him. The Rev. Mr. North Pinder, late Fellow and Tutor of Trinity, speaks of his 'diffidence and modesty'; and this testimony is the more pleasing as it is combined with other tributes from friends and brother scholars at Trinity to his energy and talent. He had the gift of popularity, and his late head master and parents watched with a certain fear the temptations to which it exposed him. Their letters of those days disclose this anxiety, and they also disclose that Wyllie's good sense and modesty steered him clear of the peril. In 1855 he obtained his first class in Moderations, and everything seemed to promise the academical successes which the head master of Cheltenham had predicted.

But in this same year (1855) the new system of appointing to the India Civil Service by open competition was inaugurated. An intimate friend of Wyllie's (a brother scholar at Trinity) succeeded in winning an appointment, and about the same time Colonel Wyllie lost the command of his brigade on promotion to the rank of major-general. John began to grow restive at the idea of continuing to be a burden, however slight, on his father, and turned his eyes wistfully to the Indian service. At any rate he thought he would like to try his luck in the open competition, and the long vacation of 1856 found him in London with that view. 'My chance,' he wrote to his mother, 'is small this time; but I have still two or three years before me in case of failure.' What between anxiety and an unfortunate period of ill-health, he, like many other young men in the same circumstances, worked his mind up to an absolute expectation of failure, and perhaps did not do so well as he might otherwise have done. However, he took a creditable place, passing eleventh out of about twenty-two men who gained appointments (æt. 21).

He sailed for India the same year, and having his choice of Presidencies, selected Bombay as that in which his father was still serving. He arrived in November 1856. At that time the young civilians in the Bombay Presidency were not, as now, appointed Assistant-Collectors on arrival, but lived under the supervision of the Collectors in various parts of the Presidency, until they had qualified in the native languages. John Wyllie easily obtained permission to reside at Satárá, where his parents were living. In this interesting district, on the inner slopes of the Gháts, he rejoined them after an eight years' separation from his father, and in the hot weather accompanied them to the Mahábaleshwar hills, the summer retreat of the Presidency. It was a happy time with him, and one to which he always looked back with fondness. He enjoyed to the full the gaieties of the hill capital, and among other developments commenced his literary career by a critical notice of Mrs. Speir's (Manning's) 'Life in Ancient India,' for the *Bombay Quarterly Review*. The article is clever and lucid, but Mr. Wyllie came to the writing of it with the usual defect of a beginner in literature, namely, an imperfect knowledge of his subject. However, the culture and general ability which pervaded the essay, covered his unacquaintance with Sanskrit, and made it one of the most popular articles in the number. It brought him into public notice, and on passing his examinations in the vernacular languages, Lord Elphinstone, then Governor of Bombay, selected him for political employment, and sent him as an Assistant to the Political Agent in Káthiáwár.

This was a little out of the usual course, young civilians in Bombay being as a rule required to go through a training in the Revenue Department before being employed in other branches. His appointment bears date January 25, 1858, and he remained an Assistant in Káthiáwár until August 31, 1860. The nature of his employment and the character of his work may be gathered from the note below.[1]

[1] Memo. of Mr. Wyllie's services in Káthiáwár furnished by the Political Agent.

'Mr. J. W. S. Wyllie was appointed Third Assistant Political Agent in Káthiáwár on January 25, 1858; promoted as Acting Second Assistant May 30, 1860; left for Oudh August 31, 1860.

'On his joining his appointment in February 1858, the Acting Political Agent sent him out into the district with the Second Assistant, in order that he might become acquainted with the nature of the duties he would be required to perform. He was subsequently chiefly employed in making translations of Gujaráti papers into English, and the then Political Agent stated that he was "always very attentive to the work he had to do, and performed it in a manner exceedingly creditable to him."

'He held the Magisterial charge of the Regulation District of Bhaunagar from June 1859 to August 1860.

'In February 1859 he was deputed by Government to meet the British and Portuguese Commissioners, to attend to their suggestions in fixing the boundary between the Junaghar and Diu territory.

'On his departure for Oudh, the Acting Political Agent brought to the notice of Government "the able and efficient manner in which he had performed his duties, and the regret he personally felt at the loss of Mr. Wyllie's valuable services."

'He prepared a translation of Colonel Lang's collection of *Mulk Sherishta*, or Common Law of Káthiáwár for Mr. Forbes, who speaks of him as "an officer whose services would be zealously rendered, and will be found most valuable."'

In June 1858 he went to Surat to pass an examination. While there he was prostrated by a severe attack of Gujarát fever, to which he nearly succumbed. It left his constitution permanently impaired, and in the opinion of those who knew him best, left the seeds which afterwards germinated so fatally. For many weeks in each subsequent year his life was a struggle with the rheumatic affections, ague, diarrhœa, and other painful and depressing *sequelæ* of an Indian fever.

Meanwhile, on his recovery, he thoroughly enjoyed the combination of open-air tent life with incisive intellectual work, which does so much to reconcile young civilians to exile and the discomforts of a tropical climate. His day-dream was employment in Persia or Afghánistán, 'Káthiáwár being in these days,' he writes to his mother, 'mild work;' with an Arabic professorship at Oxford as a 'pleasant nook to end one's days in.' His studies in Persian or Arabic were destined, however, never to go very far; doubtless choked off, as many another young civilian's aspirations after learning have been, by promotion and the ever-rising tide of official work which accompanies it.

In the more immediate duty of perfecting himself in the vernaculars, he made good progress. Up to that time no effort had been made to systematise the judicial customs and varying land-laws of the 224 native States of Káthiáwár. As late as 1863 the Political Agent (or chief British Administrator of the Province) officially declared that 'up to the present time no State in Káthiáwár has any judicial system, any written law, or any recognised civil or criminal court.'[1] In another book[2] I have narrated the measures which remedied this state of things. Mr. Wyllie contributed to the coming work of reform. During his year and a half in Káthiáwár, he

[1] Political Agent's circular to the chiefs of Káthiáwár, dated September 4, 1863.

[2] Life of Lord Mayo, vol. i. 215 *et seq.*

devoted himself with characteristic vigour to the study of native usages and rights; left behind him a body of papers which he translated from the vernacular, and prepared an English version of Colonel Lang's *Mulk Sherishta,* a Gujaráti collection of materials illustrating the unwritten laws of the 224 native States which in 1860 made up the province of Káthiáwár.[1] He did his current duties well, as the official records testify. But his bright vigour of mind, once he had got rid of the Surat fever, found for itself a hundred fresh outlets in the study of the people. On leaving the province, he published an account of it in the *Calcutta Review* (December 1860), and obtained for it a degree of public attention which aided the advocates of reform, and strengthened the hands of the Political Agent in his great settlement of Káthiáwár a few years later. Although immature in style and thought, it helped in a good cause, and will be found somewhat condensed at the end of this volume. On August 31, 1860, John Wyllie left Káthiáwár and the Bombay Presidency for service in Northern India (æt. 25).

Among the administrative reforms which followed upon the suppression of the Mutiny was the formation of the Province of Oudh into a Commissionership. This measure involved an immediate increase in the strength of the Bengal section of the India Civil Service. John Wyllie was among those who received the offer of one of the newly created appointments. A letter to his mother, dated August 20, 1860, records the conflicting considerations which determined him to accept this proposal. On the one hand there was the climate of Bengal, which he dreaded with a prophetic foresight; besides the separation from the Presidency which he had originally chosen, and which was endeared to him as the scene of his father's career and by the presence of his brother Frank, also in the Civil Service. But on

[1] The number is given at 224 by Mr. Wyllie in 1860; it is now returned at 187.

the other hand—'My chief inducement to go is of course the wider sphere which Bengal offers for action. If I am ever to do any good, or rise to any distinction in my generation, the opportunities are incomparably finer there than here. Then, too, I like the idea of Oudh ; there is real hard work to be done there, not merely routine, but such that the doer of it will leave his mark behind him, whether for good or ill, for some time to come.' Accordingly, he accepted the appointment, and with it the permanent transfer of his services to the Bengal Establishment. Henceforward his Indian career belongs to his adopted Presidency, although his name continued to remain on the Bombay List.

After a hasty visit to his brother at Tanna, he sailed for Calcutta. On his arrival in Oudh he was posted as an Assistant-Commissioner to the District of Bárá-Bănki, and was shortly afterwards transferred, in the same capacity, to Lucknow. Early in 1861 he was appointed Assistant-Secretary to Sir George Yule, then officiating as Chief Commissioner of the Province. In May 1862 the dream of his early ambition was realised. He was selected for the Calcutta Secretariat, where in one department or another he remained as Under-Secretary, and for a short time as Acting-Secretary, to the Government of India, until he finally quitted the service.

He had made his mark in Oudh, doing good official work, and shrinking from no extra duty that might come in his path in addition to his regular labours. Among other things, he had greatly exerted himself in raising subscriptions for the monument to Sir H. Lawrence, the hero of the Lucknow siege. He not only distributed circulars among Englishmen over the whole of India, but he also wrote frequent articles in the newspapers in advocacy of the scheme. His efforts were successful, and on December 31, 1861, he could write—'Rs. 15,000 (1,500*l.*) have been obtained by subscriptions, and Government will, perhaps, give as much more; so the monument will be worthy of its hero.'

With reference to his introduction to the Secretariat of the Government of India in Calcutta, he was always anxious that it should be known that he obtained it 'of his own good fortune,' and without the aid of private interest. The proposal to appoint him to officiate in the Foreign Office originated with Mr. Aitcheson and Sir H. Durand, the two officials immediately concerned, who knew nothing of him except by the reputation which he had earned in Oudh. Sir George Yule bade him good-bye in friendly words:—'If ever I get anyone again to work as well as you have done, I shall be the luckiest man in India.'

John Wyllie joined the Government of India as officiating Under-Secretary in the Foreign Department in May 1862, but was forced to go on a month's leave to the Nilgiri Hills in September, to recruit his health which had been much shaken by a fresh attack of fever. Sir Henry Durand (his immediate superior) and the Viceroy recorded their regret at temporarily losing him. On his return he officiated for a month in the Home Department, and on November 18th was appointed Under-Secretary in the Financial Department. In March 1863 he was re-transferred as Under-Secretary to the Home Office, where the work was more congenial to his tastes, and where he remained until his health compelled him to take sick leave, in 1864. The hard work of the Secretariat, and the enervating climate of Lower Bengal, seriously impaired a constitution which had already received a rude shock, and his trip to the Hills had resulted in disappointment. But whenever he was not actually ill, his high spirit carried him through everything. He thoroughly enjoyed the charms of Calcutta society, making friends, as was his wont, everywhere; and especially securing a reputation for industry and brilliancy among his immediate superiors. He thus fully accomplished what was his main object during these early days of his career, viz., to establish such a position in Bengal as would never cause him to regret having left his own Presidency. His reward was not long in coming. While he was on leave in Europe, the Under-Secretaryship to the Government of India in the Foreign Department fell permanently vacant, and although not on the spot he was at once nominated, on the recommendation of Sir Henry Durand, to that post—the one which he had been most ambitious of obtaining.

He left Calcutta on April 23, 1864, and remained at home until October 1865. He resolved to read up his old studies, and complete his residence at the University for the purpose of taking his degree. With this object he made one of an autumn reading party in Scotland in company with his friend George Trevelyan, and in October went up to Oxford and resided at his old College of Trinity, where his name still lingers among a new generation of scholars. In December he passed his examinations and took his degree, and subsequently took also his M.A. The remainder of the winter he spent in Italy, chiefly at Rome, accompanied by an old Oxford friend who had also entered the India Civil Service. In May he returned to London, which he made his head-quarters until his departure for India. In July there occurred a general election, and he managed to see both his friend, G. Trevelyan, elected at Tynemouth, and his brother-in-law, Mr. Adam, in Kinrosshire. His brother Frank also came home from India this summer, and in September the two travelled together as far as Homburg, where it was thought advisable for John Wyllie to stop a fortnight to drink the waters. While there he occupied himself in reading books on Egypt, and on continuing his journey he spent a second fortnight in that country. His special object was to visit the works of the Suez Canal, which were then unfinished, grave doubts being entertained by many persons regarding the ultimate success of the enterprise. The result of this visit was an article written to wile away the tedium of the sea voyage in the Indian Ocean, which appeared in the *Cornhill Magazine* of March 1866.

On his arrival in India, he found Sir William Muir Foreign Secretary, under Sir John Lawrence as Viceroy, and he soon established himself on good terms with his new superiors. About this time he made his first appearance as a public speaker, on the occasion of the Oxford and Cambridge dinner at Calcutta, at which he was selected to return thanks for the Civil Service. He took the precaution of learning his speech by heart, and sent home his MS. copy to his mother. It boldly uttered his dissatisfaction with the present system of competition for Indian appointments, in so far as it tends to shut out candidates from a University education. This dissatisfaction became more deeply rooted in Wyllie's mind as the number of University men year by year diminished in the list of the successful competitors, and received its final expression in a printed letter from him to Sir Charles Trevelyan. I believe that every member of the service, and indeed all who have had practical experience of the working of the system in India, take the same view. In Wyllie's case such sentiments are particularly worthy of notice ; for they are not the utterance of one who was calling up, after the lapse of a considerable interval, the transfigured memories of his undergraduate days, but of one who had volunteered to undergo his final University examinations at the mature age of thirty-one.

Immediately after his arrival the climate of Calcutta began to resume its unfavourable influence upon his health and spirits. However, on the approach of the hot weather, he accompanied the Viceroy to Simla, and while there the circumstances of his official life combined with the mountain air to restore the wonted energy of his mind. He now for the first time gained the absolute confidence of the new Governor-General. The absence of the Foreign Secretary for a few days caused some important business to be thrown entirely into his hands, and he proved himself equal to the emergency. The *Cornhill* for March reached India at this time also, and his article on the Suez Canal met with a good deal of praise. Sir J. Lawrence was glad to avail himself of the services of one who both by inner knowledge and literary talent was so well qualified to undertake in the press the defence of his foreign policy in Central Asia, which was then the object of much criticism. Accordingly, at the express request of the Viceroy, he commenced his article 'On the Foreign Policy of Sir John Lawrence,' an article destined to become in one sense the turning-point in his career. 'It is very pleasant and interesting labour,' he wrote to his aunt, Lady Hutt, on June 1, 1866, 'but rather exhausting. An article worth reading is not written easily or quickly, and the ordinary work of the office must still be carried on. So here I sit writing, without pause, day after day, from breakfast time till it is too dark to see. I leave myself barely time to dress for the ceaseless round of dinner-parties and balls, which keep one up until two or three in the morning. However, when I do get to bed, I sleep intensely hard, and the climate of the place is delicious.'

This article, it may be mentioned, was originally intended for the *Quarterly Review*. The Editor, however, refused it, on the sufficient ground that it was in direct antagonism to an article which had appeared in that Review twelve months previously, and it was immediately accepted for the next number of the *Edinburgh* (January 1867). Wyllie was now thirty-one, and 'The Foreign Policy of Sir John Lawrence' may be taken as a fairly-matured expression of his mind. It formed a skilful popular exposition of the views of those who were opposed to drawing closer the relations of the British Government in India with the trans-frontier Asiatic States ; and as a strong party will always exist in favour of this policy, Mr. Wyllie's essay has a permanent interest. At the time of its publication it won a great and deserved success, and it stands first in the following collection of his Essays.

In November 1866 Wyllie accompanied the Viceroy on his tour to Delhi and Agra. A grand Darbár was held at the latter place, all the arrangements for which fell upon the shoulders of the Under-Secretary in the Foreign Department. For his conduct on this laborious occasion, Sir William Muir, the Chief Secretary, wrote to him a special letter of thanks, adding that it was only in keeping with the able administration which had uniformly characterised his work in the office. Wyllie then returned to Calcutta and, Sir W. Muir taking a three months' leave, was appointed to officiate as Secretary in his place. On his vacating this post the Viceroy, in an official Minute, 'deemed it right to place on record his entire satisfaction with the manner in which the work had been performed by him.' It was Sir William Muir's duty to forward him a copy of this Minute, and in the private letter which accompanied it he wrote—'Even in the few days I have been back I have seen enough to convince me of the devotion, ability, and strength which you brought to bear on your working of the office.' In March, when the climate of Calcutta had again begun to tell on his health, he was allowed a month's privilege leave to Simla, and on the arrival of the Government at that place continued to conduct the duties of his office, as Under-Secretary in the Foreign Department, till November. On the return of the Government to Calcutta, Wyllie found himself compelled to accept the course which his medical advisers had pressed on him early in the year, and to take the three years' furlough, to which the length of his Indian service then entitled him. During the preceding year he had had in contemplation a great amount of literary work. In a letter, April 4, 1867, he refers to an intention of writing a sort of

Burke's Peerage of the Princes and Chiefs of India who are recognised as feudatories of the Queen of England. But these projects were beaten back by repeated attacks of ill-health; and during his last months in India poor Wyllie had to recognise that his strength was unequal to anything beyond the ordinary work of his office. He did, however, manage to send home in November an article on 'Western China,' which was published in the *Edinburgh Review* of April 1868, and procured for him the acquaintance of Sir Roderick Murchison and Lord Strangford.

The spring and summer of 1868 were spent in London, and his thoughts were speedily diverted from Indian matters by home politics. The defeat of Mr. Disraeli's Government upon the Resolutions proposed by Mr. Gladstone concerning the Irish Church, had rendered certain a dissolution of Parliament in the coming autumn. Amid the general demand at that time for new men, John Wyllie was persuaded by his uncle, Sir William Hutt, to give up his Indian career and stand for Parliament. Sir William Hutt had taken a great interest in John from early childhood; and in a matter of this kind his counsel was of great weight, for he had himself occupied a seat in the House of Commons during forty-one years, and held office as Vice-President of the Board of Trade and Paymaster-General. Acting on his uncle's advice, John Wyllie went down to the city of Hereford, where it was hoped that the second seat might be wrested from the Conservatives. The task thus marked out for him was no slight one. The sitting members, Mr. George Clive and Sir Richard Baggallay, had both considerable influence. The former, a Liberal, was the head of a county family connected with Hereford for generations, and had moreover been at one time Under-Secretary in the Home Office. Sir R. Baggallay, though not locally connected with the constituency, had made himself very popular, personally, during his four years' representation of it, and now brought with him all the prestige which followed from his recent appointment as Solicitor-General by the Conservative Ministry. John Wyllie had neither wealth, nor local influence, nor English reputation. He had never attempted to address a public audience on political questions, and like most Indian officials had enjoyed no opportunity of acquiring the art of public speaking. Moreover, he was still suffering from the effects of the Bengal climate. But he plunged into the contest with his usual energy and courage. He went down to Hereford armed with a few letters of introduction from the chiefs of the Liberal party in London, and was at once accepted, both by the local leaders and at an enthusiastic public meeting. His address attracted attention from the principles which it enunciated, and from the style in which they were expressed. Amongst other supporters, Colonel Allen Johnson, an Indian friend, and Sir Henry James, an old school-fellow, came down to Hereford to help him. And he presently found not only that his usual facility in winning friends had not deserted him, but that he had obtained a popularity with the mass of the electors which fairly astonished himself. The result of the poll was officially declared as follows:

		Votes.
Liberals	Mr. G. Clive . .	1055
	Mr. J. Wyllie . .	1015
Conservatives	Sir R. Baggallay .	983
	Major Arbuthnot .	872

John Wyllie thus achieved his first success in England with the same rapid step as he had advanced to promotion in India. But as in India, so now, he was not destined to enjoy the honours which he had won. He took his seat in the House of Commons, voted at least once, and asked a pertinent question of the Under-Secretary for India. But his Parliamentary career was speedily interrupted by a petition being presented against the return of the two members for Hereford. They were both charged with bribery and treating, and the election of John Wyllie was further alleged to be invalid on the ground that he held a place of profit under the Crown as a member of the India Civil Service.

With regard to this last ground of disability it would not be necessary to say much, as it never came up for legal decision, if it had not directly led to his resignation of the service. It suffices to mention that the Act of Queen Anne, which creates this disability, is of notoriously difficult interpretation, and that there was a precedent in the case of another member of the India Civil Service, Lord William Hay, whose election under similar circumstances had not been questioned. An Indian civilian, moreover, when on furlough, is regarded as holding no substantive appointment. The difficulty had first been suggested some days prior to the election, when Sir R. Baggallay had pledged his legal reputation to the opinion that Wyllie was disqualified, and that, consequently, all votes for him would be thrown away. John Wyllie immediately resolved, with the approval of his family, to send in his resignation, which was accepted at the India Office as from the day on which it was tendered. That day was the 14th of November, and the poll was not taken till the 17th. His case, therefore, was strong, and he was himself desirous that this point should be taken first; his opponents, however, commenced with the charges of bribery and treating, and the petition was tried at Hereford, before Mr. Justice Blackburne. All who knew either of the successful candidates were satisfied from the first of their personal innocence of any malpractices. The allegations of bribery were most satisfactorily refuted, but by a cruel fortune the excessive zeal of an indiscreet supporter had brought them within the 'treating' clauses of the Act. It was proved that a certain merchant of the city had on the polling day given a breakfast to divers electors, and then driven them to the booths to vote for the Liberal candidates. This amounted to treating, and by construction of law it was also held by the learned judge that this merchant must be considered as an agent of both the sitting members. It was in vain urged on behalf of Mr. Wyllie that he had never set eyes on the man, or even heard his name, until the election was over. It could not be denied that he had been deputed by the recognised Liberal agents to act for them in certain matters connected with the election, and that the Liberal candidates, after their return, had written him a joint letter of thanks for his services. Perhaps neither of these circumstances would by itself have been sufficient, but taken together they formed the basis of the judge's finding that the sitting members had been by their agent guilty of treating, and that their election was therefore null and void. The effect of this decision was to render the unseated members ineligible to stand for Hereford during the term of the existing Parliament. It was thought at the time by some legal critics that Mr. Justice Blackburne had laid down a hard rule. But to Mr. Wyllie's honour it should be said that on all occasions when the decision was impugned in his presence, he defended it, alike in public and in private, as a necessary and logical interpretation of the Act. He did not, however, feel the blow the less severely. It was not only that the hypersensitive purity of official life in India had ill-prepared him to endure even the shadow of a stain. He had forsaken the Indian service for a career that now sunk under him; he had burnt his ships, and could not return. Above all, he saw himself condemned to a life of inaction for some time to come, for it was beyond hope that a second seat in the Parliament then sitting would fall to him.

Before retiring into private life, he found one more opportunity of doing a service to his party, and of showing that he could work for others as energetically as he had fought for himself. A new election was forthwith ordered for Hereford. The new

Liberal candidates were Colonel Clive and Mr. Wren Hoskyns, who were returned by a majority which closely corresponded to the votes of the previous election. John Wyllie stayed at Hereford during their canvass, and by his speeches, and in other ways, contributed materially to the result. At a large meeting subsequently held in the city the Liberal electors presented him with an address, thanking him for his services to the cause, and expressing a hope that his connection with the constituency would some day be re-established.

The sympathy which he met with from every quarter,—and at this time he received letters from many distinguished persons outside the political world,—could not, however, prevent his fretting at the disappointment. Though suffering from no actual organic disease, he had never recovered the strain to which the Surat fever and subsequent attacks in India had subjected his constitution, and throughout the summer of 1869 he was in poor health. On June 2 the Crown appointed him a Companion of the Star of India, as a reward for his Indian services. It was not, however, until the winter that his spirits revived, and his interest was re-directed to Indian affairs. He now wrote his article in *The Fortnightly*, entitled 'Masterly Inactivity,' which is, perhaps, the best known of all his writings. It was signed with his name, and being no longer hampered by official responsibility, he was better able to indulge the natural brilliancy of his style. During the month of December *The Times* newspaper contained one or two letters from him on the affairs of Central Asia, and in *The Daily News* he took part in a controversy on the same subject. The companion article in *The Fortnightly*, called 'Mischievous Activity,' was also written at this time, though not published till March 1870. In a letter to his brother, dated December 10, 1869, he says, 'I shall stay in London until about the middle of January, in order to see "Mischievous Activity" through the press. Then I go to

Paris, where I mean to remain till after Easter. I shall try, if possible, to get admission to some French family, and live wholly among French people.'

This visit to Paris was carried out, but not precisely in the mode anticipated. He established himself at the Hôtel Vouillemont, Rue Boissy d'Anglas, and regularly took lessons in French. His object was not only to improve his knowledge of the language, but also to study French politics at first hand. Affairs were at that time in a very critical condition. The health of the Emperor was a constant source of anxiety; Emile Ollivier was trying his experiment of a Constitutional Government; and H. Rochefort had just been imprisoned for his writings in *The Marseillaise*. John Wyllie was a constant attendant at the debates of the Corps Législatif, and daily read and analysed the varied contents of the French press. The diary which he kept at this time is mainly composed of comments upon political subjects, but it also shows how widely his sympathies and his position permitted him to enjoy Parisian society. He made many acquaintances in the French literary world, and among others struck up a warm friendship with M. Charles Yriarte, the well-known man of letters. Introductions to Renan, Prevost Paradol, &c., brilliant dinner-parties, and receptions at the house of Guizot and elsewhere, flit through his diary. The following extracts from a letter to his brother, dated March 4, 1870, disclose his frame of mind and mode of life at this time. 'My health is infinitely better than it has been for years past; and having now got rid of my chronic diarrhœa, I hope to keep clear of it during the London season. I shall return to town about Easter, or, perhaps, not before the end of April. After the close of the season I don't know what I may do. There is not the least chance of my getting into Parliament again before the next general election. . . . . . I have been to a ball at the Tuileries, and to some other entertainments. The people are very civil, and I see quite as much society as I care for. When I am not dining out, I generally go to the table d'hôte at the Grand Hôtel, where I always come across people I know, English or others. Then men friends from town are constantly passing through Paris, and, on meeting, we make up a little party at a Restaurant.'

This was destined to be the last letter which he wrote to his brother. Before its arrival in India a Reuter's telegram had announced in the Bombay press the death in Paris of a Mr. J. T. Wylie (*sic*). The error, however, in the name scarcely deceived any of his friends. His health had long been a source of deep anxiety to them, the more so as his buoyant indifference about himself and his hunger after work tempted him to rush into new labours the moment that the pressure of actual illness was removed. A week before his death his father and mother, then in London, were not aware that he was unwell. He had always been a good correspondent, and a week's silence caused them some anxiety. Then came a letter to say that he was laid up with a bad cold. It was written by a nurse, but there was a re-assuring postscript from himself which bade them not to be alarmed for he was much better. A telegram of similar purport followed. His parents were no longer young, and his mother was in feeble health. It was thought advisable to await further news. The first intimation of his alarming state did not reach them till Monday, March 14, when there came a telegram from the medical man, saying—'Mr. Wyllie continues dangerously ill, and some one should come.' His father and mother, accompanied by his uncle, Sir William Hutt, at once started for Paris. But when they arrived all hope was gone. He was unconscious, and never fully recognised them. On the morning of Tuesday, before their arrival, he had said to his nurse, when pressed to take some nourishment, 'I cannot take any more. I should have liked to have gone to my mother, but it is too late now. Do not think that I am afraid to die. I die in Christ.' So on March 15, 1870, the first anniversary of the day on which his election had been declared void, John Wyllie finished his short life of $34\frac{1}{2}$ years.

The immediate cause of his death was a cold, caught as he came out of a hot café into the chill night air. Inflammation of the lungs supervened, then his old malarial fever, and finally inflammation of the brain. He was buried at Montmartre, with the intent to remove the body on a future occasion to England. The German war and the siege of Paris quickly followed, and it was not till after the restoration of peace that his remains were removed to their final resting place in Kensal Green.

It is not often that so young an Indian officer attracts the attention of the English public. Men who have slowly won fame in the East often come home to find themselves relegated to obscurity. The death of John Wyllie was noticed at considerable length and with strong expressions of regret by almost all the London newspapers. In Hereford, Conservatives as well as Liberals manifested their sorrow, and the city voted an address of condolence to his father and mother. The entire Indian press united in paying its tribute to his memory. A memorial tablet, erected in the School Chapel at Cheltenham, bears his effigy in marble, graven by Woolner. It is placed on one side of a doorway. On the other side is a medallion, by the same artist, in memory of the Rev. W. Dobson, the head master by whom he had been taught, and who had predicted his distinction. His friends and old schoolfellows have founded a scholarship to commemorate his career, to be held by Cheltenham boys proceeding to Trinity College, Oxford. The annual income from the fund amounts at present to 70*l.*

It would be idle to quote from the letters of condolence which from all sources poured in upon his parents. Words of sympathy and of respect, however tenderly uttered, could do little to allay that grief, nor would they give the reader a truer picture of the man than that afforded by his own works. But they disclose the loving estimation in which he was held by men and women of very diverse character, and in widely different spheres of life. The charm of his nature lay in his modesty. One felt that his brilliancy of talent and his social graces entitled him to a sort of precedence which he would never accept. The Essays now collected show him in part; but only those who personally knew him can understand why he was so loved, or how deeply he has been lamented. His was a life which only too faithfully represents the debt which India owes to England. There are many others who, devoured by their own restless energy, beat out their lives in unknown work on the burning plains or among the malaria-smitten jungles of Hindustan. His sphere of action was merely placed on a more conspicuous stage. That, however, which singled him out among his compeers, and which this slight memoir would in vain attempt to pourtray, was the tender charm which he shed upon all with whom he mingled, and the grace of his blameless life.

'*Multis ille bonis flebilis occidit.*'

CONTENTS.

ESSAYS

ON THE

EXTERNAL POLICY OF INDIA.

THE FOREIGN POLICY OF LORD LAWRENCE.[1]

THE Government of India is divided into six great departments—Foreign, Home, Legislative, Military, Finance, and Public Works. Every order issued from any of these departments runs in the name of 'The Governor-General in Council.' And in the earlier days of the Anglo-Indian empire, when all cases used to be submitted for the collective consideration of the Governor-General and each member of his Council, this formula was a cor-

[1] Edinburgh Review, Jan. 1867.

1. *Parliamentary Blue Books relating to Bhután* 1865 *and* 1866.

2. *Selections from the Records of the Bombay Government, No. XXIV. New Series.* Bombay: Printed for Government at the Bombay Education Society's Press. 1856.

3. *Diary of a Journey across Arabia in the Year* 1819. By Capt. G. Forster Sadlier, of Her Majesty's 47th Regt. Compiled from the Records of the Bombay Government. Bombay: Printed at the Education Society's Press, Byculla. 1866.

4. *Journal of the Royal Geographical Society. Volume the Thirty-fifth. Article XV., A Visit to the Wahábi Capital, Central Arabia.* By Lieutenant-Colonel Lewis Pelly, Her Majesty's Political Resident, Persian Gulf. London: 1865.

5. *Reports on the Political Condition of the Province of Turkistán, and the Financial Resources of Tashkend, from the Governor-General of Orenburg to the Russian Minister of Finance, published in the 'Invalide Russe' of the 20th November,* 1865.

rect description of the mode in which the machinery of government actually worked. But as time advanced, bringing with it additions of territory, improved administration, and better means of communication, it became impossible for so cumbrous an organisation to bear the strain of the enormously increased correspondence. At length Lord Canning remodelled the Council into the semblance of a Cabinet, with himself as president. Each member of the Government now holds a separate portfolio, and despatches the ordinary business connected with it upon his own responsibility, only reserving matters of exceptional importance for the opinion of a colleague or the decision of the assembled Council. The particular branch of administration which Lord Canning, Lord Elgin, and subsequent Governors-General have successively reserved for their own special charge, is the Foreign Office of India.

The Indian Foreign Office is entrusted with the duty of directing our diplomatic relations—first, with all neighbouring foreign Powers beyond the limits of Hindustán; and, secondly, with all the dependent princes and chiefs of India. These two functions are obviously of supreme importance, for on these more than on any other departments of the State the maintenance of peace and the general policy of the empire depend. They are, however, necessarily secret in their operation, and they usually become known to the public by their results. Indeed, it may be affirmed that a large portion of the important diplomatic transactions in which the Governor-General of India is engaged never attract the notice of Parliament or of the British public. On some of these questions we are about to lay before our readers complete information. We shall not at present enter upon the controverted subject of the relations of the Supreme Government of India with the princes and chiefs who have retained some show of independence in that country, except to remark that Sir John Lawrence is a firm adherent of the non-intervention policy of the present day. But our object is to carry the reader beyond the frontiers of India to those less known regions in which we have to encounter the independent and barbaric races of the Asiatic continent.

Of course, in dealing with independent principalities and powers beyond the bounds of India, the Governor-General must act in concert with the English Cabinet whenever he is dealing with a European State or with any oriental nation, such as Persia and China, at whose Court there is a diplomatic representative of Her Majesty. But, even subject to this limitation, the Indian Foreign Office yet remains the focus of politics for half Asia—the storehouse of the romance of all the East. Murmurs of Dutch aggression in far Sumatra, and whispers of piratical prahs lurking amid the unexplored isles of the Malayan Archipelago; rumours of French enterprise in the feverish rice-swamps of Cochin-China, and quaint glimpses of Burmese life at the Court of the golden-footed monarch of Mandalay,—such are the varied contents of a mail packet from the southern seas. Out of the west come tidings of pilgrim-caravans at Mecca, of pearl-fishers in the Persian Gulf, or of burning slave ships on the coast of equatorial Africa; the outrages of the Christian emperor in Abyssinia are not omitted, nor those of the Wahábi fanatic at Riad overlooked. North-eastward, down the Himálayan passes of Bhútán and Nepál, the life that slowly stirs among the lámás and monasteries of Thibet sends now and then a faint pulsation into Bengal;

and lately the valley of Káshmír afforded a passage to envoys from the uncouth kháns of Chinese Tartary. Finally, in the furthest north, beyond Afghánistán and the deserts of the wandering Turkomans, looms the giant form of steadily-advancing Russia. In fact, it would be hardly an exaggeration if the English viceroy's political range of vision were to be described in the sonorous syllables of Milton :—

> 'His eye might there command, wherever stood
> City of old or modern fame, the seat
> Of mightiest empire, from the destined wall
> Of Cambalu, seat of Cathaian Can,
> And Samarcand by Oxus, Temir's throne,
> To Paquin of Sinæan kings ; and thence
> To Agar and Lahor of Great Mogul,
> Down to the golden Chersonese ; or where
> The Persian in Ecbatan sat, or since
> In Hispahan ; or where the Russian Ksar
> In Mosco ; or the Sultan in Bizance,
> Turchestan-born ; nor could his eye not ken
> The empire of Negus to his utmost port,
> Ercoco, and the less maritime kings,
> Mombaza and Quiloa and Melind.'

Descending, however, to the prose of current events, we find that the questions of external policy which at present chiefly command attention from the Government of India lie in the direction of Arabia and Central Asia. These, therefore, must be the main subject of our inquiry. But before we proceed to discuss our relations with either Mr. Palgrave's interesting friends, the Wahábis, or the picturesque ruffians in Afghánistán, there is another matter which, though of less importance, deserves a cursory notice, if only that the erroneous accounts of it which have reached England may not pass altogether unchallenged. We allude to the recent war with Bhútán.

The facts are very simple. In December 1863, just a month before the accession of Sir John Lawrence to viceregal power, it was found necessary to send an envoy into Bhútán to demand reparation for a long series of injuries inflicted on our frontier villages. The mission failed; the envoy was subjected to gross insult, and compelled to sign a treaty re-adjusting the whole boundary between British India and Bhútán, and making other preposterous concessions to the Bhútán Government. This crowning outrage was more than could be endured. Sir John Lawrence instantly repudiated the document extorted from his envoy, and took measures for chastising the offenders. Of the tract of territory lying at the southern foot of the Bhútán hills, and known generally as the Dwárs, the eastern portion, or the Assam Dwárs, had hitherto been a kind of a debateable land—that is, the British Government occupied the ground, but annually allowed 10,000 rupees, or one-third of the revenue, to the Deb and Dharm rájás as their share. Sir John Lawrence now announced to the Bhútán Government that this payment, as also the rent of another patch of land held by us in farm from Bhútán, had ceased for ever. Further, he demanded the restoration of all British subjects who, within the last five years, had been kidnapped by the Bhútiás; and he threatened that, unless the demand were fully complied with by the 1st of September, it would be enforced at the point of the sword. The Bhútán Government allowed the interval of grace to pass by without taking advantage of it. Accordingly, Sir John Lawrence, who had already extinguished all Bhútiá rights in the seven Assam Dwárs, now issued a proclamation, dated the 12th November, 1864, by which the Western or Bengal Dwárs, eleven in number, were likewise definitively incorporated into the Queen's Indian dominions, and the British frontier was advanced even beyond the plains, so as to include certain hill forts, and give us the command of the passes through which the Bhútiás had been wont to descend in their predatory incursions. The proclamation was, in fact, a declaration of war. But the Governor-General still looked to peace—the final aim of every war. A well-equipped force had by this time been assembled on the frontier, but it was not allowed to move until the terms upon which Bhútán might again be received into amity had been carefully settled and fully notified to all concerned. Within six weeks of the column being set in motion, every position in Bhútán which our programme had marked for occupation was in our keeping. The Bhútiás made little resistance, and it was thought they had abandoned the contest. Suddenly, in January 1865, they debouched in force along almost our whole line. At Díwángiri the surprise was complete: an unreasonable panic arose among the garrison, and the post was disgracefully abandoned with the loss of two mountain train guns. But this disaster of a subordinate officer—the only one that occurred throughout the entire campaign—was soon retrieved in gallant style by General Tombs; and after the reoccupation of Díwángiri in April, not a Bhútiá appeared in arms against us. Upon the cessation of hostilities, the Bhútiá authorities gave frequent indications of a desire for peace. Their overtures were invariably met by a reference to the terms—still open to them—which had been offered in the previous November, and by an assurance that unless those terms were accepted before the opening of the cold season, they would see an advance of British troops upon their capital, Púnakhá.

Convinced at last, by the preparations made by Sir John Lawrence and Sir William Mansfield, that we were in earnest in what we said, they signified their willingness to treat. Their overtures were favourably received. The surrender of the treaty which had been extorted from our envoy, and a humble letter of apology for the insults to which he had been subjected, formed the commencement of the negotiations. Afterwards, on the 11th of November, 1865, a treaty of peace was concluded upon the identical basis which the Government of India had from the outset held in view. The Bhútán Government formally ceded to us all the eighteen Dwárs and the rest of the territory taken from them, and agreed to liberate all our kidnapped subjects; in return for these concessions the British Government undertook to pay the Deb and Dharm rájás annually, subject to the condition of their continued good behaviour, an allowance beginning at 25,000 rupees, and rising gradually to a maximum of twice that amount. Also, by a separate agreement simultaneously executed, the Bhútán Government engaged to procure restitution to us, by the 10th of January, of the two guns lost at Díwángiri. These guns had fallen into the possession of a powerful Bhútiá noble known as the Tongso Penlo. He refused to give them up, in the hope that, by playing upon the desire of the British Government to recover trophies of war, and upon the desire of his own Government for peace, he might get himself constituted the channel through which the British allowance to Bhútán should be paid. The Deb and Dharm rájás sincerely endeavoured to fulfil their engagement, but the coercion of their refractory vassal was beyond their ability. The task, therefore, was undertaken by a British force. Our troops started on the 3rd of February, but they had not made many marches towards Tongso when the Penlo, as had been anticipated, gave up the game, and submissively sent the guns into our camp.

So ended the Bhútán war. Its conclusion was greeted with a chorus of disapprobation from the Indian press. The honour of England, it was said, had been betrayed by a pusillanimous Government. We ought to have marched into the heart of Bhútán, humbled the rájás in their capital, and exacted a condign retribution. Instead of doing so we had slunk back to the plains foiled in purpose, and content to purchase a dishonourable immunity from future aggressions at the cost of paying black mail to a crew of barbarous caterans. Divested of all rhetoric, the accusation seems to be that the conditions of the treaty were improperly lenient to Bhútán. It has been above explained that these conditions were the same as had been offered to the Bhútiás before hostilities commenced. Sir John Lawrence, therefore, cannot be charged with having lost heart in the struggle. The utmost that can be said is, either that in the original selection of a punishment for the Bhútiás their offences were too lightly judged, or that, as the fray proceeded, it became due to the honour of the arms tarnished at Díwángiri to wreak an increased vengeance on the foe. Neither of these suppositions will stand the test of cool inquiry. With regard to the first, it is certain that, short of the absorption of their whole country, the annexation of the Dwárs was as severe a penalty as could have been inflicted on the Bhútiás. Their State had hitherto been mainly supported from this fertile tract, Bhútán Proper being a very poor country. In truth, the principal reason for allowing them to retain a beneficial interest in the Dwárs was that, unless some such substitute for their usual means of maintenance were granted, they would be driven by sheer want to the very habits of depredation which the war was undertaken to suppress. But though originating in a sentiment of humanity, the measure was also recommended to the Government by considerations of policy. It was obviously desirable to secure some guarantee for the future good conduct of the Bhútiás, and the power of diminishing or altogether withholding an allowance which was essential almost to their bare existence, offered the very hold upon them that was wanted. Accordingly it was specially provided by the 5th Article of the treaty that the British Government should be at liberty, at any time when the conduct of the Bhútiás might give cause for dissatisfaction, to suspend payment of the allowance either in whole or in part.

In reply to the second charge—namely, that the disgrace incurred at Díwángiri demanded to be wiped out in further slaughter—we prefer quoting the words of Sir William Mansfield, the then Commander-in-Chief in India:—

> 'Was it to be supposed that a people which, however barbarous and untaught, at least possessed the attribute of animal courage, would submit to the loss of a slip of territory which, in their eyes, was probably as valuable as the territory that remained to them—I say, was it to be supposed that a people in such circumstances would not stand up and fight for their own property? Surely nothing else could be expected, and the Bhútiás are hardly to be blamed on that account. Yet that was the head and front of their offending, which raised such a cry for more punishment. They stood up and fought; and I can only say that they are, in my opinion, to be respected for so doing. People clamoured for more punishment—for what? Because the Bhútiás came and reoccupied a few posts. What

really took place? The first duty I had to perform on assuming my command was to receive the reports of the heavy blows delivered by Generals Tytler and Tombs at Bálá and Díwángiri. I am justified in attributing that character to them, because, when the small number of the Bhútán population is considered, the actions they fought, with respect to the losses they incurred, must have assumed in their eyes such proportions as in great European contests would be attributed to pitched battles. This is undoubtedly true, notwithstanding that to us such actions appear as insignificant skirmishes. I say it with confidence. The numbers of Bhútiás reported to have been killed in General Tombs' affair having been reported to be 200, I ask with confidence if this was not a terrible retribution, with regard to the numbers of the Bhútán population, for the check sustained by our arms at Díwángiri? I am happy to say that such was the opinion of your Excellency's Government. If we had further pressed this miserable people, for the purpose of inflicting a still greater summary punishment, we should have laid ourselves open throughout the civilised world, both in India and in Europe, and even with those who had been most impatient at our assumed inaction, to a charge of inhuman oppression, and, I think I may say, cruelty. I am happy to think that this Government has escaped such a stigma.'

But enough of Bhútán. We must hasten to scenes of more immediate interest in Western Asia. On the moot question whether Mr. Palgrave's book added anything to the stock of information already available to the general public regarding the past history of the Wahábi power in Arabia, we have no desire again to enter. Our sympathies are certainly on the side of the author, whose amusing narrative recently drew our attention to the subject. But there can be no doubt that the contemporaneous chronicles of the Indian Foreign Office, of the local Government at Bombay, and of the Residency at Bushire, do contain materials of a more detailed and trustworthy character than any it was in Mr. Palgrave's power to consult. During the last fifty years the Anglo-Indian agent in the Persian Gulf has been in frequent contact with the Wahábis of Nejed—for the Indian Government has good reason to watch with peculiar interest the proceedings of that sect. The fact is, that the same tenets which reign at Riad in an independent monarchy are scattered through the length and breadth of India in the far more dangerous form of secret confraternities, inspired with the most bigoted detestation of the infidel Feringhi. The Ambeylá campaign of 1863 affords an illustration in point. On that occasion it cost the army 847 men killed and wounded to subdue a small band of marauding fanatics on our far north-west frontier; and it has since been conclusively established that the head-centres of the band were the Wahábi priests of Patna—men of irreproachable respectability, who had been accounted, up to the moment of their detection, among the most inoffensive citizens that the unwarlike neighbourhood of Calcutta could produce.

Presuming that Mr. Palgrave's work has rendered our readers sufficiently familiar with the story of the Arabian Wahábis, it may now be worth while to notice briefly the salient points in the past relations of British India with the Nejedi dynasty. Three different sets of circumstances have from time to time brought the two powers into contact—first, the audacious piracies carried on in the Persian Gulf, under the protection and encouragement of the Wahábis, by several maritime Arab tribes, especially the Joasmis; next, our interest in the two great invasions of Nejed by the Egyptians; and in the last place, our obligation to extend moral support to the kingdom of Oman and the chiefship of Bahrein against the encroachments incessantly directed against both of them from Dereyiyah and Riad. Throughout all these complications the distinctive principle of our policy has been a desire to have as little to do with the Wahábis as possible, consistently with the necessity of maintaining the maritime peace of the Persian Gulf; and, above all, to avoid a downright collision with them. Thus, when a naval expedition was despatched against the Joasmi pirates in 1809, the full effect of the blow was certainly marred by the forbearance which the officer in command was ordered to show towards the Wahábis. Again, when the Imám of Muscat, or, as he is more properly called, the Sultán of Oman, shortly afterwards entreated our assistance against the Wahábis, he was told that the British Government had no particular interest in the quarrel, and that he had better make what terms he could with his adversaries. Next came the first Egyptian invasion of Nejed—a cause of great relief to the Sultán. It was now the turn of the Wahábi Amír to raise signals of distress. He sent an envoy to the British Residency at Bushire, proposing to enter into a treaty of amity and free trade with us. But his suit was as unsuccessful as that of the Sultán had previously been; we politely declined giving him any countenance. When the news reached India, in 1818, that Ibrahim Pasha had captured and destroyed Dereyiyah, and was meditating an advance to the shores of the Persian Gulf, the Marquis of Hastings conceived the design of allying the English arms by land and sea with the Egyptian conqueror, and so making a clean sweep of all the littoral nests of piracy, whether Joasmi or Wahábi. Captain Sadlier, of Her Majesty's 47th Regiment, was the officer selected to conduct the necessary negotiations with Ibrahim Pasha. In quest of the Pasha, whose camp was at Medina, and afterwards in his company, Captain Sadlier, as is well known, traversed the breadth of the Arabian peninsula —from Katif, on the Persian Gulf, to Yambo, on the Red Sea. Politically, however, the enterprise was a failure. Ibrahim Pasha, so far from desiring to push his conquests further east, was content to rest on his laurels, and had, in fact, begun his march homewards before Captain Sadlier arrived. He sailed from Jeddo for Suez at the same time that Captain Sadlier, *re infectâ*, took his departure for Bombay. The year 1834 brought a renewal of the question[1] whether our treaty engagements with the Sultán of Oman did not demand the interposition of British force to save him from the Wahábis. Lord William Bentinck repudiated any such liability. He even went so far as to contemplate, unmoved, the contingency of the Wahábis seizing the port of Muscat and making it a base for the renewal of piracy in the Gulf: 'It would be much easier,' he said, 'and cheaper to chastise them then, than to take up the matter as it stood, and constitute ourselves the guardians of the Sultán's possessions against all comers.'

Once more, the aid which the Sultán could not obtain from England, came to him indirectly through an Egyptian diversion. Khurshid Pasha in 1836 advanced with a large force from Medina, and in two years made himself master of all Nejed, Hasa, and Katif. But this time India had no welcome for the Egyptian commander. The policy of the Indian Government was no longer coloured by exclusively oriental considerations, but had to take its tone from Lord Palmerston, who at this junc-

[1] By Article II. of the Treaty of 1798, the friends and enemies of either Government are to be the friends of the other. But in practice this provision has always been a dead letter for both parties.

ture was carrying through, in conjunction with the Northern Powers, his determination to reduce Muhammad Alí, the too powerful Pasha of Egypt, to subordination as a vassal of the Porte. That ebullition of hostility to Egypt and to France produced a singular indirect result on the politics of Arabia. Instead of viewing the downfall of Wahábi fanaticism, and the rise of semi-civilised Egypt in its stead, with complacency, the Indian Government omitted no effort of diplomacy to counteract Khurshid Pasha's progress. Strong remonstrances were addressed to Muhammad Alí by the English Consul-General at Cairo. The result was, that in May 1840 the Egyptians yielded to our pressure and evacuated Arabia. Within three years after their departure the Wahábis were once more an organised power under their rightful Amír, Faizul.

One of Faizul's first acts was to address a communication to the Resident at Bushire, begging for the friendship of the British Government. His advances met with a civil reply; but it was at the same time significantly remarked that our presence in his vicinity had no other object than the preservation of peace on the waters of the Persian Gulf. Almost simultaneously with the exchange of these barren courtesies, the preponderating influence which Faizul had acquired at Bahrein and elsewhere on the coast began to inspire the Bombay Government with uneasiness. But Lord Ellenborough, to whom the question was referred, declined to interfere, and in 1844 his successor, Lord Hardinge, took the same view. The latter, however, consented, the following year, to a naval demonstration off the Batinah coast on behalf of the Sultán of Oman, whose territories had been invaded by the Wahábis in considerable numbers. Not a shot was fired from the British ships, but their presence enabled the Sultán to purchase peace from Faizul at the cost of an annual tribute.

Similar demonstrations were made for the protection, in 1851, of Bahrein, and, in 1853, of Oman for the second time. The invasion, checked in the latter instance, was of a very serious character. It was led by Faizul's son, Abdullah, who did not retire until he had extorted from the Sultán a large sum of ready money, and an agreement to pay double the former tribute. In 1859 it required the presence of the whole English squadron before Katif to induce Faizul's deputy at that place to abandon his designs on Bahrein and sue for pardon; but on this, as on previous occasions, a threatening attitude proved sufficient for our purpose. Once only—in 1861—did the British Government commit itself to actual hostilities with the Wahábis, and even then it was rather the semblance than the reality of war that we displayed. Faizul, influenced probably by sentiments of Arab hospitality, had refused to comply with our demand that he should expel from his fort at Daman a political refugee, whose intrigues for sixteen years had kept Bahrein and all its neighbourhood in a ferment. The Resident, therefore, proceeded to obtain satisfaction by force. An hour's distant firing from a steamer, to which the twin forts of Daman and Katif made no response, and which terminated without a man being touched on either side, gave the Wahábi Governor a decent excuse for expelling the obnoxious chief; and there the dispute ended. This incident gave rise to a remarkable proceeding on the part of the Turkish Governor-General of Bagdad. That functionary entered a formal protest against the Resident's conduct, on the ground that Faizul was only the Porte's vicegerent in Nejed, and that the fort of Daman was an integral part of the Turkish empire. The protest was disallowed by the English consul-general at Bagdad; for, although it is not improbable that since the second Egyptian invasion the Wahábi Amír has remained tributary to the Turkish authorities at Mecca—the tribute being regarded as an offering to the head of his religion—there is no controverting the fact that the practical authority of the Porte in Nejed is *nil*. The incident, however, is deserving of remark, because the Wahábis, when it suits their purpose, are rather given to making parade of their nominal dependence on Constantinople.

We now proceed to narrate transactions of a more recent date, to which the foregoing occurrences formed a necessary introduction. In the interior of Oman, about 100 miles west of Muscat, there is a fort and district called Rostak, the charge of which, two years ago, was held by Sayyid Ges, a kinsman of the Sultán. Sayyid Ges becoming restive, the Sultán marched out of Muscat to coerce him. Opposition was offered, and while the Sultán was still besieging the fort, Turkí bin Ahmad Sadairi, the commandant of the Wahábi stronghold at Bereymah, came up in force, and insisted on the contending parties accepting his mediation. The Sultán was consequently obliged to abandon the siege, and return humiliated to Muscat. No sooner had the troops of Oman disappeared than the Wahábi seized the fort he professedly had come to rescue, ravaged the surrounding territory, killed some of the inhabitants, and extorted from the rest a large pecuniary ransom. Intelligence of this outrage reached Bushire in December 1864. The Residency was at that time, and is still, held by Colonel Lewis Pelly, an officer who, during his previous employment in Sind, had acquired the entire confidence of the Governor of Bombay, and also was not unknown to the Anglo-Indian public—for the two dissimilar reasons, that in 1858 he wrote a foolish book, and in 1860 had the enterprise to travel from Teheran through Herat, Kandahar, and Beluchistán, to the British frontier in Sind. Colonel Pelly now, on his own responsibility, determined to visit the Wahábi Amír at Riad. He started from the Port of Koweit on the 18th of February, 1865, accompanied by a naval officer, Lieutenant Dawes, and the Residency surgeon, Dr. Colvill. Faizul received the party civilly, and during their short stay at Riad, Lieutenant Dawes succeeded in ascertaining the latitude and longitude of the city, and Dr. Colvill, we believe, procured some interesting geological and botanical specimens. But otherwise the expedition was without any result. Returning from the interior, Colonel Pelly emerged[1] on the 18th March near Bahrein, and from thence embarked for Bushire, where he arrived before the end of March. Very soon afterwards he came to England on leave for six months. During his absence fresh indignities befell the Sultán of Oman. First of all, a delegate from Faizul arrived at Muscat, demanding four times the amount of the usual tribute. Then Abdul Azíz, a brother of the Sadairi,

[1] The security with which Colonel Pelly visited Riad has at times been quoted in disparagement of Mr. Palgrave's adventures. Some critics have even gone so far as to imply that there was no necessity for Mr. Palgrave to have stooped to the immorality of disguise. These people forget that Colonel Pelly travelled with all the prestige attaching to the well-known office of Resident at Bushire, and that it is not given to everyone to enjoy so redoubtable an advantage. Besides, even if, for argument's sake, it be conceded that Mr. Palgrave, in a shooting coat, would for twelve months have been as safe as Colonel Pelly was for one month in a scarlet uniform, there needs very little experience of the East to know that no recognised European ever has a chance of obtaining such an admission to the inner life of the people as it was the principal object of Mr. Palgrave's wanderings to obtain.

who in the preceding year had harried Rostak, made his appearance as a Wahábi agent among the Beni Bú Alí and Jenubah tribes in the southern province of Jaalan, and, with the assistance of these disaffected Arabs, besieged and captured Súr, a port about 80 miles below Muscat, plundering the bazaar and shooting some of the inhabitants. Lastly, a threatening cloud of Wahábis gathered about Ras-úl Khaimá in the Joasmi territory, north of Oman. In short, when Colonel Pelly returned to India towards the close of 1865, there was a general disorder along the whole frontier, and the Sultán's prospects looked as gloomy as they had ever been during the Wahábi irruption of 1853.

Colonel Pelly arrived at Muscat on the 25th November, bringing with him apparently *carte blanche* from the Bombay Government to do whatever he might think best for the Sultán's protection. The first intelligence that reached him was that Faizul, the famous Wahábi Amír, was undoubtedly dead, though Abdullah, who had succeeded to the throne, was doing his best to keep the event secret. The Government of Nejed was still carried on in Faizul's name, and Abdullah even shrank not from the irony of putting his father's seal to despatches which declared the writer to be, 'by the blessing of God, in good health.' Faizul's disappearance from the scene was unquestionably a great point in the Sultán's favour. Colonel Pelly urged the Sultán to take advantage of the confusion to which it had given rise among the enemy. Bereymah was the keystone of the Wahábi power for annoyance, and this place Colonel Pelly thought the Omani troops might take by land, while by sea English co-operation might perhaps undertake the blockade of the Wahábi ports. The latter part of the scheme was not, however, easy of execution. Irrespective of the Resident's steam yacht, the 'Berenice,' there was only one English man-of-war in the Gulf—the 'Highflyer'—and Captain Pasley, who commanded the latter vessel, was under orders to return to Bombay as soon as possible. Under the pressure of this difficulty, Colonel Pelly conceived that he had no alternative but summary action, such as he had not at first contemplated. He addressed a communication to the Amír of Nejed, demanding in peremptory terms a written apology for the late Wahábi outrages in Oman, and also payment of 27,700 dollars as compensation for the Hindu-British subjects residing at Súr whose property had been plundered by Abdul Azíz. This ultimatum was delivered by Captain Pasley to the Shaikh of Katif on the 12th of January for despatch to Riad, and seventeen days from that date were allowed for compliance with the terms. On the 30th the 'Highflyer' returned to Katif for an answer. The Shaikh had no answer to give; and thereupon, in accordance with instructions received beforehand from Colonel Pelly, Captain Pasley commenced hostilities against the place. The shallow waters of the bay refused admittance to his ship, and his heavy boats were unable to approach within 1,200 yards of the shore. The native agent, however, who, in Colonel Pelly's absence at Muscat, acted as political adviser to the expedition, assured Captain Pasley that the fort of Daman was defended by only twelve men; and, upon this representation, it was determined to take the crews of two light cutters to the assault. Even these boats grounded a long distance from the beach, so that Lieutenant Long and his thirty gallant followers had to wade through 300 yards of mud and sand before they found themselves in the presence of the enemy. They carried the lower storey of the fort with a rush, but this success only showed them that to attempt anything more was hopeless. Gates and walls, manned by marksmen far more numerous than their own small party, still separated them from the principal towers. There was nothing to do but to retire to the boats. They did so in good order, but with a loss altogether of two seamen killed, and one officer and two seamen wounded. After this affair, the unfortunate issue of which must be ascribed to the deficiency of the local information at Captain Pasley's command, and to the imprudence with which the enterprise was attempted, the 'Highflyer' returned to Muscat, and being there joined by the 'Berenice,' the two vessels proceeded southwards to Súr, the scene of the Jenubah insurrection. Arriving at Súr on the 11th of February, Colonel Pelly gave six hours' notice to all non-combatants to clear out of the forts and the neighbourhood of the shipping. The 'Highflyer,' then opened fire, and after three hours' bombardment, reduced the forts to ruins. The next morning her boats went up the Súr creek, and destroyed or confiscated every vessel belonging to the Jenubahs. With this measure of chastisement, active operations terminated. The 'Highflyer' started for Bombay on the 13th, and Colonel Pelly the same day returned up the Gulf towards the telegraph station at Cape Mussendom.

That very day there was enacted at Sohar a tragedy, before which, to borrow an expression from Colonel Pelly, the horrors of Macbeth must pale. Sohar is on the Batinah coast, north of Muscat, and not far from the inland fortress of Bereymah. Mr. Palgrave's friends will remember it as the port of his departure on the unlucky coasting voyage in which he was wrecked. Hither had come Sultán Thoweyni, in order to organise a campaign against the Wahábis at Bereymah. On the fatal 13th of February he lay down in an upper chamber to sleep—his 'custom always in the afternoon.' Stealing upon his secure hour, his son, Sayyid Salím, with a Wahábi attendant named Besharí, crept up the staircase, entered the chamber, and silently closed the door from the inside. Besharí drew a double-barrelled pistol from under his cloak. Salím signalled him to fire. But Besharí handed the weapon to the prince, and drew his dagger, intimating by a noiseless gesture that if the pistol failed to do its work, he would 'mak' sikker' with cold steel. Salím then fired both barrels into his father's forehead, and all was over. Thoweyni had passed from sleep to death without a struggle. The murderers threw a sheet over the corpse, and hurried downstairs. Their first care was to seize Sayyid Turkí, the late Sultán's brother, and throw him heavily ironed into a dungeon. It was then given out in the town that Thoweyni had died of fever. At nightfall the body was secretly buried under the floor of an inner room, and the parricide rode off with his accomplices to take possession of the kingly power at Muscat.

Vague rumours of what had happened at Sohar reached Colonel Pelly at Cape Mussendom on the 20th. He lost no time in coming to see for himself how matters stood at Muscat. Calling at Sohar on his way, he succeeded in effecting the release of Sayyid Turkí. At Muscat, where he arrived on the 2nd March, he found everything in confusion. Sayyid Salím had thrown himself into the hands of the Wahábi faction, and was the mere creature of their behests. On the 6th, Colonel Pelly obtained intelligence that the Salím had a plot on foot for suddenly attacking the 'Berenice' that night, as she lay at anchor. Whatever may have been the amount of truth in this report, there is no doubt that the 'Berenice' had not the means of defending herself if attacked, and that all the Hindus of Muscat were in utter panic. Colonel Pelly therefore acted as prudence dictated, and, after having taken on board all persons who had any claim to British protection, steamed quietly out of the harbour.

All these events—from the first appearance of the 'Highflyer' in the Gulf up to the 'Berenice's' retirement from Muscat—had followed one upon another in such quick succession, that there had been little time for the Bombay Government to refer for instructions to Calcutta. In judging, therefore, of Sir John Lawrence's foreign policy, it must be understood that he is not responsible for any of Colonel Pelly's proceedings. But we must be permitted to observe that the British agent at Bushire appears to have not always acted with discretion; and it is painful to reflect how little control it is possible for the Government of this country or of India to exercise over its officers in these remote regions, while perhaps irreparable mischief has been done. The very first opportunity that the Government of India obtained for interposing its authority arose out of the arrival at Bombay of envoys from Sayyid Salím. These envoys were the bearers of a letter, in which their master protested against the recent deportation of Hindu merchants from Muscat in the 'Berenice,' and pointed to the perfect safety of all the property which had then been abandoned as a proof that he had been unjustifiably discredited by Colonel Pelly's apprehensions. Sir John Lawrence decided that this letter should be answered in terms of frigid civility. It was impossible to continue to Sayyid Salím the relations of personal friendship which our officers had cultivated with his father; but it was equally undesirable that the diplomatic relations of two States mutually necessary to each other should be suddenly and completely broken off for the crime of an individual. It was no part of the duty of the British Government to avenge the death of the late Sultán of Muscat, or to punish the guilt of his successor.

While this question was being discussed in India, affairs in the Gulf had righted themselves with singular rapidity. The inducements which usually led the British Government to assist, and the Wahábis to attack, Oman, had alike been much weakened by recent events. The new ruler had no title to our regard, while, on the other hand, he was the publicly declared ally of the Wahábi Governor at Bereymah. A further reason why the Wahábis should, for a time at any rate, show a peaceable bearing to their neighbours, was the fear lest our unsuccessful attack on Katif might only be the prelude to more serious hostilities. The Amír Abdullah regarded this contingency with alarm. He took early measures for averting the storm by the despatch of two emissaries from Riad—one to entreat the mediation of his suzerain at Constantinople, and the other to patch up a peace with the English representative at Bushire. The first messenger, though he carried with him two Nejedi horses as a present for the Sultán, advanced no further than Bagdad, being turned back by the Turkish Governor-General of that province. The second has recently (1866) engaged in negotiations with Colonel Pelly, and the conciliatory spirit he displays gives reason to hope that the several causes of dissatisfaction which the British Government has against the Amír of Nejed are in a fair way of adjustment. It only remains to be added that all is quiet again at Muscat, and that the traders who fled have now returned to their former avocations.

From the glittering waves of the Persian Gulf we must now take flight to the bare steppes and snow-capped mountains of Central Asia. In that inhospitable region, the State which, from its geographical position, must always be viewed with the greatest interest by England, is Afghánistán. This kingdom, during the last years of Dost Muhammad's reign, presented the appearance of as compact and independent a government as even the authors of the Afghán war could ever have hoped artificially to create on our north-west frontier. Dost Muhammad's last feat, performed when he must have been close on eighty years of age, was to wrest Herat from Persian influence. He died on the 9th June, 1863, twelve days after he had taken the city by storm. From that moment the Nemesis of Muhammadan polygamy, in the usual form of children by different mothers scrambling for the inheritance, has laid its curse of anarchy and civil war heavily on Afghánistán.

The old Amír left sixteen sons. Four of these were too young at the time of his death to have acquired any personal influence; but of the elder twelve, every single man aspired, if not to sole supremacy as his father's successor, at any rate to a separate principality independent of any brother's control. Those whose ambition aimed at the entire kingdom were five in number[1]—

[1] The most prominent of the seven chiefs figuring as partisans rather than principals were Wali Muhammad, Faiz Muhammad, and Aslam Khán. In this same class may be also ranked two grandsons of Dost Muhammad,

namely, Afzal and Azím Khán, sons of one mother; and Sher Alí, Amín Khán, and Sharíf Khán, sons of another and more highly-born lady.

Afzal Khán, aged fifty-two, the eldest of Dost Muhammad's sons, bore the reputation of being also the bravest; his conquests in the north had added considerable territory to the Afghán dominions, and for some time past he had been governing with vigour and popularity the whole tract lying between the Hindu Khúsh and the Oxus. (This province, known to the Afgháns as Túrkistán, we shall prefer to speak of as Balkh, in consequence of the Russians having appropriated the former name for the districts of their southern frontier.) The head-quarters of Ufzal Khán's Government were fixed at Takhtapul, a city which has risen on the ruins of the ancient and more familiar Balkh, or Bactra. Perhaps it was this proximity to Bokhara that first suggested the matrimonial connexion subsisting between his son and daughter and a daughter and son of the King of Bokhara. Afzal Khán was still at Takhtapul when Herat fell and Dost Muhammad died.

Azím Khán is described by Dr. Bellew, who saw him in 1857, as a middle-aged man of very tall stature and herculean frame, with a dignified and commanding mien. Little, if at all, inferior to Afzal Khán as a soldier, he was incomparably Afzal Khán's superior in statecraft. Without any real love for the English, Azím Khán had yet established a strong claim upon our goodwill by the

Fathi Muhammad and Jalál-ud-dín Khán, sons of the famous Akbar Khán, who murdered Sir William Macnaghten. Fathi Muhammad had courage and ability, and Jalál-ud-dín Khán deserves notice because a recent journey through India to Mecca and Constantinople had inspired him with apparently a sincere regard for the English, such as no other Barukzai sardár pretended to feel.

course he adopted in 1857, when the whole Afghán nation clamoured to be led down the passes that they might join the mutineer sepoys in a meritorious extermination of the infidel English. Dost Muhammad would perhaps have been unable to resist the popular cry but for Azím Khán's steadfast and openly declared advocacy of the English cause. The eastern districts of Khúrm and Khost, bordering upon the Indian frontier, were Azím Khán's charge, but he had left them to follow the Afghán army to Herat.

All the three princes forming the second group of competitors had likewise accompanied their father to Herat. The youngest of the trio, Sharíf Khán, aged thirty, held the south-western districts of Farrah and Ghirishk. Not wanting in military courage, he probably shone best as a civil administrator. He had somehow accumulated more treasure than any of his brothers, but he marred this important advantage by a fickleness of spirit extraordinary even in an Afghán; unstable as water, he was the Reuben of these Beni-Israel, foredoomed not to excel.

Very different in character was Amín Khán, Governor of Kandahar, in the south—a bold impetuous man, who always took the shortest road to his object, and suffered no temptation or obstacle to baulk his purpose.

Sher Alí, forty years of age, was perhaps not equal to Afzal Khán as a general, or to Azím Khán as a statesman, but he was, nevertheless, an adept in the arts both of peace and of war, as understood among his countrymen; and if it had not been that his many fine qualities were alloyed by an ungovernable temper, which at times entirely swamped his judgment, he might well have been recognised by others besides his father as the flower of the family. Sher Alí's political proclivities had hitherto been towards a Persian rather than an English alliance.

Sher Alí it was whom Dost Muhammad, some time before the expedition to Herat, had publicly selected as his successor, passing over the claims of both the elder princes, Afzal Khán and Azím Khán. The selection, according to family custom, was authoritative. Sher Alí ever since had borne the designation of heir-apparent; and when Dost Muhammad died, none ventured to question his title to succeed. Even Azím Khán himself in that first hour of confusion was fain to join in the general homage due to Sher Alí as rightful Amír of Afghánistán.

Signs of disaffection to the new ruler soon showed themselves. First Amín Khán, then Sharíf Khán, and lastly Azím Khán, abruptly quitted Herat, and retired to their respective fortresses in Kandahar, Ghirishk, and Khúrm. The Amír himself began his return march towards Kabul on the 5th of July, leaving his third son, Yakub Khán, as Governor of Herat. He reached Ghazní on the 24th of August, and halted there in order to ascertain what Azím Khán was about in the neighbouring district of Khúrm. His inquiries elicited very unsatisfactory intelligence. He therefore diverged eastward with his whole force into Khúrm, and compelled Azím Khán, who was hardly prepared for such prompt action, to tender a formal submission. The two brothers then embraced: Azím Khán swore fealty to the Amír, and in return obtained a confirmation of all the dignities and emoluments he had enjoyed during the late reign. The Amír, having thus scotched his snake, recommenced the march to Kabul, which city he finally reached on the 9th of September. Before the end of the year he had the satisfaction of receiving regular recognition from the British Government as successor to Dost Muhammad's vacant throne.

The winter passed away without any event of importance; even Barukzai restlessness is not proof against 'the mesmeriser snow.' But with the first genial breath of spring both Afzal Khán and Azím Khán were up and doing. The former, notwithstanding that he had begun by sending in letters to Herat replete with protestations of the most devoted loyalty to Sher Alí, now scrupled not to proclaim himself throughout Balkh as Amír of Afghánistán: indeed, his preparations for making good the claim by force of arms were already well advanced. The latter was busily organising an insurrection in Khúrm; but he hesitated to engage in any overt outbreak, being anxious that all the odium of the intended rupture might fall upon the Amír. With this object he left his fort of Gurdez with a garrison so insufficient as to invite attack. The bait took. One of the Amír's officers indiscreetly pounced on the fort in his sovereign's name, and Azím Khán was at once provided with a pretext for rebellion. The Amír met the double danger boldly. On the 20th of April 1864, he despatched the best soldier in his kingdom, Muhammad Rafik, to crush Azím Khán in the south-east, while he himself marched northwards to meet Afzal Khán's more formidable invasion. Fortune favoured his tactics. As soon as Muhammad Rafik entered Khúrm, Azím Khán's venture utterly collapsed. Abandoned by his troops, Azím Khán on the 16th of May fled for refuge into British territory, and became a pensioner of Sir John Lawrence at Ráwal Pindí.

In the meantime the armies of the Amír from Kabul

and of Afzal Khán from Takhtapul had come face to face in the mountain defiles of the Hindu Khúsh near Bamian. On the 3rd of June an indecisive but hotly-contested action took place between the advance guards of either host, at a place called Bajgah. The Amír's troops in this engagement were commanded by his eldest son, the heir-apparent, who displayed great gallantry, killing two of the enemy with his own hand. Two days afterwards the Amír was reinforced by the arrival of Muhammad Rafik with the troops which had been employed in suppressing Azím Khán's disturbances in Khúrm. Such a concentration of the Amír's whole strength was more than Afzal Khán was prepared to meet; he had calculated that Azím Khán would have found full employment for half the Kabul army. On the other hand, family traditions, as well as the nearly equal strength of the opposing force, disposed the Amír to avoid further bloodshed. With these sentiments prevailing in either camp, the natural result was peace. The Amír and Afzal Khán publicly embraced one another on the 29th of June; and the reconciliation which followed was, to all outward appearance, perfect. It was agreed that the two armies should proceed peaceably together into Balkh, and that, after having seen something of the province with his own eyes, the Amír should then define Afzal Khán's future position in the State. In pursuance of this arrangement, the brothers proceeded harmoniously to Tashkurghan, a town about forty miles south-east of Takhtapul. Here, on the 9th of August, Afzal Khán's claims were settled to his satisfaction by nearly the whole of his former government being restored to him. For yet another fortnight all went merry as a marriage bell, and then came a sudden crash. The conduct at Takhtapul of Afzal Khán's son, Abdul Rahmán, having given rise to some suspicion, the Amír summoned the young chief to his presence. Abdul Rahmán, instead of obeying the summons, fled across the Oxus into Bokhara. Perhaps the Amír wanted an excuse for long-meditated treachery; perhaps his ordinary principles of action were overwhelmed in a sudden tempest of anger; but whatever may have been the motive, he visited the sins of Abdul Rahmán on his father, Afzal Khán. In public darbar he called up one of his kinsmen, gave him a pair of leg-irons, and bade him seize and fetter Afzal Khán. The Sardár had the independence to remonstrate, and begged that, if the Amír persisted in his determination, some one else might be found to do his bidding. Almost beside himself with passion, the Amír turned to a more complaisant courtier, General Shaikh Mír, and insisted on being obeyed. The general took the irons and repaired with them to Afzal Khán's quarters. Placing them respectfully before the old prince, he informed him of the Amír's order. Afzal Khán said, 'It is God's will;' and, spitting three times on his own beard, stretched out his legs, when the general affixed the irons and left him.

Intense excitement followed this *coup d'état.* The Afghán nobles had seen the Amír only two days previously at the tomb of one of their holiest saints swear fidelity to Afzal Khán solemnly on the Kurán; and the fresh remembrance of that scene effectually destroyed their faith in the Amír, and devoted all their sympathy to his wronged prisoner. Several of them hurried across the Oxus to join Abdul Rahmán in Bokhara; others fled to Amín Khán at Kandahar; those that still stayed by the Amír held aloof from personal contact with a temper which they had now greater cause than ever for mistrusting. As for the gallant army which, under Afzal Khán, had so well held its own against the Amír in the passes of the Hindu Khúsh, it melted away like a snowdrift. Some small portion accepted a service of doubtful fidelity under the Amír, and one body of 800 regular troops made good its retreat to Kandahar; but the majority dispersed in plundering parties over the northern districts. From Tashkurghan the Amír proceeded to Takhtapul. There the confiscation of Afzal Khán's property, and the deportation of his zanáná to Kabul, occupied some time. Early in October, the Amír appointed his nephew, Fathi Muhammad, Governor of Balkh, and turned his own steps southwards to the capital. He entered Kabul in triumphal procession on the 14th of November.

Meanwhile the fugitive Abdul Rahmán had been received with open arms by his father-in-law, the King of Bokhara. The tale of Afzal Khán's wrongs, confirmed as it was by the production of the Kurán bearing the seal of the perjured Amír, moved general indignation. The King laid the case before his College of Divines, and when the learned men replied by pronouncing sentence of excommunication against the Amír, he declared to the assembled Court his royal intention of espousing Abdul Rahmán's quarrel at the head of an army of 10,000 men.

Nor was it from the north alone that danger threatened the Amír. The signs of the times were equally menacing in the south. Amín Khán for months had been exerting all his energies to put Kandahar in a state of defence, and now, just as his plans for throwing down the gauntlet to the Amír approached maturity, he obtained the important assistance of Sharíf Khán's money bags. Sharíf Khán and he, with their nephew, Jalál-ud-dín, as a subordinate member of the triumvirate, entered into a compact to stand by each other against the Amír to the last extremity.

It must have been an anxious time, therefore, that winter of 1864-65, at Kabul, though the severity of the Afghán climate guaranteed the Amír immunity from any immediate attack. Snow still lay deep over all the country, when the ball was opened in the Kandahar direction by a forward movement on the part of Jalál-ud-dín to capture the important fortress of Khilat-i-Ghilzai, on the road towards Ghazní and Kabul. The attempt was unsuccessful; Jalál-ud-dín, after a six weeks' siege, being obliged, on the 28th March, 1865, to abandon the siege and fall back on Julduk, a place thirteen miles to the south. But as a signal for malcontents to bestir themselves, Jalál-ud-dín's efforts were by no means labour lost. Azím Khán, whose intriguing correspondence with the Kandahar chiefs had been a source of incessant trouble to his hosts throughout the ten months of his sojourn in British territory, now recrossed the border; and betaking himself to his old haunts of Khúrm and Khost, raised a standard of revolt, to which numbers of the wild Wazíri tribe were very soon attracted. He had already received considerable aid in money from Afzal Khán's wife, a princess of masculine courage and energy; and about this time she sent him 25,000 rupees, with a message that now or never was the time to show his manhood; if he had none to show, he had better spend the present remittance in buying a shroud, for he would get no more from her.

Still the Amír rose to face his various foes undauntedly. Recurring to the plan of campaign which last year had served his turn so well, he dispatched Muhammad Rafik against Azím Khán, with instructions to disperse the Khúrm insurgents as soon as possible, and then join the main army, which he intended himself to lead against Candahar.

Muhammad Rafik, thus limited as to time, was unable to accomplish much in Khúrm. Azím Khán at his approach fled to the Wazíri Hills, and the Amír's orders allowed no leisure for a pursuit. All that Muhammad Rafik could do was to offer a large reward for the capture of the rebel prince, hastily pacify the disturbed tract, and then make the best of his way to the Amír's camp.

He effected a junction with the Amír at Mukhar, forty miles south of Ghazní, on the 28th of May, and the united army reached Khilat-i-Ghilzai about the 3rd cf June. By this time Jalál-ud-dín had been joined by the other confederate sardárs, Amín Khán and Sharíf Khán, and from Julduk the entire Kandahar force had advanced to a position within two miles of Khilat-i-Ghilzai. A collision was therefore imminent, and the chances seemed not to be in favour of the Amír; for, although the two belligerent parties were about equal in point of numbers (say 12,000 men with 20 guns on either side), the Kandahar troops were better fed than those of Kabul, and their *morale* was unquestionably superior. The battle took place at Kujhbaz on the 6th of June. One wing of the Amír's army, under the command of his eldest son, attacked Amín Khán's battalions, while Rafik Khán led the other against Sharíf Khán. After four hours' fighting the Kandahar troops had gained ground considerably, and were pressing their advantage with vigour. At this moment the Amír dashed up to his son's side, and taunted him with incapacity for command. Stung by such a reproof, the gallant heir-apparent put himself at the head of his men, and led a charge of desperate valour, which carried everything before it. In the *mêlée* the prince found himself face to face with Amín Khán. A hand-to-hand combat ensued between the uncle and nephew, each giving and receiving some severe sword cuts. Suddenly Amín Khán drew a pistol from his girdle and shot the heir-apparent through the head. Five Kabulis at once avenged their leader, and Amín Khán fell, riddled with bullets, by the side of his brother's son. This was the turning-point of the battle. The Kandahar army wavered, broke, and fled, and the day was gained for the Amír. Eighteen guns and many prisoners (including Azím Khán's eldest son, Surwar Khán) fell into the Amír's hands. But, in the words of his own despatch from the field of battle, grief for the loss of his son 'clouded all the joy of victory.' For four days the Kabul troops remained inactive, allowing Sharíf Khán and Jalál-ud-dín to take back their shattered force to Kandahar without molestation.

Nevertheless, the blow at Kujhbaz had been decisive. When the Amír at length advanced on Kandahar, the two rebel chiefs, with their principal adherents, came out to meet him: all surrendered their swords, and prayed to be forgiven. So, without any further contest, the Amír entered the city a conqueror on the 14th of June. We may pause here for a moment to remark the rapidity and completeness of the Amír's success. A year ago he had been encompassed by four powerful rivals, any one of whom might have been backed to oust him from his inheritance. Where were they now? Afzal Khán a captive, Sharíf Khán a defeated suppliant for pardon, Amín Khán slain, and Azím Khán a hopeless refugee among the hills on the Indian frontier.

Fortune, however, was not always to smile on the Amír. Already her face was darkening for him on the northern horizon, beyond 'the broad, clay-laden, lone Chorasmian stream.' Abdul Rahmán, with the nucleus of an invading army procured under the auspices of his royal father-in-law, left the Bokhara Court on the 22nd of June, and reached the banks of the Oxus about the 15th of July.[1] Faiz Muhammad, the commandant of Akcheh, first allowed him to cross the river unopposed, and then openly declared in his favour. Fathi Muhammad, the Governor of Balkh, hastened out of Takhtapul to retrieve Faiz Muhammad's treachery; but the discipline of the Balkh troops, numbers of whom had belonged to Afzal Khán's old army, went to the winds in the presence of Afzal Khán's son sounding in their ears

[1] In what strength Abdul Rahmán re-entered Afghánistán is uncertain; but the constitution of his force suggests a reminiscence of Mr. Matthew Arnold's 'Sohrab and Rustum:'—

> 'The Tartars of the Oxus, the King's guard,
> First, with black sheepskin caps and with long spears;
> Large men, large steeds; who from Bokhara come
> And Khiva, and ferment the milk of mares.
> Next the more temperate Toorkmuns of the south,
> The Tucas and the lances of Salore,
> And those from Attruck and the Caspian sands;
> Light men, and on light steeds, who only drink
> The acrid milk of camels and their wells.
> And then a swarm of wandering horse, who came
> From far, and a more doubtful service own'd;
> The Tartars of Ferghana, from the banks
> Of the Jaxartes, men with scanty beards
> And close-set skull-caps; and those wilder hordes
> Who roam o'er Kipchak, and the northern waste,
> Kalmuks and unkemp'd Kuzzaks, tribes who stray
> Nearest the Pole, and wandering Kirghizzes,
> Who come on shaggy ponies from Pamere.'

the popular war-cry of rescue for Afzal Khán, and vengeance on the perfidious Amír. They rose in mutiny, compelled Fathi Muhammad to fly for his life to Kabul, and *en masse* transferred their allegiance to the invader. Thus Abdul Rahmán, without a blow, found himself master of all Balkh. Flushed with success, he began preparations for an immediate descent on Kabul, leaving the security of his base to the charge of Faiz Muhammad.

Now, Faiz Muhammad was full brother to Wali Muhammad, whom the Amír, when starting for Kandahar, had appointed Governor of Kabul. And Wali Muhammad's own conduct had of late not been altogether above suspicion. The Amír, therefore, had good ground to be alarmed for the safety of his capital. His measures, however, were not equal to the occasion. Grief for the loss of his heir had deadened his perception ; and instead of himself hurrying to the scene of action, he remained sunk in supine gloom at Kandahar, and deputed the duty of defending Kabul to his second son, Ibrahim Khán, and his well-tried general, Muhammad Rafik.

These joint commanders, bringing with them a large portion of the Amír's army, arrived at Kabul on the 5th of September, and Ibrahim Khán immediately relieved Wali Muhammad in the office of Governor of the city. Ibrahim Khán's position, with troops clamouring for arrears of pay, an empty exchequer, and not an adviser near him on whose loyalty he could rely, would have tried the resources of the most fertile genius ; and Ibrahim Khán was essentially dull and irresolute. Plan after plan for stemming Abdul Rahmán's advance was devised only to be laid aside ; detachments started for the passes of the Hindu Khúsh only to be recalled ; and at last all hope of any greater strategy than a stand at bay before the walls of Kabul was abandoned. As if to omit no chance of ensuring his own ruin, Ibrahim Khán must needs take this opportunity to give mortal offence to his colleague, Muhammad Rafik. Twenty-four hours after the receipt of the insult, Muhammad Rafik rode out of the capital with a large band of retainers to cast in his lot with Abdul Rahmán. So dangerous a defection moved the Amír even in his lethargy at Kandahar. He sent off reinforcements to Kabul under the command of the now pardoned Sharíf Khán; not that Sharíf Khán was altogether trusted; the Amír seems rather to have hoped, than to have trusted, that he would act faithfully. Sharíf Khán reached the environs of Kabul on the 30th of November.

That same day Azím Khán, who for the last six months had been condemned by bodily sickness and want of funds to lie quiet in his mountain retreat among the Wazíris, made his appearance in the camp of Abdul Rahmán at Bamian, where for some time past he had been eagerly expected. The aid in men or money which Azím Khán could bring to the cause of the invaders was insignificant; but his commanding ability and the prestige of his name at once gave him the lead in their councils, even to the supersession of Abdul Rahmán.

Supposing Sharíf Khán had been quite sincere in his new attachment to the Amír, it still would have been but a poor fight that he and Ibrahim Khán could make, when pitted against such antagonists as Azím Khán and Muhammad Rafik. But Sharíf Khán had no intention of fighting. He deserted to the enemy ten days after his arrival. Ibrahim Khán, thus left completely in the lurch, was fain to have recourse to negociation. And he was more fortunate in his efforts than might have been expected. The bitter cold of December stood him in good stead. The Balkh army, though now within ten miles of Kabul, and numerically far superior to Ibrahim Khán's garrison, had suffered severely from frost and snow, and, so far from being in a condition to undertake the siege of a large city, it urgently needed rest and shelter; consequently Azím Khán was almost as desirous of an armistice as Ibrahim Khán could be. Between them it was soon arranged that there should be a suspension of hostilities until the 19th of February, during which time the Balkh army was to remain undisturbed in winter quarters in the neighbourhood of Kabul, and Ibrahim Khán was to use his best endeavours to obtain the release of Afzal Khán and the other state prisoners whom the Amír had in confinement at Kandahar.

This lull in the troubled affairs of Kabul was employed by Sharíf Khán in a succession of extraordinary intrigues. He began by deserting from the confederates back again to Ibrahim Khán. Then he made a dash at Kabul on his own account, and, being detected in the attempt, was expelled the city. His wealth enabled him to obtain readmission, and eventually he settled down as a nominal supporter of Ibrahim Khán, maintaining at the same time the closest relations with the enemy outside the walls. Ibrahim Khán, for his part, beset by treason in the palace, mutiny and desertion among the troops, and anarchy and famine throughout the city, spent the interval in despatching repeated entreaties to his father either to release the state prisoners without delay, or to repair in person to Kabul for the rescue of the sinking kingdom. Querulous and futile orders to act more energetically against the foe were the only answer he ever received. Nothing would induce the Amír to stir from

Kandahar. Buried there in the seclusion of inner chambers, he admitted none but a few personal attendants within his sight ; and if at intervals he broke silence, it was only to wish, with a burst of Nero-like ferocity, that he could cut the throat of every man in Kabul and Kandahar, or to declare in utter despondency that he should depart out of Afghánistán, and learn to forget his home and people in England, Russia, or the holy land of Arabia. One night he jumped into a tank, and began groping under water in search of his dead son ; his guards rescued him, but he remained insensible for some time afterwards. Altogether, there was only too good ground for the rumour then prevalent throughout all the bazaars of Central Asia, Persia, and India, that Sher Alí of Afghánistán was mad.

The 19th of February, 1866, the day fixed for the termination of the armistice, arrived, and Azím Khán sent a herald into Kabul to notify to Ibrahim Khán that, as the state prisoners were still unreleased, hostilities must recommence. As the Balkh army approached, Ibrahim Khán's outposts, one after another, were treacherously surrendered ; and on the 22nd the main body of his troops abandoned their camp, and dispersed, some to their homes, and many more to a career of brigandage. Azím Khán took possession of the city of Kabul on the 24th, Ibrahim Khán retiring with a handful of faithful followers into the citadel of the Bálá Hissár. After some days' bombardment, a guarantee of personal safety and freedom induced Ibrahim Khán to capitulate ; and Azím Khán, now completely master of the whole capital, entered the Bálá Hissár under a salute of forty-three guns on the 2nd of March, and held a public darbár in the Royal Garden.

The fall of Kabul electrified the Amír. Roused in a moment from his disastrous stupor, he addressed himself to the recovery of his long-lost kingdom with a fire and determination which showed that he was thoroughly himself again. Not a trace of his late eclipse hung about him, except the deep mourning which he still continually wore. The districts of Kandahar, Farrah, and Herat supplied him with troops and money, and from morning to night through all the month of March he laboured at the equipment of his army.

At Kabul, the allied princes, Azím Khán and Abdul Rahmán, showed no backwardness in preparing for the encounter. Strategic points of obvious importance were the historic fortress of Ghazní, on the road to Kandahar, and the town of Shaikhábád, lying midway between Kabul and Ghazní. Troops were therefore promptly thrown forward to besiege Ghazní, while the bulk of the confederate army took up a strong position at Shaikhábád.

The Amír arrived at Khilat-i-Ghilzai, with a force of 9,000 infantry, 5,000 cavalry, and 25 guns, about the 20th of April. At his approach the enemy's corps before Ghazní raised the siege of that city, and fell back on their supports at Shaikhábád without firing a shot. The Amír entered Ghazní on the 1st of May, and halted there for a four days' rest. His star apparently was again in the ascendant. Fathi Muhammad, of whom we last heard as being driven out of Balkh by Abdul Rahmán's invasion, and who subsequently had obtained the government of Jalálábád, was now in arms for the Amír, marching manfully against Kabul from the east, and raising all the adjacent clans in his progress. But even more important than Fathi Muhammad's diversion was the jealousy and contention prevailing among the heads of the hostile camp. Abdul Rahmán could not forgive Azím Khán for having jockeyed him out of the leadership. Muhammad Rafik sighed for the superior power and consideration he had formerly enjoyed in the Amír's darbár. And the minor Sardárs, such as Wali Muhammad and Aslam Khán, chafed under the limitations newly imposed by Azím Khán on their rapacity and ambition, and were only biding their opportunity to change sides. The universal expectation was that in the coming struggle the Amír would win. Veering as the wind blew, that shameless weathercock, Sharíf Khán, briskly turned his back on the confederates and faced about for the Amír: a pity he was not acquainted with the old French proverb, 'Il n'y a rien de certain hors l'imprévu.'

Leaving the state prisoners, Afzal Khán and Sarwar Khán, at Ghazní, the Amír marched northwards on the 5th of May. He came up with the enemy at Shaikhábád late in the afternoon of the 9th. A cannonade was immediately opened between the two armies, which continued without much result till nightfall. Azím Khán, with the last detachment sent out from Kabul, was still nine miles to the rear of the confederate camp; but, warned by the distant booming of artillery, he pushed on with all speed to join Abdul Rahmán and Muhammad Rafik, and arrived in time to take part in the critical engagement of the following day. Early in the morning, the Amír led in person a general assault against the entrenchments behind which the northern army lay. The latter were kept within their defences, and ordered not to throw away their fire. In spite of this wary generalship, by which the assailants were more than once repulsed with heavy loss, the impetuosity of the Amír and of that portion of his troops recruited from Herat and Kabul might yet have carried the day, when suddenly, at his greatest need, the whole of the men from Kandahar abandoned their position, and went over in a body to Ismail Khán, a prince who held high command in the confederate army, and who, as being the late Amín Khán's son, had special claim to the attachment of all Kandaharis. The Amír now saw that his chance was gone. He turned his horse's head, and fled with four or five hundred Herat horsemen towards Ghazní. Sharíf Khán accompanied his flight. Almost all the rest of the southern army made their submission to Abdul Rahmán. The Amír's guns, elephants, and entire camp equipage became prize of war to the victors.

As soon as the issue of the battle became known at Ghazní, the false-hearted garrison released the state prisoners who had been committed to their charge, and shut their gates in the face of the Amír. The fallen king had to pass on without drawing rein. He halted at last at a small town called Nanní, twelve miles further south. Here the country people brought him provisions, and he was joined by straggling relics of his defeated force, to the number of 2,500 men—Kabulis, Heratis, and Kandaharis. He could put no trust in the Kandaharis; but, calling the others round him, he told them, in tones of more than usual dignity, that what had happened was God's will, and that he knew not what might be in store for the future; that he was satisfied with their services; but that any who wished had his free permission to return to Kabul. For himself, he added, he was still Amír of Afghánistán, and would relinquish the right only with his life. The next night when the moon rose he resumed his flight towards Khilat-i-Ghilzai and Kandahar.

The confederate army made no attempt to follow up their victory. Only Abdul Rahmán, with a thousand horsemen, hurried forward immediately after the battle to meet the liberated state prisoners, and bring them in triumph to the camp.

With Afzal Khán's resurrection to political life, the constitution of the northern faction passed into a new phase. Both Abdul Rahmán and Azím Khán were content to compromise their mutual jealousies, and to waive their respective pretensions to the leadership, by recognising as a common superior this third prince, who stood in the relation of father to the one, and elder and full brother to the other. The subaltern chiefs had no choice but to follow suit, and the order of the day was very agreeable to the veteran battalions from Balkh. By reason of these influences, Afzal Khán passed at a bound from captivity to kingly power. He received the congratulations and homage of the assembled Sardárs at Shaikhábád on the 16th of May, and then the camp was broken up, and the whole army returned to Kabul. Afzal Khán was installed in the Bálá Hissár as Amír of Afghánistán on the 21st of May amid much clangour of kettle-drums, a general illumination of the city, and a salute of one hundred guns.

In the meantime the Amír Sher Alí made good his retreat to Kandahar. He was well received by the inhabitants, and, nothing daunted by his recent defeat, he forthwith set to work collecting a fresh army for the renewal of the contest. He has been incessantly engaged upon this task during the past year (1866), and talked with confidence of being able to take the field again in two months' time. All the south and west, including the districts of Khilat-i-Ghilzai, Kandahar, Ghirishk, Farrah, and Herat, were still in his possession. Sharíf Khán was with him, and provided the sinews of war liberally. His second surviving son, Yakub Khán,[1] could be reckoned on to furnish a stout contingent from Herat. Half the chiefs in Kabul continued in secret correspondence with him. And, above all, the reputation of being the ally of the British Government was a tower of strength to him; for though, since the commencement of the strife, innumerable proofs have been given of our determination to let the Afgháns fight out their own battles without the grant of a single musket or rupee to one side or the other, Sir John Lawrence has taken no less pains to let it be known throughout the length and breadth of Afghánistán that England does not depart lightly from her engagements, and that no pretender can hope for any countenance from her, so long as the prince whom she has once recognised as sovereign retains any material hold upon the country.

At Kabul nothing of any importance occurred after the installation of the rival Amír, Afzal Khán. But the prospects of the party have sensibly deteriorated in the interval. They hold nothing now but Kabul and Ghazní (1866); for Faiz Muhammad, who was last year left in charge of Balkh when the rest of the confederates marched

[1] This is the young chief who, penetrating Dr. Vambéry's disguise as a pilgrim from Constantinople, denounced that courageous traveller as an Englishman. The incident occurred in November 1863, and Vambéry, in mentioning it, portrays his interlocutor as 'a good-humoured, inexperienced child.' During the three eventful years that have since elapsed, Yakub Khán has fairly won a title to higher estimation. Not only has he securely maintained himself in his difficult position as Governor of a newly-conquered frontier city, but, whenever called on, he has always been able to spare troops for his father's assistance. The fact is, the political atmosphere of Afghánistán, surcharged with vicissitude and peril, acts as a forcing-house on the intellects of the young Barukzais: they shoot up into statesmen and soldiers before they have ceased to be boys.

to the capture of the capital, took advantage of the crisis to declare that he holds that province independent of any master. Afzal Khán himself, demoralised by his long captivity, yielded to the temptation of sensual enjoyments, and from four in the afternoon till next morning was too intoxicated to be seen by anyone. All power centred in the hands of Azím Khán, who ruled with a tight hand, feared by many and loved by none. Abdul Rahmán especially chafed under his uncle's arrogance, and it was even reported that he had quitted Kabul in disgust, at the head of a force with which he meant to wrest Balkh from Faiz Muhammad's grasp.

While the relations of the British Government with the Amír Sher Alí remain, as we have already indicated, on the old footing of mutual trust and goodwill, the attitude Sir John Lawrence holds towards the opposite faction at Kabul is equally clear and simple, though at times it has been obscured by Azím Khán's pertinacious efforts to lure us from our fidelity to the Amír Sher Alí's cause. Every wile within the compass of Azím Khán's crafty character has been exhausted in this attempt. His first move, essayed immediately after the capture of the capital in March last, was to work on the fears of the Indian gentleman who, though a mere news-writer, holding no diplomatic powers of any kind, is, after a fashion, the representative of the Governor-General at the Court of Kabul. In full darbár, this Munshí being present, Azím Khán made it a practice to rail in unmeasured language against the inhospitable and ungrateful English, and to declare his intention of seeking an alliance through Bokhara with Russia. The grudge of which he made such parade, he was far from really feeling ; he knew well that our policy, during his sojourn in British territory, in limiting the number of his followers, and insisting that he should not abuse the privilege of asylum by intrigues across the border, had proceeded, not from any lack of goodwill to himself, but from a sense of duty towards the established government of Afghánistán. His two youngest sons were in fact still in the enjoyment of British hospitality and protection. But he calculated that by an affectation of deep resentment he might possibly entrap us into a policy of conciliation terminating in actual alliance. And the ruse was not a bad one. With the British Munshí it entirely succeeded. Fired with the ambition of doing a brilliant stroke of diplomacy for his employers, the Munshí opened negociations with Azím Khán, and the latter, after some show of coy reluctance, consented to make overtures of amity to the English Government. Sir John Lawrence, however, was not so easily intimidated or hoodwinked. Under his instructions, Azím Khán's letter was answered by the officer to whom it was addressed (the Commissioner on the Peshávar frontier), in that tone of unmeaning courtesy which flowery Persian is well adapted to convey; and the Munshí received a severe reprimand, coupled with a warning that the next time he stepped beyond his letter-writing *rôle* he would infallibly be recalled to India. In justice, however, to the Munshí, it must be added that he was not the only one on whom Azím Khán's vapouring imposed. The rumour of Russian influences in the Kabul darbár spread through Meshed to Teheran, and the tale, as told in Persia, was that Abdul Rahmán had obtained, through the mediation of Bokhara, recognition from the Russian Government as Amír of Afghánistán, on condition of vassalage to the Emperor Alexander. The credulous Persians accepted this story, ignorant of the intense jealousy with which every native statesman in Central Asia views the advance of Russia; ignorant also that for ten months past Abdul Rahmán had not been north of the Oxus; and forgetful that Bokhara, through whom the unnatural alliance was said to have been cemented, was at that very time locked in a death-struggle with the battalions of the Czar. Azím Khán renewed his manœuvres as soon as the successful issue of the battle of Shaikhábád left him once more at liberty to play on the Munshí's feelings. This time he alternated direct offers of assistance with threats of downright war. First he pointed out the expediency of an alliance between England and Bokhara against Russia, and volunteered his services as a go-between to bring about the arrangement. And then again he would drop hints of having received an embassy from the Akhund of Swat (that mysterious 'old man of the mountain' on the Indian frontier) urging him to proclaim a religious war against infidels in general and the English in particular. But his promises and his threats were alike thrown away. Sir John Lawrence would not hold up a finger for Bokhara; and as for Azím Khán presuming to fly in the face of England and lead a fanatical descent upon Pesháwar, at a time when the Amír Sher Alí was still unconquered at Kandahar, and Faiz Muhammad in open insurrection at Takhtapul, the idea was simply laughable. Foiled at all points, Azím Khán was in the end obliged to have recourse to a more straightforward proceeding. He caused a letter to be written in the name of the titular Amír Afzal Khán to the Governor-General, making a plain demand for the friendship of the British Government. Sir John Lawrence's reply was as follows:—

'*To His Highness Sardár* MUHAMMAD AFZAL KHÁN, *Wali of Kabul, dated Simla, 11th July,* 1866.

'I have received your Highness's friendly letter, giving an account of late events in Afghánistán. It has been to me a source of sincere sorrow that misfortunes such as your Highness describes have befallen the great house of the Barukzais, and that calamities so heavy and protracted have been experienced by the people. It was, and still continues to be, the hearty desire of the British Government that the Afghán nation should remain under the strong and united rule of the Barukzai family, and that this family, endowed by the Creator of the world with wisdom to be at peace among themselves, should be respected both in their own country and by surrounding nations. Wherefore it has been a source of distress and anxiety of mind to me that strife and division have arisen among the members of your Highness's family.

'My friend! your Highness alludes to the friendship which existed between your Highness's renowned father and the British Government, and your Highness says that from this Government your Highness expects similar treatment. It is the earnest wish of the British Government that that friendship should be perpetuated. But while I am desirous that the alliance between the two Governments should be firm and lasting, it is incumbent on me to tell your Highness that it would be inconsistent with the fame and reputation of the British Government to break off its alliance with Amír Sher Alí Khán, who has given to it no offence, so long as he retains his authority and power over a large portion of Afghánistán. That Amír still rules in Kandahar and in Herat.

'My friend! the relations of this Government are with the actual rulers of Afghánistán. If your Highness is able to consolidate your Highness's power in Kabul, and is sincerely desirous of being a friend and ally of the British Government, I shall be ready to accept your Highness as such; but I cannot break the existing engagements with Amír Sher Alí Khán, and I must continue to treat him as the ruler of that portion of Afghánistán over which he retains control. Sincerity and fair dealing induce me to write thus plainly and openly to your Highness.'

It remains to be seen what effect this frank avowal of a preference for the Amír Sher Alí will have in the Kabul darbár. Possibly Azím Khán may yet, in desperation, make those advances to Russia which hitherto he has only bragged of making. But we doubt his doing so; and we are confident that, if he does, he will gain nothing by his motion beyond fair words. The Russian outposts, even if they had reached Samarcand, would still be 500 miles from Kabul, and the Czar, for the present at any rate, seems neither inclined nor prepared to push a man beyond the Oxus (1866).

Such, then, is the present condition of Afghánistán, and of England's relations with the Barukzai chiefs contending for her favour. The State which, after Afghánistán, has the best claim on English attention, is Bokhara; but before we cross the Oxus to peer into the field of Russia's principal activity, it may be worth while to spare a glance sideways at Chinese Tartary. This region, lying east of Afghánistán and north of the British dependency of Káshmír, is separated from the latter by the almost impassable barrier of the Kuen Lún Mountains, and from the former by the Pamir Steppe—an extensive tract of elevated table-land, known also as the Bam-i-duniyá, or Roof of the World, and occupied by the black tents of the pastoral and freebooting Kirghizzes. The vast level valley of Chinese Tartary, irrigated by rivers and canals, and rich in various minerals, including gold and coal, contains four provinces—Kashgar, Yarkand, Aksu, and Khoten. The population is composed for the most part of a mixed breed, half Kirghiz and half Persian; besides these there are Kalmucks, Chinese, and a race called Túnghánis, who, though by extraction Chinese, are by religion Muhammadans: all, as a general rule, occupying fixed habitations and following agricultural pursuits. On Kashgar, which from its geographical position is marked out as a great centre of future trade, the Czar's Government has long fixed a covetous gaze; and although the aggrandisement of our powerful neighbour in this quarter is not likely to react injuriously on the British tenure of India, we must still confess to a certain interest in the progress of events, all steadily tending to pave the way for Russia's appearance at the northern foot of the Kárá Koram Pass. Early in 1863 the Túnghánis of Khoten rose upon their Chinese masters, massacred numbers, and compelled the remainder to become converts to Islam. Their example was soon followed by the Muhammadans of Yarkand, Aksu, and other cities, and in this way the rule which the Court of Pekin had exercised for a century was suddenly annihilated: Chinese Tartary is Chinese now only in name. Kashgar has fallen into the possession of a party of Kipchak refugees from Kokand, who were driven from their home across the mountains in the year 1865, when the King of Bokhara overran Kokand and set up a nominee of his own in the government, by way of counterblow for the Russian capture of Tashkend. Yarkand is in a state of utter anarchy (1866), the refugees from Kokand and Andijan contending for the mastery with the native Túnghánis. Khotán alone seems not to have suffered from the expulsion of the Chinese: it boasts a settled government, conducted despotically, but not unwisely, by the old chief who originated the revolution. This Khán Bádsháh, as he styles himself, has recently been interchanging communications with the British Government. Hearing last autumn that there was an

English officer (Mr. W. H. Johnson, of the Trigonometrical Survey) employed on scientific investigations along the Káshmír frontier, he sent him an invitation to come to Ilchi, the capital of the province. Mr. Johnson, regardless of the fate which met the unfortunate M. de Schlagentweit at Kashgar in 1857, boldly accepted the invitation on his own responsibility. He met with a cordial welcome from the Khán Bádsháh, and after a stay of sixteen days (during which the people of Yarkand sent a deputation to him entreating him to come and be their king—so wearied are they of their intestine strife and confusion!) he[1] returned over the mountains in safety to Káshmír. The Khoten chief's object had been to obtain troops and arms from India wherewith to defend himself against the much-dreaded encroachments of Russia, and failing to find his hopes in any way furthered by Mr. Johnson's visit, he despatched a special envoy to the Governor-General of India. The envoy arrived at Calcutta in

[1] Mr. Johnson's Report (No. 102, dated 22nd April, 1866, 'to the address of the Superintendent of the Trigonometrical Survey') has recently been brought under the attention of the Royal Geographical Society. But there are two odd circumstances connected with Mr. Johnson's visit, which, as they find no mention in that very interesting paper, we may casually notice here. In the first place, a Persian Jew sought him out, and, professing to have authority for the purpose, offered to provide him employment as a Russian spy. And, secondly, Mr. Johnson imagines that the Islamised Hindu whom he found at Khoten in command of the Khán Bádsháh's infantry, is capable of identification as the infamous Náná Sáhib of Cawnpur. Mr. Johnson appears to have jumped to this belief from altogether insufficient premises, but it is not beyond the bounds of possibility that he is right. There is good reason for doubting whether the report of the Náná's death, circulated in 1858, had any foundation; it seems more probable that he escaped from Nepál into Thibet. And if he reached Thibet, he certainly might have wandered on into Chinese Tartary. We may also take this opportunity to observe that a valuable map of Central Asia, based on the most recent surveys that have been made by British and Russian officers, has just been issued by Colonel Walker, R.E., F.R.S., from the office of the Indian Trigonometrical Survey.

February 1866, bearing proposals for a defensive alliance against Russia and China, and begging that artillery-men, English officers to drill the native troops, and artificers skilled in casting guns and making swords and muskets, might accompany him back to Khoten; he was also very desirous to obtain the aid of European engineers competent to work the valuable mines of his master's country. But the requests of the poor Khán Bádsháh were not preferred at a favourable time. Other viceroys might perhaps have been dazzled at the sight of potentates from the end of the earth suppliant at their footstool; but Sir John Lawrence was used to strange embassies of this kind. Already more than once it had been his lot, either as Chief Commissioner of the Panjáb or in his present more exalted capacity, to give audience to semi-barbarian deputies from Central Asia, entreating to be saved from the clutches of the all-absorbing *Rús;* and to every such appeal, even though some of them came before him during the excitement of the Crimean war, he had, from motives of policy, persistently turned a deaf ear. It was not likely, therefore, that he would take other than a practical view of this latest application. He dismissed the unlucky envoy with a civil but absolute refusal on all points.

Turning our back now on Chinese Tartary, we may proceed in a north-westerly direction over the Alai Mountains into the Máwar-u-Nahr, or the territory between the rivers Oxus and Jaxartes, belonging to Kokand and Bokhara. In the immediate vicinity, but on the left bank of the Oxus, is Khiva. The three Usbeg lie together, as it were in a semicircle, with Bokhara southernmost in the concave centre of the arc, Khiva at the north-western extremity, and Kokand at the north-eastern. All three, but especially Khiva and Kokand, retain an independent existence only so long as Russia pleases (1866). Two hundred navigable miles of the Oxus are all that separate Khiva from the Russian flotilla on the Aral Sea; and Kokand, at the other extremity, is not a hundred miles from the large Russian garrison at Tashkend. Bokhara, if it had behaved with common prudence, might have remained unmolested for some time to come; but, unfortunately, the King of Bokhara pretends to rights of sovereignty acquired by recent war over a great portion of the Kokand principality, including the town of Tashkend, and he has not had the sense to accept the inexorable logic of facts by which Tashkend, from being Kokanian, has become Russian.

In July 1865, a month after the Russians had captured the city, the King sent in an arrogant letter to General Tcherniayeff, the military governor of Turkistán, calling on him to withdraw from Tashkend or accept the alternative of a general war to be waged in the name of the faith by all the Muhammadans of Central Asia. At the same time he marched an army into the province of Kokand, expelled the chiefs of the Kipchak tribe from the capital, and delivered the government to Khudá Yár Khán, a prince who, he thought, might be trusted to keep Russian diplomacy at arm's length. These inimical demonstrations were met at Orenburg by the detention of a caravan of Bokhara traders. The King then in turn retaliated on a Russian caravan. As if to hedge, however, against a rather doubtful issue, he qualified his challenge by despatching an ambassador named Najum-ud-dín Khán with valuable presents to St. Petersburg, to demand the release of the Bokhara subjects. He also addressed a letter to General Kryjanovski, the Governor-General of Orenburg, informing that officer of the despatch of the embassy, and proposing that, until the Czar's reply should be received, the Russian troops at Tashkend should not cross the river Chirchik. This endeavour to temporise altogether miscarried. The Russian general was in no mood to recognise the King's assumption of lordship over Kokanian territory. Besides, the rich transfluvial fields were really wanted as a means of providing grain for the garrison of Tashkend. A tract, therefore, of about twenty miles square on the southern bank of the Chirchik, including the forts of Kiriuchi, Niazbek, and Chinaz, was promptly occupied by the Russian troops, without any regard for the wishes of the Bokhara darbár. Nor did the embassy to St. Petersburg at first obtain any better treatment. Najum-ud-dín was put under restraint as a hostage at Fort Cazala, and kept there several weeks.

All at once a change came over the spirit of the Russian policy towards Bokhara. Perhaps the generals at Orenburg and Tashkend on reconsideration concluded that it would be both desirable and possible to convert Bokhara into a friend; perhaps their natural restlessness felt the check of the Emperor's sincere desire for a period of repose on the southern frontier. But whatever may have been the cause, the defiant attitude of Russia was transformed towards the close of the year into one of conciliation. Notwithstanding that Russian traders were still in confinement at Bokhara, and that the suspension of traffic between the two countries continued in full force, Najum-ud-dín was released from Cazala and allowed to proceed on his way through Orenburg to St. Petersburg; and in November a Russian officer, with seven European attendants, arrived at Bokhara charged with a mission to remonstrate against the King's proceedings in Kokand, and to make arrangements for a treaty of amity and peace. Now, considering the dubious character of the relations at the time subsisting between Bokhara and Russia, and the notoriously small sanctity which any ambassador's person has in the eyes of a Central Asiatic despot, we doubt whether General Tcherniayeff was altogether justified in staking several valuable lives and all the prestige of the Imperial Government upon the chances of the King of Bokhara's temper. At any rate, the measure turned out ill. And if there is any truth in the assertion of the 'Journal de St. Petersbourg,' that General Tcherniayeff's action in this matter was precipitated by the receipt of intelligence that there were English emissaries at Bokhara intriguing to secure an alliance prejudicial to Russian interests, no better proof could be found that Russia no less than England might be saved from many a blunder, if on the common ground of Central Asia the political intentions of either party were more clearly understood by the other. There was no foundation whatever for the Russian general's apprehensions. Since the day in June 1842, when our ill-fated countrymen, Stoddart and Conolly, were murdered by a former king, there has been no English agent invested with diplomatic authority of any kind at the Court of Bokhara, nor, so far as the present affords a guide for the future, is it likely that there ever will be one. India, whatever her rulers may once have thought, has neither part nor lot in Bokhara. The errand of the Russian ambassador, M. Struve, who for some time past had been employed in the double capacity of astronomer and political agent on the southern frontier, was, so far as it might be intended to counteract the imaginary machinations of the Anglo-Indian Government, as unnecessary as for the reasons above-mentioned, it assuredly was hazardous. The King of Bokhara, uninfluenced in the slightest degree by England, rejected the Russian approaches, and announced his determination to keep the ambassador a prisoner at Bokhara until his own representative, Najum-ud-dín, should return in safety from Orenburg.

General Tcherniayeff, on learning this result, threatened that unless the members of the Russian mission were at once voluntarily set free, he would come and deliver them by force. Still, the Bokhara Court persisted in its contumacy; whereupon the Russian general proceeded to put his threat into execution. The troops with which he started from Tashkend at the beginning of February 1866, numbered 14 companies of infantry, 600 Cossacks, and 16 guns, with 1,200 camels carrying provisions for a month. On the 16th of February, as he neared Juzak, a town fifty miles north of Samarcand, the King of Bokhara sent him a letter dated from Samarcand, consenting to yield up the captives, and assuring him that they had already started from Bokhara, and would reach Samarcand on the 17th. There was no truth in this communication; for, as we shall presently show, the envoy and his suite were still detained at Bokhara. It had the effect, however, of inducing General Tcherniayeff to halt for a time where he was. On the third day, finding that his expectations of obtaining supplies of firewood and forage by peaceable purchase from the inhabitants of Juzak were vain, and that the troops were suffering severely from the want of these necessaries, he sent out a small column, composed of two companies of infantry, 400 Cossacks, and two guns, towards the outskirts of the town, with instructions to help themselves to wood and hay, but not to use their arms unless forced into an action. The contingency he was anxious to avoid came to pass. The Bokhariot garrison of Juzak gave battle to the foraging party, and drove it back to camp with the loss of six men killed and nineteen wounded. This disaster, taken with the insufficiency of his commissariat arrangements, compelled General Tcherniayeff, on the 23rd of February, to begin a retrograde movement towards Fort Chinaz, without further waiting for the promised surrender of the Russian prisoners. For the first few miles of the retreat, swarms of Bokhariot horsemen hung about his flanks and rear, but occasional round shot kept them at a respectful distance, and on the 26th the Russian field force reached the banks of the Jaxartes in safety after an absence of about three weeks. This account of the bootless expedition to Juzak we have taken from the columns of the 'Journal de St. Petersbourg,' and we see no reason to question its candour and general correctness. The reports which have reached India direct from Central Asia are so manifestly exaggerated that we cannot afford them any credence.

Meanwhile, as may readily be imagined, the position of the unfortunate Russians at Bokhara had not been improved by General Tcherniayeff's ineffectual effort to enforce their liberation. Up to the 1st of February the ambassador and his suite had been kept within the four walls of their residence, but otherwise they had encountered no indignity. On that day they were requested to deliver up their arms. They refused. In the evening the city magistrate surrounded the house with troops, and repeated the demand. The small party of Russians, with more gallantry than prudence, declined to submit, and in the fracas which ensued, the magistrate and five other Bokhariots were severely wounded, and one of the pugnacious diplomatists was hurt. Attracted by the disturbance, the populace assembled in crowds about the house, and clamoured for the destruction of the infidels. The Russians were then in imminent danger of being torn to pieces by the mob. They escaped this fate by at last making timely surrender to the constituted authorities. The following day they were sent off manacled in a cart to Samarcand, where the King had already taken up his quarters at the head of a considerable army.

On these events becoming known at St. Petersburg, the Czar, we believe, expressed his strong disapproval of the line of conduct pursued by his enterprising lieutenants; he despatched a special aide-de-camp to Orenburg to insist on the adoption of a less ambitious policy; and both General Kryjanovski at the central seat of government, and General Tcherniayeff in Turkistán, were recalled from their respective commands. The months of March and April appear to have been spent by the King of Bokhara in braggart proclamations of a religious war, so that the Russian outposts south of the Chirchik were kept in a state of continual alarm. On the 12th of April a reconnoitring party, which General Romanovski, the successor of General Tcherniayeff, had sent out twelve miles on the road to Khojend, encountered a body of some 400 Bokhariot horsemen, escorting large flocks of sheep towards Oratepe. The Bokhariots were routed, and their sheep, to the number of 15,000 head, carried off as prize of war by the Russians. Beyond this insignificant skirmish there seems to have been little or no fighting in April. By the commencement of the following month the Russian preparations for retrieving the laurels lost by General Tcherniayeff were complete.

According to the Russian official account of the campaign, the estimate of 53,000 men given by the 'Levant Herald' as the strength of General Romanovski's army proves to be a considerable exaggeration. The battle in which the King of Bokhara was routed took place on the 20th of May; and the Russian troops engaged in it consisted only of a detachment from Fort Chinaz, numbering 14 companies of infantry, 500 Cossacks, and 20 guns. The Bokhariots were totally defeated; all their artillery was captured, and the King fled in panic to Samarcand. The Russian loss was twelve men wounded. The scene of the engagement was Idjar—a place not, as we had been led to believe, on the road to Juzak and Samarcand, but on the left bank of the Jaxartes, thirty miles above Chinaz. From Idjar General Romanovski, reinforced by a detachment from Fort Kiriuchi, advanced up the river, and captured, on the 26th May, Naou, and afterwards the important city of Khojend, thereby completely isolating Kokand from the sister state of Bokhara, and establishing eighty miles of the Jaxartes, from Chinaz to Khojend, as a frontier in advance of Tashkend. At this point the expedition terminated. The Russian envoy, M. Struve (who seems to have been detained at Samarcand until after the battle of Idjar), was given up, and the King of Bokhara sued for peace. Our latest intelligence is that M. Struve has returned to the scene of his seven months' captivity in order to settle what the terms shall be, and that the terrified King of Bokhara has despatched envoys to Calcutta and Constantinople, in the vain hope of obtaining help from the English and Turkish Governments (1866).

After the extraordinary stories which have appeared in the Indian newspapers of the capture of Samarcand, and the presence of Russian troops as far south as Sháhr-i-sabz and Karshí, it is curious to find that General Romanovski's operations were confined to the valley of the Jaxartes, and that he has throughout been separated from Samarcand by about 150 miles of country, including a long waterless steppe and the Ak Tau Mountains. Russia clearly has no present wish to annex any part of Bokhara. Her next appropriations will probably be Kokand and Andijan, so as to reach the Thian Shan Mountains south of Lake Issyk Kúl, and give the province of Turkistán its natural development over that space between the meridians of 68° and 76°, in which the most recent Russian maps leave the boundary of the empire still a blank. They are based on reports received through Afghánistán—a channel which, under existing circumstances, cannot be altogether depended on for either fulness or accuracy of intelligence. The Afghán chiefs, wrapped up in their own internal quarrels, have no leisure to inquire about the blaze in their neighbour's dwelling; and what little news dribbles down spontaneously to Kabul, Azím Khán takes good care to manipulate before passing on to the Indian Munshí. The party now in power at Kabul is, as we have already explained, bent on enticing the British Government into an alliance; and in this spirit it is Azím Khán's regular practice to paint the progress of Russia in portentous colours, and scatter mysterious insinuations as to her widespread plots for the conquest of India.

Is it then potent still, this phantom of a Russian invasion, that Azím Khán should choose to conjure with it? Are Englishmen still haunted by the vague alarm which a quarter of a century ago hurried us into the blunder, guilt, and miserable discomfiture of the Afghán war? We answer that the old feeling still undoubtedly survives in the minds of many of our countrymen. The class fortunately is more numerous in India than in England. It includes, besides 'the panic-mongers of the press,' military men whose professional instincts lead them to snuff the battle afar off, and to mistrust our existing frontier line, whether along the Indus or at the foot of the Khaibar and Bolán Passes beyond that river, as false to the principles of the art of war. These are they who, to prove the possibility of invasion, cite the conquests of the Macedonian Alexander, of Timur, and of Nádir Sháh, and who, in the so-called will of Peter the Great, the traditional policy of his successors, the treaty with Napoleon at Tilsit, and the immense development southward which the Siberian boundary has undoubtedly received, find cumulative evidence of Russia's determination to make the possibility an accomplished fact. According to these alarmists, what we have to expect is as follows:—In a very short time the Russians will have military colonies on the Oxus at Charjui and at Takhtapul. From Charjui troops will be thrown across the desert to Merv, and from Merv the fertile banks of the Murgab offer easy access to Herat. Simultaneously a smaller column will proceed through Takhtapul and the defiles of the Hindu Khush to occupy Kabul. Persia, of course, will act in alliance with the invaders, and at Herat the force from Charjui will be joined by large Russo-Persian reinforcements marching in from the shores of the Caspian Sea and the districts of Khorasan. Some delay must occur at Herat, for that city, as the key of the position, will have to be fortified and provisioned, and a chain of smaller forts on either side will have to be established, stretching as far as Takhtapul in the north and Lake Seistan in the south. But the interval will be well redeemed by disarming the hostility and securing the co-operation of the Afgháns. The darling dream of the whole nation is to plunder India, and Russia will offer them that guerdon, and the restoration of their old provinces of Pesháwar and Káshmír to boot. Then some fine morning in early spring —unless timely measures of prevention are adopted on a scale far above the present Government's capacity to comprehend or courage to undertake—forty thousand disciplined troops of Russia and Persia, in conjunction with a countless horde of wild Afghán auxiliaries, will be launched, resistless as an avalanche, upon the doomed plains of the southern El Dorado, and there at once is an end of our Eastern empire. Language like this is, we can assure our readers, by no means uncommon in India; and the practical remedies recommended by such speakers extend to an immediate reoccupation of all Afghánistán.

Politicians of another and far higher stamp, while they see clearly that any immediate or even proximate danger of a Russian invasion is chimerical, nevertheless look forward with uneasiness to the inevitable day when the Russian and English empires shall be conterminous, and the presence of a first-class European state on our border shall have power at any time to fan into a flame those elements of sporadic disaffection which of necessity are ever smouldering in any country won and held, as India was and is, by an alien sword. For political reasons of obvious weight, they believe that it would be in the last degree dangerous, should war arise, to have

India as a battle-field; and on grounds of military strategy, they are convinced that, sooner or later, we ought to occupy certain positions beyond our present frontier as outworks of the empire. Therefore, advancing from Jacobábád, which now is our uttermost station on the Scinde border, they would proceed up the Bolán Pass through Shawl into Afghánistán, and, leaving Kabul and Ghazní untouched, they would take possession of Kandahar and eventually also of Herat, and establish at these two points fortresses of exceeding strength, to be to India what the Quadilateral has been to Venetia, strongholds such as no invader would dream of trying to mask. And the long process of a regular siege would, it is argued, be an almost hopeless undertaking in consequence of the natural poverty of the country, the distance of the enemy from their base, and the previous destruction of the crops by the besieged. These opinions deserve to be received with the greatest respect, for they have been advocated not only by high authorities like Sir Justin Sheil and the late General John Jacob, but also, we believe, by Sir Henry Rawlinson, who, besides his large general experience of war and policy in the East, stands *facile princeps*, as Dr. Vambéry has justly testified, among all who profess a special knowledge of the present condition of Central Asia.

The majority of the British public appear to favour a third view of the question. Under the inspiration of a generous optimism, rather than from any discriminate appreciation of the dangers to which the Indian empire is exposed, they scout Russophobia as an exploded fallacy. In the interests of humanity they rejoice that a dayspring of Christian civilization is spreading through the horrible blackness of barbarism in which Central Asia has hitherto been wrapped; and they positively grudge the interval that must yet elapse before India can have a neighbour whose dealings with her will be conducted on the clear principles of European good faith, and whose settled government will offer new openings for trade. Their vision of the future is the Cossack and the Sepoy lying down like lambs together on the banks of the Indus.

Lord Lawrence, the Governor-General of India, has been steeped too long in the rough practice of actual statesmanship to have much faith in the advent of that political millennium when

> 'The common sense of most shall keep a fretful realm in awe,
> And the kindly earth shall slumber, lapt in universal law.'

But his opinions with respect to Russia, so far as they can be inferred from his public acts, tend clearly towards the conclusion which the quietists would advocate—a masterly inactivity. And we are rejoiced that this is the case, for any other course, we are convinced, would be inappropriate to the requirements of the occasion.

Were the Russian frontier pushed forward from the line of the Jaxartes to the foot of the Hindu Khush—were there war in Europe between England and Russia, or even if both these contingencies came upon us at the same time, there still would be many grave reasons for pausing before we fairly committed ourselves to the project of defending the British boundary by means of an advance into Afghánistán. In the first place, there is the nature of the country and its inhabitants, both so untractable that, except in the last resort, the task of dealing with them had far better be left to a rival or an enemy than undertaken by ourselves. It is a land, in Lord Wellesley's contemptuous phrase, of 'rocks, sand, deserts, ice, and snow;' and the men it breeds are warlike, turbulent, fanatical, and perfidious. Take a small force into the country, and you are beaten; take a large one, and you are starved. Then there is the financial argument to be considered. The army that made its way up the Bolán Pass in 1839, all counted, was only 19,000 strong; yet the Afghán war cost us from first to last fifteen millions sterling. Whence is to come the money for a repetition of the experiment? As it is, the finances of India are with difficulty kept at a bare equilibrium, and the ways and means for any extraordinary expenditure could only be provided either by an increase of taxation, or an addition to the public debt. The latter alternative manifestly hampers the resources of the empire for a future time of, perhaps, sorer need; and the dangers of popular discontent arising from the former are so great that, sooner than incur them, Lord Canning declared his readiness to dispense with the services of 10,000 English soldiers. Lastly, there can be no question that, however desirable from a strategical point of view the establishment of outworks at Kandahar and Herat might be, there are, *per contra*, certain solid advantages in the present concentration of our strength on the hither side of the passes which would be forfeited, and some perilous responsibilities which would have to be incurred, in connexion with the proposed advance. For instance, the troops now quartered on our frontier are available equally for the repulse of foes from without, and for the suppression of insurrection from within; whereas every red-coat despatched beyond Jacobábád, and committed a hostage to fortune among an unfriendly race, would be so much strength taken from, so much anxiety added to, the internal garrison of India. That garrison would have to be largely increased. And whence are the men to be obtained?

It is no easy matter to find sufficient recruits for the English army on a peace footing, and we may well doubt whether England at any time, much less with a war on her hands in Europe, could afford to add a unit to the 70,000 men who constitute the standard of India's requirements according to existing arrangements.

But in the recent proceedings and present position of the Russians we can see nothing to call for a counter-demonstration from the Indian Government. We believe that the Emperor Alexander, apart from the necessities for quiescence imposed on him by an embarrassed exchequer, discontent in Poland, and the difficulties of carrying through the emancipation of the serfs, is positively desirous of refraining from further conquests, in order that he may have time for the consolidation of his power throughout the vast area stretching from the Aral Sea to Lake Issyk Kúl. At all events, the imperial professions of a wish for peace have been openly vindicated by the disgrace of the two generals who contrived that war with Bokhara should be unavoidable. After General Tcherniayeff's repulse from Juzak and the imprisonment of the ambassador at Bokhara, Russia had no choice but to take active measures for the redress of the national honour; and the march of General Romanovski to Juzak is no more to be wondered at than our own advance two years ago, under somewhat similar circumstances, into Bhután. From the slender data at our command it would be idle to speculate on the extent of the penalty which General Romanovski is likely to inflict on Bokhara; but we should not be surprised if he retired to Tashkend without insisting on any considerable cession of territory. Perhaps it may be objected that our view of Russia's pacific tendencies is good only for the life of the present autocrat.

The objection cannot be gainsaid; and, when another Emperor may arise, reproducing possibly the traditions of the ambitious Nicholas, we shall be prepared to admit the necessity of keeping a jealous watch on Russian doings. But in the meantime we would deprecate the exhibition of a temper unwarranted by the aspect of the actual conjuncture. Moreover, if we may venture to add our contribution to those forecasts of the future which time invariably belies, we must confess to a certain scepticism as to the probabilities, at any period within the coming half-century, of Russia's penetrating south of the Hindu Khush, either in warlike or peaceful guise. If we in India find it difficult, expensive, and dangerous to advance further from our resources, so must Russia. In the desolate sandy plains of Turkistán, and among the Usbegs of the Máwar-u-Nahr, she has a more awkward country in which to operate, and poorer and fiercer people with whom to deal, than we have in India. She cannot afford to subsidise, and she must tax, if it is only to feed her soldiers. All the passions and prejudices of Islam are arrayed against her, and the nearer she approaches India, the worse will be her entanglement. Even those to whom she is the greatest bugbear admit by implication that it will be impossible for her to reach Herat in any appreciable strength without the active assistance of Persia, and to our thinking the day when the Sháh shall have been induced into so suicidal a course will not be seen in the present generation. These difficulties must be as patent to Russia as to ourselves. Neither can she forget that, though by a concatenation of favourable circumstances, she might succeed in landing a well-ordered army at Kabul and Kandahar, nothing up to that point would have been gained but the ill-will of

England and the presence perhaps of English fleets in the Baltic and Black Seas. Between Russia and those rich plains, the hope of which could alone make it worth her while to enter Afghánistán, there would still be a *chevaux de frise* of bayonets, wielded by the same men who gave her a taste of their quality not long ago at Alma and at Inkermann, and who this time would be fighting on their own ground and with the perfection of military appliances at their command. Therefore we think it unlikely that for many years to come so much as a solitary Cossack will be seen across the Oxus. Should Russia still be possessed with the earth-hunger of which she has been accused, and seek to obtain an expansion of territory for Siberia towards the genial south, we imagine that she will prefer to advance on China from the seaboard, and from the line of the Amur, rather than on India. In the one case she will find an easy, in the other a very tough morsel to digest.

We do not shrink from the conclusion to which these arguments all point. We believe that with respect to Central Asia the Indian Government can do no wiser thing than fold its hands and sit still. By all means let it obtain information, detailed and accurate, regarding the course of events beyond the mountains; but let no decisive action of any kind be taken until England can see more clearly what there is that she should do. The materials are not wanting for the formation of an effective intelligent department. There is the news-writer at Kabul, whose diaries, on the whole, give a faithful picture of all that passes in Afghánistán; and, as regards tidings from the other States of Central Asia, there are Panjábi merchants and travellers, whose somewhat hyperbolical accounts can from time to time be checked by the despatch of specially selected scouts. Presuming that Lord Lawrence must have already pressed these sources of information into his service, we think there is nothing more at present to be done. We would be quiet now, in order that we may act with greater vigour when the time for action comes. Every day of peace and economy that India enjoys strengthens our moral and material hold on the country; and England may be congratulated that Sir John Lawrence has clung to this truth through good report and evil report. His policy is of too sober and practical a complexion to hit the taste of our impetuous countrymen in the tropics, who freely charge him with ignorant indifference to the perils gathering against the State in Chinese Tartary, in Afghánistán, and in Russia. But inaction in this instance is not identical with unconcern.

NOTE BY THE EDITOR.

Bhútán, the first of the States of which the foregoing Essay treats, soon settled down into undisturbed relations with the British Government; and the territory whose annexation Mr. Wyllie describes, has remained a part of the British Empire. In the Persian Gulf, the second subject of the Essay, affairs are still liable to periodical complications. The Wahábís continue to give trouble; and for several years the fanatics of the same sect in India proved a source of serious disquiet. The recent history of Afghánistán, the third question dealt with, will be continued in the following Essay. The relations of Russia with Khiva and Bokhara are now matters of European rather than of Indian diplomacy, and the results of the late Russian Expedition, ending with the fall and temporary occupation of Khiva, are sufficiently well known. In Kashgar, now generally spoken of as Eastern Turkistán, the Muhammadan ruler has established himself on a strong *de facto* basis. He has been recognised by the Government of India; and after sending a mission to the Viceroy, a return Envoy, in the person of Mr Douglas Forsyth, C.B., of the Civil Service, was despatched with a well-appointed suite in 1873 to conclude a mercantile treaty. Mr. Forsyth was well received, and has successfully accomplished his work. The text of the Treaty has just been published, and the Envoy is now (April 1874) on his journey back to India.—W. W. H.

MASTERLY INACTIVITY.[1]

1869.

FEW regions in the world have claims on our interest comparable in extent and variety to those which Central Asia possesses. As the eye travels southward from Orenburg to Pesháwar, there is a fresh picture at every stage of the country. First, steppe and desert, scanty herbage or deep sand, vast expanses vexed by mirage and simoom; the home of marauding nomads, in whose hordes survive unchanged the Mongols of Chinghiz-Khán, the Túrks of Atilla and Timur-Lung, myriads of barbaric horsemen, ready as ever, if civilisation would but give them the chance, to again obliterate all the kingdoms of Asia in ruin, again surge in resistless tumult to the shores of the Baltic and the Danube. Then, rivers, the ancient rivers Oxus and Jaxartes, rolling, turbid and yellow, through shifty channels to their rest in the Aral Sea. And between these fertilising floods, like 'a jewel set in sand,' the oasis-lands of the Máwar-u-Nahr, teeming with every crop and fruit that a temperate climate, kindly soil, and abundant irrigation can produce; rich too in the renown wherewith bygone dynasties and the fanaticism of modern Islam have combined to clothe the names of Bokhara and Samarcand, of Ferghana and Kharesm. Lastly, Afgháni stán, a mass of barren rocks for the most part, and stupendous mountain-ranges crowned with eternal snow, yet rejoicing here and there in green-

[1] 'The Fortnightly Review,' December 1, 1869.

wood valleys, lovely as a dream; its people, the physical perfection of humanity, and bearing in their faces strange confirmation of the tradition that refers a part at least of their lineage to Jews of the Dispersion, transported hither from Babylon by successors of Nebuchadnezzar. In Central Asia philology has discovered the cradle of that great Indo-Germanic race, from which conquering Anglo-Saxons and conquered Hindus are equally descended. In Central Asia, Alexander of Macedon founded a sovereignty, the traces of which are locally extant to this day, as well in the freshness of the great 'Sikandar's' fame, as in the Greek characters inscribed on the old coins which a Túrkish beauty strings round her neck. Across Central Asia, as neutral ground, the Romans of the Byzantine empire stretched a hand to the Chinese monarchs of the Han dynasty, and the recollection of that period serves to explain the historic awe with which every Tartar still turns to Constantinople—'Rúm' or Rome still in his phraseology—as the seat of an omnipotence not to be gainsaid. Central Asia, in the eighth century, became the eastern terminus of Saracenic conquest; here the idolatry of China and the monotheism of Arabia met in sanguinary collision; and each prescribed bounds not to be trangressed by the other. Central Asia, in the middle ages, held so large a leaven of Christianity, according to the Nestorian form, that Popes busied themselves in quests of an imaginary priest-king, whose odd cognomen of Prester John sends a vague familiar echo even to the ears of the present generation. Christianity nowadays has wholly disappeared from the scene, but not so the clash of rival empires contending for supremacy. Two powers at this moment are again in motion, mightier than any that have preceded them in the same field; and on the issue of their meeting hang consequences most momentous, not only to the continent of Asia but to all mankind. One of these powers is Great Britain; her antagonist is Russia.

The approach of Russia's Siberian frontier towards India, has for half a century filled English statesmen with alarm. To fend it off by artificial barriers, innumerable schemes of diplomacy have been woven, and repeated wars with Afghánistán and with Persia have been undertaken, costing thousands of valuable lives, and over twenty millions of money. In this cause was encountered the greatest disaster which has ever befallen the British arms. The shock which the Kabul massacre gave to our prestige in India remained vivid enough sixteen years afterwards to inspirit discontented Sepoys into mutiny, and even now has not altogether been forgotten. Yet, despite of all our efforts, Russia's progress has not been arrested by one inch of space, or for a single hour of time. On the contrary, the strides of her southward march, since the Crimean war, and especially during the last five years, have been enormous. At present (1869) her troops are in occupation of Samarcand, and dominate all the three Khanates of the Máwar-u-Nahr. Her influence extends to the Oxus, and nothing now remains to separate the Cossack from the Sepoy save only Afghánistán. Hence to us the importance of that territory—through it we feel the palpable presence of Russia. Hence also our communications with Afghánistán are no longer matter of local Indian politics, which the British public may incuriously leave to fortune for settlement. They now touch the relations subsisting between the imperial cabinets of

London and St. Petersburg, and may at any time produce some 'question' in which Parliament and the people shall find themselves very deeply concerned.

On this ground I venture once more to invite popular attention to recent events in Afghánistán. Hitherto, I am aware, the majority of my countrymen has been much of a mind with Goldsmith's squire, who 'no more troubled his head about Hyder Ally, or Ally Cawn, than about Ally Croaker.' It is a natural aversion, nor should I care to brave it but for a sustaining sense that the uncouth names of men and places in which my chronicle deals represent forces charged with mischief to the national peace. Ordinarily, the intestine brawls of a nation of poverty-stricken and semi-savage mountaineers would be of little interest to anyone; but when they come to affecting the course of English policy towards one of the greatest military powers of Europe, the warning, '*tua res agitur*,' may well be impressed on exery tax-payer.

The death, in 1863, of the famous Dost Muhammad was followed, as every student of Afghán affairs had predicted it would be, by a fierce scramble among his sons for the inheritance. The earlier incidents of this fratricidal contest have been already described.[1] I resume the tangled thread of the story from the issue of the battle on the 10th May, 1866. In the pause that then ensued, the position of the principal competitors was as follows:—Sher Alí, Amír of Afghánistán by the double right of paternal selection and of the acknowledgment which all men, including his rival brethren, had in the first instance accorded to his accession, was at

[1] 'Edinburgh Review,' January 1867, which forms the preceding Essay in this volume.

Kandahar, still reeling under the disastrous recoil of the blow at Sayyidábád, by which he had vainly hoped to recover possession of his lost capital. Afzal Khán, also calling himself Amír of Afghánistán in virtue of primogeniture and of his occupation of the royal citadel, was at Kabul, having by his side his son, Abdul Rahmán, and his full-brother, Azím Khán, by whose allied arms he had been recently rescued from Sher Alí's grasp. Beyond Kabul, in the territory lying between the mountains of the Hindu Khush and the river Oxus, which may best be described by the name of Balkh, a new potentate had unexpectedly sprung into existence in the person of Faiz Muhammad, a younger prince of the Barukzai house, who aspired to convert the lieutenant's commission he held over that country into an autonomy, independent of any control, whether from Kabul or from Kandahar. The conclusion, therefore, to which matters appeared for the time to have arrived was a dismemberment of Afghánistán between three separate powers; the north to Faiz Muhammad, centre to Afzal Khán, and south with west to Sher Alí. But this superficial view needs certain corrections. We must note that Faiz Muhammad had not in himself strength to maintain his bold attitude of isolation for any considerable period; and, in the next place, that Afzal Khán, in spite of the outward observances of sovereignty which surrounded him, was in truth a nonentity, set up by Azím Khán as a convenient and decorous screen to cover the motive power of his own superior will. These deductions made, we find the factions in the field reduced practically to two; one headed by Sher Alí at Kandahar, the other by Azím Khán at Kabul. In the rivalry between these two parties, Sher Alí's right pitted against Azím Khán's ambition, the whole civil war of Afghánistán has almost from the outset been comprised.

Absolute and complete as Sher Alí's late defeat had been, he neither despaired, nor had any need to despair, of his fortunes. The wholesome spur of adversity had quickened his sullen nature, and he applied himself with resolute activity to the task of organising a force for the prompt renewal of hostilities. Besides Kandahar, he still held the whole westward country up to the Persian border; and even towards Kabul, whence his danger lay, the fortress of Khelát-i-Ghilzai was yet in his possession, constituting for him an outpost of greater natural strength than that of the enemy at Mukhar, which it faced. At Herat he could depend upon his second son, Yakub Khán, a youth of remarkable shrewdness and energy, to send him every man that could be safely spared from the garrison of that important city. Present with him in Kandahar he had his full-brother Sharíf Khán, fickle and untrustworthy in temper, but not without value as a source of pecuniary loans, and as an instrument of extorting revenue from the people. From Balkh he justly calculated on obtaining, sooner or later, Faiz Muhammad's active co-operation; and in Kabul itself there were not a few persons of great influence corresponding with him regularly, and only biding their opportunity to rejoin his cause. Above all he held distinct assurance that the Anglo-Indian Government, though on terms of civil communication with his foes, had hitherto refused to recognise any one but himself as Amír. On the other hand, almost all his guns had been captured, and he was in great straits for small-arms and for money. New cannon he might certainly get cast, after tedious delay, by the artificers at Kandahar; but for the other two essentials of a campaign, where was he to turn? He had already tried the English. One of the first acts of his reign had been to send an envoy to Pesháwar, praying for a grant of muskets. And the prayer had been rejected, notwithstanding that he had then been undisputed sovereign of all Afghánistán, and that Oriental custom would have justified the British Government in regarding his recent accession to the throne as a fit occasion for the issue of exceptional presents. There was little likelihood of his being more successful now when half his kingdom was rent from him, and round him bickered a flame of war, from which the English Viceroy insisted on keeping aloof. Remote, however, as the chance appeared of obtaining help from India, in no other direction was there any chance at all. This forlorn hope, therefore, Sher Alí determined again to essay. What his reasons may have been for taking a circuitous path towards his object, instead of writing directly to the British authorities at Pesháwar, it is unnecessary to inquire; suffice it, that he selected our news-writer at Kabul as the depositary of his desires.

The position of the functionary thus brought upon the stage was an anomalous one, hardly justifying Sher Alí's choice. The right vested by treaty in the Governor-General of deputing a native of India as envoy to the court of the ruler of Afghánistán, had been in abeyance since January 1864, when the last Vakíl returned to India, leaving a Munshí, or clerk, behind him to carry on the minor duties of the office. Difficulties arising from the civil war which immediately followed, and the fall of the capital into the hands of the insurgent faction, had prevented the despatch of a regular successor; and, meanwhile, the clerk-substitute continued sole representative of our power at Kabul. For his own safety this Munshí had regularly to make his obeisance at the Darbár, in which the usurping brothers, Afzal and Azím Khán, held on most afternoons a reception of chiefs, city notables, and newly-arrived travellers; but his place in the assembly was merely that of a simple news-writer. By such visits to the Bálá Hissár, by the exchange of private civilities with the principal inhabitants, by rambles through the public bazaars, and by resort generally to every available centre of information, he was expected to gather materials for a diary in the Persian language, which, twice a week, he transmitted by courier to our frontier officers at Pesháwar. Diplomatic powers he had none, though the temptation to assume them must at times have been irresistible.

In June and July, Sher Alí wrote three successive letters to the Munshí, asking him to explain to the British Government the extremity of his need, and the gratitude with which he would receive a gift of 6,000 muskets and a proportionate supply of money. His first letter was turned back by the enemy's line of sentries at Mukhar; the second, delayed for two months between Kandahar and Kabul, did not reach India till after the third; and both the second and the third were viewed and treated by the authorities in the Panjáb as forgeries, contrived by Azím Khán for the purpose of obtaining an insight into the British Government's real sentiments towards his rival. Consequently no reply was sent to the application. This, we must allow, was an unsatisfactory conclusion; but the doubts which dictated it were neither unnatural nor unreasonable. One letter was written in a combination of Persian language with English characters, and was without Sher Alí's seal of signature.

In both cases it was incomprehensible why Sher Alí, if he really were the author, instead of writing, as afterwards he actually did write, directly to the Commissioner by the short road which he commanded to our frontier, should have preferred to betake himself to the unusual intervention of a news-writer, and the long war-blocked route through Kabul. The fact of our Munshí having forwarded the letters as genuine proved nothing; in the perilous position he held at Kabul, bolder men than himself, and owning a higher stake in our interests, might have seen through a ruse of Azím Khán's without daring to expose it. Several months elapsed before the authenticity of the documents came to light. The regrettable part of the incident is that Sher Alí, who had anticipated nothing better than an explicit refusal, and who was ignorant of the suspicions attaching to his missives, seems to have allowed himself to interpret the Viceroy's silence in a sense too favourable to his own hopes.

Turning now to the head-quarters of the opposition at Kabul, we light upon a scene of still greater perplexity and trouble. Afzal Khán, the titular Amír, was rapidly drinking himself to death; and between the two other members of the triumvirate, quarrels were vehement and interminable. Abdul Rahmán, the Hotspur of the party, conscious of military services at least equal to those of his uncle, ill brooked the state of pupilage to which Azím Khán's assumption of superior wisdom would have consigned him. His father vainly tried to be peacemaker: maudlin entreaties that State affairs might all be left to Azím were not calculated to allay the young man's indignation. Nothing could have kept his reluctant neck in the yoke but the inexorable necessity of the times. For, notwithstanding their victory at Sayyidábád, the confederates were beset by danger on every side. Accounts of Sher Alí's preparations and capacity for a new campaign came to them with all the exaggerations of Eastern rumour. Faiz Muhammad they had hoped to cajole or coerce by the hold they had on his full-brother, Wali Muhammad, in Kabul; but day by day this hope diminished, and it soon became clear that they would have to face a coalition between him and Sher Alí, the one descending against them from the north, the other simultaneously marching up from the south. Between the two fires their case looked critical indeed. Even the territory they called their own was held with difficulty; for the Ghilzai tribe about Jalálábád had risen in insurrection, declaring for Sher Alí, and the disturbances reached within five-and-twenty miles of the city of Kabul. Worse still, they were short of money, and the arbitrary measures they adopted to remedy the deficiency, irritated every class of the community against them. Nobles, whom Sher Alí's haughty demeanour and ungovernable temper had stung into revolt, discovered that Azím Khán could be not less overbearing in manner, and that, if Sher Alí had been quick to resume, and loth to make grants of the crown lands, these tempting objects, the promised rewards of treason, were now retained by Azím Khán in a gripe quite as miserly, and additionally odious by reason of its ingratitude and fraud. Priests murmured against the diversion of their religious endowments to purposes of State. Soldiers, to whom a year's pay was due, were obliged to take half that amount in quittance of the claim; nor was the edge of their discontent the less keen for a belief, likely enough to be true, that at their expense, and out of the public coffers, Azím Khán was laying by a private provision for himself against a rainy day. Agriculture fell under assessments, heavy in amount, and collected before harvest. Traders, already hard hit by Faiz Muhammad's detention in Balkh of caravans which they expected from beyond the Oxus, were subjected to double customs duties, an endless succession of forced loans never to be refunded either in interest or in principal, and an indiscriminate impressment of the camels on which they depended for the carriage of their goods. The poorer people starved under a monopoly of grain, which raised the necessaries of life to famine prices. Robberies in the open street, and burglaries at night, were frequent; assassinations were not uncommon. No one looked for justice; might was the sole measure of each man's right. A few ambitious spirits found their interest in the continuance of such disorder; but generally the inhabitants were weary of war and its accompaniments.

So matters stood when Sir John Lawrence's letter of the 11th July reached Kabul.[1] This, it will be remembered, was in reply to a communication, nominally proceeding from Afzal Khán, but inspired of course by Azím Khán, in which the British Government was invited to extend its valuable friendship to the writer. The Governor-General's letter commenced with an expression of profound regret for the dissensions by which the great house of the Barukzais was torn, and professed strong desire for the maintenance of good-will between the Afghán and English nations; but in substance it was a very clear and emphatic refusal to break off our alliance with Amír Sher Alí.

The arrival of so important a despatch necessarily caused deep sensation in Kabul. In the palace it produced consternation and bitter resentment; but in all

[1] See *ante*, p. 48.

other quarters there was universal glee over the discomfiture of the tyrannical rulers. Azím Khán was at no pains to conceal his anger. He sent for our news-writer, and straightly cross-questioned him as to the Viceroy's intention in addressing Afzal Khán as *Sardár* only, or Prince, instead of *Amír*, or King. Upon this text he launched on to a furious tirade against English ingratitude and selfishness. The Munshí bowed in silence before the storm; he had no authority to explain any passage in the Viceroy's letter.

Azím Khán's wrath was not of the kind that evaporates in mere words. He looked round for a victim on whom his fury might be more safely indulged than on a British subject. Out of the Barukzai family the foremost man in Afghánistán was Muhammad Rafik. Generally it may be taken for granted that any prominent leader in Afghán politics must of necessity be either a son or grandson of Dost Muhammad—so completely has the strength of the country been absorbed into that house. Muhammad Rafik's unique position, in exception to the rule, came from his being the best soldier, the best statesman, the best diplomatist of his time. It was his defection from Sher Alí's cause in the preceding autumn that first and most powerfully turned the tide in favour of the confederates. He had done nothing in the interval to forfeit the confidence of Azím Khán. The blandishments by which Sher Alí had striven hard to win back his allegiance had been wasted on him. He told his friends that the breach between the Amír and himself was irreparable. Unconsciously foreshadowing his doom, he said that he would die sooner than return to his former lord. But he was known to be a warm admirer of English ways, and this, to the passion-blinded eyes of Azím

Khán, was in itself a crime. Some childish notion that the laying low of so illustrious a head might awe the English into a more deferential attitude towards himself, seems also to have had a share in deciding the direction of the despot's ferocity. The blow fell without a word of warning. On the morning of the 27th of August, Muhammad Rafik stood secure in his place, chief pillar of the State; at noon he was seized and hurried to prison; before one o'clock he was dead, strangled. His body was thrown naked on a dunghill, and lay there for four days, none daring to touch it. His wives and daughters, with unveiled faces and bare feet, were driven from their home into the streets. All his property was confiscated, and one of his followers, supposed to have knowledge of a secret hoard, was tortured to death.

Muhammad Rafik and his household, though the first, and probably the most innocent, were not the only sufferers at this crisis. Azím Khán's hand, once raised, was not to be lightly stayed. Soon he had as many as a hundred and fifty persons in his prisons, suspected, more or less justly, of intriguing with the enemy; and the penalty of death, which he freely administered, sometimes to batches of several at a time, had in his hands a secrecy and an absence of preliminary trial which, among civilised communities, would have earned for it a harsher name than execution. He established a reign of terror at Kabul.

Meanwhile the Amír at Kandahar was again speculating on assistance from British India. On the 10th of September Sher Alí addressed direct to the Commissioner of Peshávar a letter, which was at once recognised as genuine, repeating his original prayer for six thousand muskets, and cash in proportion. The Commissioner replied, saying that he had forwarded the letter for the Viceroy's orders, which, when received, would be duly communicated to the Amír. But the Viceroy, in his turn, postponed issuing orders of any kind on the subject, and hence Sher Alí's appeal remained practically unanswered. It may well be asked why Sir John Lawrence in this instance departed from the outspoken frankness which had so markedly characterised all his previous dealings with Afghánistán. The answer is easily given. Sir John Lawrence abided as firmly as ever by his determination to abstain from aiding either Sher Alí against Azím Khán or Azím Khán against Sher Alí, so long as each of them respectively maintained a similar quiescence towards British India. But Azím Khán had of late assumed an air so offensive that it began to be doubtful whether the principle of self-defence might not ere long compel us, however reluctantly, to act against him by extending some help to his rival. It was not merely that he made a habit in the Kabul Darbár of railing against the British Government in a strain of unbridled insolence and vindictiveness; verbiage of that kind might be overlooked with contempt; but he was doing his best by actual deeds to stir up against us, in an organised league of holy war, the numerous predatory and fanatical tribes whose mountain-fastnesses overhang our north-west frontier. Sir John Lawrence had little fear that this effort of spite would be successful; but there was none the less need to be on the watch for its issue, and to reserve in readiness the means of checking it, which Sher Alí's application offered. Still no inkling of the new contingency was, or could be, given to Sher Alí. His request was not directly negatived; but this was all: it received not the faintest sign of encouragement.

Both the contending factions in Afghánistán occupied the autumn and early winter in equipping and despatching reinforcements for the positions from which their respective armies confronted each other. The Kandahar troops at Khelát-i-Ghilzai grew steadily in numbers, discipline, and confidence; for Sher Alí was able to concentrate all his energies on a single point. The progress of the enemy's camp at Múkhar was feebler and more fitful; a spirit of disaffection, desertion, and mutiny kept thinning the ranks of Kabul, and the attention of the confederate leaders was distracted by the revolt of the Ghilzais in the east, and yet more by Faiz Muhammad's threatened descent from the north. Between these later sources of anxiety, Azím Khán's son, Surwar Khán, was left for months hovering with divided aim. Before he could effect more than a skin-deep settlement of the disturbances around Jalálábád and Kúnar, he was hurriedly recalled to undertake the more arduous task of defending the passes of the Hindu Khúsh against Faiz Muhammad; and his back was no sooner turned on the Ghilzais than they again broke out in more serious insurrection than ever.

By November all the elements of retributive violence, which had been long gathering round Kabul, were simultaneously astir, but the supreme peril lay in the combined action of Sher Alí and Faiz Muhammad. Impelled from opposite bases to a common goal, the forces of Kandahar and of Balkh, two moving masses of menace, seemed closing in on the vessel of the confederates' fortunes with fatal precision. To complete the horror of the situation, rumours darkened the air that England's patience had been at last exhausted, and that she was now permitting Sher Alí to recruit his invading strength from the arsenals and treasuries of India. Afzal Khán gave himself up to despair; and even the stubborn spirit of Azím Khán was so far shaken as to consent to a parley. Messengers were sent to Sher Alí, proposing peace on terms of a partition of the country—Sher Alí to retain Kandahar and Herat, and the confederates to keep Kabul with Balkh added. A marked improvement at the same time came over Azím Khán's demeanour towards the British Government. He soon ascertained by inquiry from our news-writer that the report of British intervention in Sher Alí's favour was baseless, and now, with the chance before him of becoming once more a fugitive adventurer, he could no longer afford the luxury of a one-sided enmity with his powerful but placable neighbour. Moreover, if it be true, as there is reason for supposing, that an emissary, whom he had three months previously despatched *viâ* Kúndúz to ask assistance from the Russian general at Tashkend, returned just at this period with an unsatisfactory answer, such a rebuff from one of the two great European Powers, between which his political loves and hates were perpetually oscillating, would naturally set him in motion with unabashed assurance towards the other. Dangers and disappointments were bringing out the prudent side of the Afghán character in Azím Khán. He was by no means cowed, however. He still turned upon his foes with a courage and vigour which it is impossible not to admire. Ignoring the lateral diversion offered by the turbulence of the Ghilzais, and abandoning Kabul to such protection as Afzal Khán's presence might afford, he absorbed every fighting man for field service at one or other of the two points where a stand was essentially necessary, viz., at Bamian against Faiz Muhammad and at Múkhar against Sher Alí. By this means the strength of Surwar Khán's camp at the former place was brought up to 7,000 men, while that of the southern force, which was to be commanded jointly by Azím Khán himself and by Abdul Rahmán, rose to 9,000—numbers in each case inferior to those of the invader, but eked out by compensating circumstances. At Bamian the mountain defiles afforded special facilities for defensive warfare, and at Múkhar there was a better park of artillery than could be opposed to it from Kandahar. If therefore Surwar Khán could only keep the Balkh army in check for a time, Azím Khán hoped that his own generalship and Abdul Rahmán's gallantry might suffice to give a good account of Sher Alí in the interval. The game he saw, though running against him, was not yet lost. He pacified the discontent of the soldiery by a timely issue of pay, and assumed the chief command at Múkhar about the 20th December.

On the other side Sher Alí did not personally take the field so soon as had been expected. He was detained in Kandahar till Christmas Day. The last weeks of the Amír's stay in that city were clouded by the sudden defection of his brother, Sharíf Khán. One more change of sides perpetrated by a chieftain whose inconstancy, even among Afgháns, was already a by-word, would not under ordinary circumstances be worth noticing; but in this instance the direction of Sharíf Khán's flight gave an adventitious importance to his eccentricities. He came southward into Beluchistán, and sought asylum from the Khán of Khelát at Quettá, thereby disquieting the British frontier in Upper Sind.

It was at this juncture that the Government of Bombay submitted for the consideration of the Government of India proposals of such magnitude as to demand record in their place of chronological order, let the inroad on the continuity of Afghán history be what it may. The spectacle of Sher Alí and Azím Khán, each in full spring at the other's throat among snows soon to be reddened by decisive battle, must be set aside for a while that we may pause in the serene atmosphere of British council-chambers. The question of the occupation of Quettá implies nothing less than a revolution in the system of India's military defences.

The plan originated in 1856 with the late General John Jacob, an officer whose assumption of infallibility did prejudice to his unquestionable talents, his sleepless devotion to the public service, and his real knowledge of the Belúch border. At that time Persia, either with or without instigation from Russia, had just seized the Afghán fortress of Herat, and England was about to embark on the campaign which ultimately extorted from the Sháh a restitution of the so-called 'Gate of India.' General Jacob availed himself of the opportunity to offer suggestions to the then Governor-General, Lord Canning, for the better protection of the frontier. He declared that if the red line of England's boundary was to retain its position on the map, there was absolute necessity for our occupying posts in advance of it. 'A war,' he said, '*within* our own territory with a European army might be ruinous to our reputation, and might entirely undermine our strength, although that strength might have sufficed successfully to meet a world in arms in a field *beyond* our own boundary.' His argument proceeded,—that there were but two great roads by which a modern army could invade India from the north-west, viz., the Khaibar Pass and the Bolán Pass; that our existing outposts were on the hither or Indian side of both these passes—at Pesháwar as regards the Khaibar, and at Jacobábád in respect of the Bolán; that at Pesháwar we might well remain as we were, watching the mouth of the defile, but that from Jacobábád we were in self-preservation bound to advance. The first step would be to take advantage of that article in our treaty with the Khán of Khelát which permits the cantonment of British troops in any part of his territory, and immediately to occupy Quettá; connected with which measure, as necessary consequences, would come a continuation of the Sind railway to the foot of the Bolán Pass, and the construction of a good road through the pass. Next, we should take a body of Belúch irregulars into our pay, who, politically, would be useful as a link of connection with the native inhabitants, and who, in a military capacity, might be to us what the Cossacks are to a Russian army. Having thus quietly established ourselves in Beluchistán, we should subsidise the Afgháns, and pave the way for a peaceable occupation of Herat. With a proper garrison at Quettá, and a fortress held by 20,000 men at Herat, we should not only block the Bolán route, but operate with destructive effect on the flanks and rear of any invader attempting to proceed by way of the Khaibar. And then 'India would be as firmly locked in our grasp as if surrounded by the ocean.' Such, briefly stated, was the project, now, after ten years' suspension, revived in official form by General Jacob's pupil and successor on the Sind frontier, Sir Henry Green. Since its original publication it had been the theme of endless controversy in the pu' lic press, and its general principles had secured the favourable opinion of such weighty authorities as Sir Henry Rawlinson and Sir Justin Sheil. Thus a special responsibility, over and above that arising from the intrinsic importance of the subject, attached to the Governor of Bombay, when, by seriously recommending that Sir Henry Green should be allowed to take preliminary action, he identified the dignity of his government with the furtherance of a scheme widely known, generally popular, and strong in the sanction of great names. Sir Bartle Frere's proposal on reaching Calcutta was immediately laid by the Viceroy before his council. Sir John Lawrence explained that he had for years been familiar with General Jacob's arguments, that he had never recognised their validity hitherto, and that he saw nothing in the present condition of Central Asia to lead him to a different conclusion now. If the strategic advantages of occupying Quettá were doubtful, some of the political disadvantages were obvious. The expense would be enormous, and he should alarm the jealousy, not only of the Afghán as a nation, but of the Persian Court also. Besides, it would always be open to us to occupy Quettá and subsidise the Beluchís at any future period, when the imminence of a real danger to our power might render such a step expedient. 'In the meantime,' Sir John concluded, 'I am absolutely opposed to this undertaking.' The discussion was taken up by two councillors, whose opinions on such a topic were entitled to the utmost respect. Sir William Mansfield united to the military talents which had raised him to the chief command of her Majesty's army in India, a statesmanlike comprehension of the internal condition and prospects of our Eastern Empire, some knowledge of Russian policy derived from diplomatic employment at Constantinople and at Warsaw, and an intimate personal familiarity with the Afghán frontier, acquired when he was winning his spurs as a regimental officer at Pesháwar. Similarly, the brilliant reputation which Sir Henry Durand had won in many an Indian Darbár and battle-field was enhanced by his particular experience in the affairs of Afghánistán. Years ago, as a young engineer of Lord Keane's force, he had laid the powder-bags which blew open the gates of Ghazní; and, more recently, as Lord Elgin's Secretary for Foreign Affairs, he had taken a large share in the direction of our later relations with the Barukzai dynasty. Both these distinguished officers gave hearty support to the view taken by the Viceroy. Sir William Mansfield calculated that the occupation of Quetta, necessitating as it would the maintenance of communication with the Indus by posts at Dádar and Jacobábád, and probably at some intermediate places, could not be safely carried out 'with less than 3,000 British infantry and artillery, 4,000 native infantry, and 2,000 cavalry, including a regiment of dragoons—9,000 in all, or 7,000 in excess of the force which is now found to be more than ample for the defence of the Sind frontier, the same being all native, and therefore comparatively of a cheap description.'

Moreover, a fort would be needed at Quettá to cover the magazine and treasure, and to be a *point d'appui* in case of accident, pending the arrival of reinforcements. Taken altogether, these arrangements represented an amount of expenditure so embarrassing to the finances of India, that to incur it, even in counteracting a Russian occupation of Kabul and Kandahar, would, in the Commander-in-chief's opinion, be of doubtful propriety so long as peace continued between England and Russia. And if war should arrive, was it certain, as a matter of pure strategy, that an advance to Quettá would be incumbent on us in that extremity? For his own part, Sir William was inclined to say :—

'The side whence to defend the Bolán Pass is not the western extremity, where the British cantonment would be cut off by a defile sixty-six miles long, through which its supports would have to advance, after a painful and exhausting march from the Indus and across a desert, but rather at the eastern extremity. For there a hostile force could be struck on the head before it could have time to deploy with the heavy *matériel*, without which a modern army cannot move, or hope to move, against such forces as we should array against it on any field we might choose between Shikárpur and Dádar. The desert would be in this manner turned into our most useful ally, instead of being a formidable difficulty. The latter would be the case if General Jacob's plan were adopted.'

Sir Henry Durand travelled to the same practical result as his colleague by a different route. He could easily 'conceive circumstances which might combine to render the partial or the entire occupation of Afghánistán necessary as a theatre for offensive operations on our part, in aid of Afghán resistance to invasion from the westward.' It was a region admirably adapted by nature for giving the fullest effect to the destructive warfare which Afgháns thus supported could wage, with small loss to themselves.

'I know,' he continued, 'that we could again seize Afghánistán, if it were advisable or necessary, and that, with our Indus frontier complete in its communications, parallel and perpendicular, no power on earth could shake us out of that country. I know, too, that, with the Afgháns friendly and cordial, we could, without the actual seizure of the country for ourselves, organise its defence in a most destructive manner against hostile invasions. But neither alternative is at present imposed on us as of the smallest necessity. . . . Any intervention now would be ill-timed, and is wholly uncalled for. It will be all that political and military considerations demand, if our lines of rail and river communication on the Indus frontier are rendered as perfect as it is easily in our power to make them ; so that, without our at present incurring the risk of complications with Afghán and Belúch tribes and politics, it may yet be in our power rapidly to mass, and securely to feed and support our forces, whether intended for operations above or below the passes. . . . If our position on the Indus frontier be one of unmistakable strength, it will long paralyse aggressive presumption.'

The remaining members of the Viceregal Council tendered their adhesion with the good-will that flowed from a similar conviction. And so the proposition from Bombay was unanimously rejected. But let no one suppose that this rejection gave a final quietus to the movement for the occupation of Quettá. Vigorous in the vitality of popular error, it to this day remains at the root of every discussion on Central Asia.

Another episode of the Calcutta cold weather of 1866–7 may also be fitted into its place here, before we return to the seat of war in Afghánistán. The intercourse of the British Government with that of Bokhara has not been so frequent or so amicable that the appearance of an ambassador from the Úsbeg metropolis, the head-quarters of Muslim bigotry, should be regarded as an ordinary event. Indeed, the past relations between the two powers might almost be summed up in the fact that two British officers, Colonel Stoddart and Captain Conolly, who had been sent to Bokhara during the Afghán war of 1839–42, to bar Russian progress by the organisation of a Tartar confederacy under the headship of Amír Nasr-ullah of Bokhara, had been barbarously seized by that Amír, and, after a long and cruel imprisonment, brutally murdered. The whirligig of time had now brought about its revenge; behold Nasr-ullah's successor, Muzaffar-ud-dín, spontaneously seeking the English as his only means of rescue from

Russian invasion! Utterly defeated at Idjar, on the 20th May, 1866, and expelled from Khojend on the 5th June, the Amír Muzaffar-ud-dín, in August, offered submission to Generals Kryjanovski and Romanovski with one hand, while with the other he sued to Sir John Lawrence for an offensive and defensive alliance against his conquerors. The person whom he selected as his representative on the latter mission was named Khojá Muhammad Parsá, and occupied at Bokhara the exalted office of Chief Muftí, or expounder of the law. This emissary, passing through Kabul, where he had a grand comparison of political notes with Azím Khán, reached Pesháwar on the 11th November, attended by twenty-two followers, and bearing letters and presents not only for the Lieutenant-Governor of the Panjáb, and the Governor-General of India, but also for their Majesties, the Queen of England and the Sultán of Turkey. The presents, though favourable specimens, probably, of the staple products of Bokhara, were more curious than valuable: They consisted of silk in pieces and in shawls, skins of kid and ermine, woollen rugs, and a few horses. The letter to the Lieutenant-Governor contained nothing beyond the usual civilities of Oriental correspondence, and a request that the bearer might be assisted on his journey. Proceeding to Calcutta, the envoy was admitted to the Viceroy's presence on the 9th January. Partly oppressed by the wonders of the civilisation which had whirled him down by rail from Delhi, a thousand miles in thirty-six hours, but still more haunted by doubts whether the deaths of Stoddart and Conolly might not be avenged on his own person, he had at first some difficulty in preserving the air of impassive tranquillity proper to his character. Quickly recovering himself, he delivered to Sir John Lawrence the letter intended for the Queen, as well as that addressed to Her Majesty's Vicegerent in India. In the one a hope was expressed that the Governor-General would interfere 'to relieve Muhammadans from Russian oppression,' and a pledge was added that the writer would follow any advice which his Excellency might be pleased to give. In the other, the Amír complained bitterly of Russian aggression, treachery, and violation of international law, as shown by the unprovoked seizure of Tashkend and other territory, and by the detention at Orenburg of one of his servants bearing the sacred character of an ambassador: he was determined, he said, to resist the enemy, by force of arms, to the utmost, but at the same time, in compliance with the Kurán's injunction, 'to consult with others and take advice,' he looked to her Majesty for advice and aid towards the expulsion of the Russians. Both these communications having been perused, it appeared odd that the envoy, while making no attempt to conceal the alarm with which his countrymen viewed the Russian advance, nevertheless abstained from any allusion to the request for British assistance which was so specifically urged in his credentials. At last, when pressed to name the precise object of his quest, he declared that he wanted nothing. The explanation soon followed. In journeying through Pesháwar he had met an agent of the Khán of Kokand, who had been despatched three years previously on a mission identical with his own, and who was then returning home. From him he had learned that nothing but disappointment was to be expected, whether at Calcutta or at Constantinople. Acting, therefore, on the discretionary power with which he believed himself to be vested, the envoy withdrew the prayer for help contained in his master's letters, and professed that he had no other object but to communicate sentiments of general friendship from the Bokhara Darbár to the British Government. Before the close of the audience the Viceroy, touched on the murder of Stoddart and Conolly, stigmatising it as a deed which covered the Amír of Bokhara with infamy in the eyes of all honest people. The envoy replied that the murder, if indeed those officers were murdered, was a very unworthy act, but that, for his own part, he at the time must have been quite a young man, with no official position, and that his master, the present Amír, must also have been a youth, and had not then succeeded to the sovereignty of the State. So terminated an interview possessing singular interest in the annals of Central Asia. Some days afterwards Sir John Lawrence issued to the envoy, for transmission to Bokhara, return presents of the usual kind, and a letter, in which the communication he had himself received from the Amír was answered as follows:—

'It is with much regret that I hear that your Majesty has been at war with the Russians, and that you believe that you have grounds for complaining of their oppression. But Bokhara is so distant from the confines of India, and the difficulties of communication which the intervening country presents are so formidable, that hitherto they have proved a bar to any freedom of intercourse, not only between our respective subjects, but also between your Majesty and the Government of India. I am, therefore, neither sufficiently well acquainted with the causes which have unfortunately produced a state of hostilities between Bokhara and Russia, nor with the present state of your Majesty's affairs, to be in a position to give your Majesty useful advice. And, therefore, though I am willing to be on friendly terms, and am desirous of the peace of your dominions, and am anxious to hear of the prosperity of your Majesty's rule, I am not able to render you effective aid, either by advice or in any other form. May God direct your Majesty in the proper course to pursue, and keep you in safety! Your Majesty's letter to the Queen of England and India shall be sent on.'

The promise conveyed in these concluding words was duly fulfilled. The appeal to Her Majesty reached its destination, but, as hardly needs to be added, it elicited no response of any kind. The British Government's position in regard to the war between Russia and Bokhara had already been sufficiently defined in the Viceroy's reply, and there was nothing in the past conduct of Bokhara or in her rank among the kingdoms of the East which at all entitled her ruler to the rare honour of an English Queen's sign-manual. No hopes of such condescension were held out to the envoy. He lingered in Calcutta sight-seeing till the 19th of February, and then proceeded to Bombay, whence he was to make his way to Constantinople for the prosecution of that part of his mission which was addressed to the Sublime Porte.

From these digressions regarding Quettá and Bokhara we must now revert to the scene of conflict in Afghánistán.

The new year opened brightly for Sher Ali's prospects. On the 6th of January, 1867, his ally, Faiz Muhammad, descending from Balkh, forced the defensive position occupied by Azím Khán's son, Surwar Khán, and drove the Kabul army back in demoralised rout on Bamian. There can be little doubt that if Faiz Muhammad had followed up this success immediately, he might without difficulty have swept through the passes, overwhelmed all opposition, and captured Kabul. Instead, he halted to check a disturbance in his rear, created by Azím Khán's staunch partisan, the Usbeg chieftain of Badakshán. Surwar Khán thus obtained breathing-time to re-form his shattered forces and make a second stand for the defence of the capital. Faiz Muhammad, when he again advanced, had lost his opportunity without knowing it. He anticipated an easy repetition of his victory over Surwar Khán, and a triumphant meeting with Sher Alí under the walls of Kabul; but, in the midst of these flattering fancies, his foot was stayed and his hand unnerved by intelligence from the south too disastrous to be readily credible.

It was true, nevertheless. The stars in their courses had once more fought against Sher Alí. That unlucky prince had issued from Khelát-i-Ghilzai at the head of his army on the 12th of January, and on the 16th he had sustained a crushing defeat from Azím Khán.

The details of the engagement are not worth our attention. There seems to have been more treachery than fighting, and the loss on either side was trivial; but the result, for all that, was quite as decisive as any amount of heroism could have made it. Sher Alí abandoned Khelát-i-Ghilzai to its fate and fled to Kandahar. He paused at Kandahar for one day only, and then evacuated that city also, without a blow. Attended by a mere handful of troopers, he continued his flight towards Herat, now the only direction—setting aside Faiz Muhammad's ambiguous allegiance in Balkh—where the vestiges of sovereign authority were yet preserved to him. Azím Khán and Abdul Rahmán entered Kandahar as conquerors on the 26th of January, and were joined there by the turn-coat Sharíf Khán, whose departure for this purpose from Quettá was a welcome relief to the Belúch border. All central and southern Afghánistán was now in the possession of the confederacy, and the north might be expected to follow, for, in Sher Ali's present disability to resume the offensive from Herat, Azím Khán's whole strength was free to cope with Faiz Muhammad on advantageous terms, and compel a surrender of Balkh.

The first use which the confederates made of the new position they had attained was to send formal announcement of their successes to the British Government. Their letter, running in the name of Afzal Khán, as Amír of Afghánistán, and dated February 3rd, was substantially a challenge for the Viceroy's congratulations. In forwarding it to Calcutta, the Lieutenant-Governor of the Panjáb added his opinion that 'the concession of the title of Amír in our correspondence with Afzal Khán should no longer be withheld.' Sir Donald Macleod was clearly right in this matter. The time had come when, unless we recognised Afzal Khán as Amír, our news-writer would be turned out of Kabul, and we should be at open rupture with the party then uppermost in Afghánistán ; that is, we should be landed in the dilemma either of actively espousing Sher Ali's cause, and forcing his supremacy on a people three-fourths of whom disowned it ; or of tamely renouncing all hold on a country in whose destinies much of our own future was involved. But the Lieutenant-Governor's suggestion has its importance as proving that Sir John Lawrence, so far from being ahead of all the world in eagerness to recognise the *de facto* rulers of Kabul—an accusation which has been often made—actually on this point lagged behind his most responsible adviser. In the Viceroy's reply to Afzal Khán, dated February 25th, that chief was styled Amír, not of Afghánistán at large, but only of Kabul and Kandahar, the territories actually in his grasp ; also the congratulations addressed to the conqueror were tempered with a regret and even a preference for his rival so nakedly declared that the records of diplomacy might be searched in vain for a parallel. The most important clauses were as follows :—

'My friend! The British Government has hitherto maintained a strict neutrality between the contending parties in Afghánistán. Rumours, I am told, have reached the Kabul Darbár of assistance having been granted by me to Amír Sher Alí Khán. I take this opportunity to request your Highness not to believe such idle tales. Neither men, nor arms, nor money, nor assistance of any kind have ever been supplied by my Government to Amír Sher Alí Khán. Your Highness and he, both equally unaided by me, have fought out the battle, each upon your own resources. I purpose to continue the same policy for the future. If, unhappily, the struggle for supremacy in Afghánistán has not yet been brought to a close, and hostilities are again renewed, I shall still side with neither party. My friend! as I told your Highness in my former letter, the relations of the British Government are with the actual rulers of Afghánistán. Therefore, so long as Amír Sher Alí Khán holds Herat, and maintains friendship with the British Government, I shall recognise him as ruler of Herat, and shall reciprocate his amity. But, upon the same principle, I am prepared to recognise your Highness as Amír of Kabul and Kandahar, and I frankly offer your Highness in that capacity, the peace and the good-will of the British Government.'

The letter concluded with a proposal that a Muhammadan gentleman of rank and character should at once be deputed to Kabul as British representative, in relief of the news-writer whose temporary and imperfect occupation of the post has already been explained.

Concurrently with this interchange of state papers between the British Viceroy and the Kabul rulers, a minor and indirect correspondence was also in progress between the same potentates through the channel of our news-writer. It has been already explained that Azím

Khán, at the time when he was preparing to march out of Kabul, with small hopes of a successful issue to the campaign, had hedged against the probability of defeat by forswearing his former rancour against the British Government and adopting instead an ostentatious desire to conciliate. In this game he had played the old traditional opening of Afghán craft. He had written a note to our Munshí on the 15th of November, dwelling on the victorious advance of Russia, affecting alarm for the independence of Afghánistán, and looking to England for rescue. The reply which Sir John Lawrence instructed the Munshí to make reached Kabul on the 14th of February, when, in consequence of the absence at Kandahar of both Azím Khán and Abdul Rahmán, the capital was in fact as well as in name under the administration of Amír Afzal. The Munshí told Amír Afzal 'that the most friendly relations existed between the British and Russian Governments, and that there was no reason to apprehend that Russia had any wish to molest those who were in friendly relations with Great Britain.' This message was immediately communicated by the Kabul Darbár to that of Bokhara. Afzal Khán was bound to the royal house of Bokhara by old political intimacy and the domestic ties of intermarriage, and therefore it was not only natural that he should advise the Úsbeg court on such a subject, but also probable that his advice would be inspired by perfect good faith. What he is alleged, upon credible authority, to have written is that, as far as he could make out, if the Russians took all Bokhara to-morrow, the English would be rather pleased than otherwise; and that, therefore, the best thing for Bokhara would be to make peace as soon as possible with Russia, and desist from futile embassies to Calcutta and Constantinople. Evidently Afzal Khán's interest in the matter was strong; for, after brooding over it for some days, he asked our news-writer what the British Government would have him do in case his old friend at Bokhara asked him for assistance against Russia? The question almost carried its own solution. The Afgháns had too much on their hands to be able to spare one man or one rupee for any external ally, however hard pressed. Nevertheless, it was no evasive answer which the Kabul ruler received. He was informed, through the Munshí, that the British Government, though always happy to receive any information he might have to supply regarding current events in Bokhara, recommended him to abstain from any proceeding calculated to involve him in the disputes of that State with Russia.

But the correspondence of our officers during the early months of 1867 was not confined to the winning side in Afghánistán. We were in communication with Sher Alí as well. The fallen king, shortly after his defeat at Khelát-i-Ghilzai, had sent a trusted kinsman and namesake of his own into Sind to lay a fresh entreaty at the feet of the British Government. This he described as his ultimatum. If England still withheld her helping hand from his distress, he was bound to look for friends elsewhere—to Persia and to Russia. In one way or another he was resolved to recover his lost kingdom. Our commissioner in Sind listened with commiseration to the piteous tale, but he could do nothing to relieve it. The policy of his Government, as proclaimed in the Viceroy's recently-published letter to Amír Afzal Khán, was rigid neutrality between the belligerent parties. The messenger received a copy of that letter, and then retired in dejection to join his master at Herat.

Of affairs at Kandahar throughout the spring it is enough to say that Azím Khán and Abdul Rahmán were there in conjunction. That implies a monopoly of authority by the former, and ebullitions of jealous anger from the latter, with the usual consequences to their subjects; *delirant reges, plectuntur Achivi.* Uncle and nephew equally saw that one of them must remain in Kandahar to keep a firm hold on the chief city of the Dúráni race and the surrounding country; but each was resolved that he would not be that one. Each strove to return with all speed to Kabul, where Amír Afzal's failing health might at any time leave the succession to the Afghán capital a prize for whichever of the two could contrive to be on the spot. Both endeavoured to obtain letters of recall from Amír Afzal, whose voice, under the pressure of these rival bids for his good word, suddenly rose to an unwonted importance in the state. Driven to make choice between his son and his brother, the bewildered referee decided in favour of the former. Abdul Rahmán was to come back to Kabul, while Azím Khán stood fast at Kandahar. The competition, however, was still at see-saw on the 30th of March, when Azím Khán received from Kabul a copy of Sir John Lawrence's letter of the 25th of February. Afzal Khán, though delighted with the Governor-General's recognition of his title, had not felt competent by himself to compose a reply, and had referred the duty to his cleverer brother at Kandahar. Azím Khán drafted the necessary answer, and sent it to Kabul to be signed and forwarded to India by the nominal sovereign. It merely reciprocated in general terms the friendly feelings of the Viceroy, and consented to receive the Vakíl, or native envoy, whom Sir John Lawrence proposed sending to Kabul as representative of the British Government. So far the action taken by the confederate brothers on Sir John Lawrence's famous letter was all that could be desired; but secretly they had another use for it. With a duplicity amusingly characteristic of the nation, they transmitted a copy of it to the Russian governor at Tashkend.[1] Amír Afzal, in whose name of course the communication was made, informed General Romanovski that he had no confidence in the 'Lord Sáhib's' fine professions of friendship, and that he was disgusted with the British Government for the ingratitude and ill-treatment shown towards his brother Azím. He looked upon the Russians as his real and only friends, hoped soon to be able to send a regular ambassador to the Russian camp, and would at all times do his utmost to protect and encourage Russian trade.

All this while Faiz Muhammad, with the Balkh army, was hanging motionless about the high passes of the Hindu Khúsh, where his descent on Kabul had been arrested by the news of Sher Alí's defeat and flight. It was for some time doubtful whether, in the altered circumstances of his position, he might not draw in his horns, and accept the liberal terms of accommodation which the victorious party would have been glad to offer him. But eventually he declared for the bolder alternative of going through with what he had begun. He sent messengers to Herat assuring Sher Alí of his unchangeable devotion to the royal cause, and begging the Amír to come with all speed and join him in Balkh. Nor did he wait for this invitation to take effect before adding the proof of deeds to his protestations of fidelity. Surwar Khán's was still the only force opposed to him, and that,

[1] The name of the bearer was Hákím Kamrudín, and he reached Tashkend on June 5, 1867. He was a merchant of Kokand, trading with Kabul, and this was not the first occasion on which he acted as letter-carrier between the Russian camp and Kabul.

strange to say, remained unaugmented by any of the reinforcements which the result of the battle of Khelát-i-Ghilzai might have been expected to produce, and which, even with allowance made for the necessity of keeping an eye on Sher Alí's movements across the Helmand, might certainly have been spared by Azím Khán from the garrison of Kandahar. All that Faiz Muhammad had before him was an ill-fed and half-hearted rabble. He attacked and almost annihilated it on the 23rd of April at a place called Bájgah. The poor remnant, pursued as far as Bamian, fled on without stopping till the neighbourhood of Kabul was reached. At Charikar, Surwar Khán made some attempt at a rally, but he had no heart for the task, and soon committed it to other hands; he betook himself to Kabul, entering the gates in silence and alone, sheltered from mocking eyes by darkness, on the night of the 27th. Now for the second time Faiz Muhammad had the capital of Afghánistán at his mercy, and for the second time he let the golden opportunity slip. He advanced no further than Bamian. Leaving a strong detachment at that important point, and dropping by the way supports for it at Seghán, Bájgah, and Roèe, among the mountains, he withdrew the main body of his army back to Ibak, in Balkh. Nothing more would he do until he had, face to face, effected a personal league with Sher Alí. The desired meeting took place at Takhtapúl, where Sher Alí, preceded by his son, Ibrahim Khán, arrived from Herat on the 9th of May. Faiz Muhammad welcomed the Amír with every demonstration of joy and reverence, and the Amír responded by lavishing marks of honour on Faiz Muhammad. By-gones were by-gones between them. It was understood that in the civil administration of Balkh and in the control of the Balkh troops the king's presence was to detract nothing from the king-maker's independence of action; and this understanding was not the less cordial for being veiled under much outward deference to the royal supremacy. The conjoined forces numbered 16,000 men with sixteen guns. They ought to have been led, without a day's further delay, to the assault and recapture of Kabul. That great prize was still within the grasp of the northern invaders, for the panic caused by Surwar Khán's defeat at Bájgah had not yet subsided, and the earliest instalment of the reinforcements sent for from Kandahar did not reach Kabul, under command of Abdul Rahmán, till the 22nd of May. Sher Alí, however, and his colleague, for some unexplained reason, would not put out their hands to take what fortune so invitingly offered. They wasted the whole summer in ruinous sloth at Takhtapúl, each day as it passed tending to introduce some strain or rift in the artificial framework of their compact. They were waiting, they averred, to be joined by more soldiery from Herat; but the pretext is inadmissible. A more likely theory is that Sher Alí sacrificed this precious interval to seeking from Russia and Persia the help that British India had denied him. In Balkh he possessed special facilities for communicating with the Russian commanders across the Oxus, which he is not likely to have neglected; and his overtures to Persia were made too openly to admit of any concealment.

The part played by the Sháh of Persia in this matter is most creditable to his Majesty. For purposes of religious pilgrimage, but also, probably, with some ulterior idea of overawing the unquiet Turkomans, he happened this summer to be at Meshhed, on the eastern frontiers of his kingdom. Thither came to wait upon him Sher Alí's son, Yakub Khán, Governor of Herat. The Afghán prince, who was received by the Sháh with all the honour due to his birth and office, proposed that in return for a subsidy to be immediately granted to his father, he should for the future hold Herat as a fief of the Persian crown. In former times, and up to a recent day, no surer bait could have been dangled before the rulers of Persia, whoever they might have been. The present monarch, however, alive to the danger lurking within this gaudy fly, refused to bite. He replied simply that he was bound by express treaty with the British Government not to interfere in the affairs of Afghánistán, and that he felt no inclination to break the engagement. Yakub Khán obtained honourable dismissal back to Herat; his mission had been a total failure.

Sher Alí's mortification, when he found Persia thus breaking under his hand like a bruised reed, was heightened by a misgiving lest shattered hopes might not represent the full distress of his predicament; how if his attempt to seduce Persia into an infringement of treaty should have given umbrage to England? To get out of this scrape he did not hesitate to volunteer an elaborate fib. Recurring to his old method of circumlocution, he wrote to our Munshí at Kabul; but, being far too wily a practitioner to commit dubious words to the enduring test of paper, he put nothing in his note (dated Takhtapúl, August 11th) save an innocent request to be supplied with the last news from India. The statement he really wanted to make he entrusted to the bearer of the note in the form of a verbal message for the Munshí's private ear. It signified that in sending his son, Yakub Khán, to Meshhed, he had been actuated, not by any political motive, but by a simple desire to show proper respect to the Sháh, when accident had brought his Persian majesty so close to the Herat frontier; further, that he had neither concluded nor desired any alliance with Persia, his old alliance with England being the only one on which he set the slightest store. Poor Sher Alí might have saved himself the trouble of this ingenious endeavour to mystify the British Government; all the details of the Meshhed conference were already known in India, having been duly reported to Sir John Lawrence by our minister at Teheran.

Yet, to do Sher Alí justice, any liberty he may have taken with the truth of Yakub Khán's abortive excursion to Meshhed, was far surpassed by his rival's manipulation of the same fact. As the former had striven to explain away the circumstance into nothingness, so the latter, writing on the very next day, strove to bring out its purport and consequences in the blackest relief. Azím Khán's version was that Yakub Khán had led back a Persian army to Herat, which had occupied the place and planted two standards on its walls, one Persian the other Russian. This story he sent by express to Kabul, desiring his brother to communicate it to the British Munshí as news of the gravest urgency. Simultaneously he wrote direct to Sir Henry Green on the Sind border, urging that, as his enemies, by throwing themselves into a Russo-Persian alliance, were now our enemies also, he reckoned with confidence on our granting him support against them. Of course neither of these overtures obtained the slightest notice from the better informed Indian Government.

The time which Amír Sher Alí and Faiz Muhammad squandered, as we have seen, in fruitless applications to

Russia and Persia, was put to better purpose by their opponents at Kabul. After the first reinforcement brought up by Abdul Rahmán from Kandahar, others followed. Two camps were formed, at Gardandiwár and Charikar, for the protection of the city on its northern face, and every exertion was used to improve the discipline and revive the confidence of the soldiery. A threatened outbreak of the Ghilzais was nipped in the bud. Chieftains of the Kohistán, suspected of a secret understanding with Sher Alí, were soothed into neutrality. Even the harshness of the bit upon the urban population of Kabul was in some degree relaxed, thanks to the more humane policy which Abdul Rahmán's presence inspired. In truth the condition of the citizens was so forlorn that the sternest heart might have been touched by some compunction. War, famine, tyranny, and anarchy had already scourged them to the limit of human endurance, and now they were overshadowed by the wings of the pestilence. Cholera broke out on the 23rd July, and in four days took five hundred victims. Everybody that could, fled into the country; the rest cowered within closed doors. The streets were deserted; the daily Darbár at the palace was discontinued; Kabul seemed a city of the dead. A heavy fall of rain quenched for a time the virulence of the plague, but soon it again burst forth, and, in gusts that rose and fell with fitful vehemence, clung scathingly about the doomed habitations throughout the month of August. Barukzai princes, however, reck little for a murrain among their subjects: at present their whole thoughts were pre-occupied by the impending vacancy on the cushion of the Bálá-Hissár, and the fair vista for their ambitious fancies opening out of that contingency. Ever since his return from Kandahar, Abdul Rahmán had affected the state, and pressed for the title, of heir-apparent to his father's dignity. Afzal Khán could not be induced to confer the coveted distinction. As the disease under which the Amír was sinking gradually gained ground, he began to repent him of the absence at Kandahar of the keen brain and quick hand on which he had been accustomed to depend; and at last, in spite of his son's passionate remonstrances, he recalled his brother to his side. Azím Khán, on receiving the summons, saw his advantage, and used it brutally. He was not, he replied, the Messiah that by coming to Kabul he could put fresh life into a dying man; and, as for the portentous invasion from Balkh, Abdul Rahmán, he imagined, was soldier enough to cope with that. He refused to stir from Kandahar until he should have been relieved in his duties there by his son, Surwar Khán. Amír Afzal eagerly complied with the condition. Surwar Khán was sent to Kandahar, and assumed the government of that place and its dependencies. Then Azím Khán set out on a leisurely progress to Kabul, reviewing and re-arranging, as he went, the civil administration of Ghazní and the other interjacent districts. His new plan was to leave to Abdul Rahmán all the danger and responsibility of a collision with the Balkh army, and not himself to reach Kabul until the decisive overthrow of one or other of the two combatants' hosts should leave his own course clear. He had tried waiting tactics before now, and found them profitable.

The event to which Azím Khán looked forward seemed at last to be really imminent. On the 23rd August the long-delayed advance on Kabul had actually been begun by Sher Alí and Faiz Muhammad, and to repel their progress Abdul Rahmán was leading a reorganized army back to the old fighting ground, the scene of Surwar Khán's defeats, in the passes of the Hindu Khúsh. The invaders numbered nearly twenty thousand men, but they marched in two columns, separated by a considerable interval. Thus, on the 17th September the leading column, under Faiz Muhammad, had reached the boundaries of Ústur-Karram, in the Kohistán, while Sher Alí's battalions were away at Panjsher. With the quick eye of a good soldier, Abdul Rahmán pounced on the opportunity which this blunder afforded. He charged Faiz Muhammad's corps, without allowing it time to obtain support or co-operation from Sher Alí's division. Fortune seconded his strategy. A chance shot, early in the action, struck down Faiz Muhammad, and at once all was over. The Balkh troops, whose attachment was not to Sher Alí or the royal cause, but to Faiz Muhammad and regular pay, immediately ceased fighting, and surrendered.

Faiz Muhammad's body was brought into Kabul, in a horse litter, on the 17th September. The Barukzais, free as they are with the blood of all the world besides, have traditional scruples, partly of religion, though more, perhaps, of selfish policy, about taking the life of a brother Barukzai; and in the worst heat of their interminable family quarrels, they seldom push revenge to the point of outraging in the public eye the respect they consider due to the meanest of their name. Full funereal obsequies were therefore granted to the remains of Faiz Muhammad; and the illuminations which the first news of so famous a victory had prompted the slavish inhabitants of Kabul to prepare, were countermanded by special instructions from the Bálá-Hissár. '*Felix opportunitate mortis*,' may be Faiz Muhammad's epitaph. Frank, gallant, and generous, he had lived long enough to win the affection of his fellows and a commanding position in the country, while the romantic circumstances of his death induce a large indulgence for the versatility of temper, which was rather the fault of his country and of his time than of the individual.

When one, and that the better, half of the invading army had ceased to exist, it was hardly to be expected that the other would cohere. The news of the catastrophe at Kilá Alládád smote the camp at Panjsher with dissolution. Deserted by most of his troops, Sher Alí was in a few days obliged to abandon his guns, and make the best of his way, with the 3,000 men that alone remained faithful to their colours, back through Inderab to Takhtapúl.

Azím Khán, now that all difficulties had been removed from his path without any exertion on his own part, entered Kabul on the 21st September. He was just in time. Amír Afzal Khán died on the 7th October, and Abdul Rahmán was ready in Kabul to dispute the succession, having hurriedly returned for the purpose from his encampment on the border of Balkh. Three days were given up nominally to mourning for the deceased Amír, who, unlike Faiz Muhammad, had lived too long for his reputation. People forgot the glories of Afzal Khán's military manhood in the fresh recollection of his nonentity as a ruler, and no one really regretted him. The practical use of the interval was to test the relative strength of the two claimants to the vacant title. On the fourth day Abdul Rahmán succumbed. In a solemn Darbár he made over the sword of the late Amír, his father, to Azím Khán, who thereupon was saluted by all the assembled nobles and chiefs as lord paramount of their fortunes. It must have been gall and wormwood to Abdul Rahmán thus publicly to make cession of his birth-right to the uncle whom he abhorred; but he went through the ceremony with a good grace, laying it up in his heart as matter for which, with the help of time, he might yet exact satisfaction. The mask of placid obsequiousness which he for the present wore, he is said to have borrowed from the advice of his step-mother, Afzal Khán's principal widow. The tale is likely enough. In Afghánistán, as elsewhere, the course of male politics largely takes its bent from the invisible occupants of the Zanáná, and the influence of Bibí Marwaríd, in particular, had long been a distinct power in the land.

Quietly Azím Khán stepped into possession of the prize to which, through much dirt and after many a downfall, his indomitable perseverance had at last conducted him. He was Amír, if not of Afghánistán, at least of Kabul and Kandahar. Whatever validity there had been in Afzal Khán's title was assuredly his now by legitimate process of succession. The fact, he felt, ought to be recognised by the British Government, and the sooner the better. Accordingly, he took early occasion to hint in roundabout fashion to our Munshí that he expected from the Governor-General some expression of condolence for the death of his brother, Amír Afzal. The moment at which he gave this intimation was propitious to his wishes, in a way and to an extent of which he could not be aware. For the last six months Sir John Lawrence had been most anxious to accredit a regular Vakíl to the Court of Kabul. Important interests demanded, and the express provision of a treaty sanctioned, our having a representative resident among the

Afgháns. The experiment, which the distracted and dangerous condition of the country had induced us to try, of limiting our representation to the person of a simple news-writer, was proved by three years' facts to be impracticable. The Munshí was constantly found, from no fault of his own, to be dabbling in business of delicate diplomacy, quite foreign to the sphere of duty for which he had been selected, and to which it was desirable he should be confined. Manifestly the office needed as capable and dignified an occupant as her Majesty's native service of India could supply. Just the man for the purpose was ready to our hand in Atá Muhammad Khán, a Patháan of good birth, tried loyalty, considerable military knowledge, and perfect familiarity with all the various intricacies of the Afghán character. As far back as in the month of May—immediately, that is, on receipt of Amír Afzal's assurance that our Vakíl would be welcome—this gentleman had been warned to hold himself ready for service at Kabul. His actual despatch thither had remained in abeyance, pending the issue of the Balkh campaign. The reason for awaiting that event had been that the Governor General, foreseeing how the *gobe-mouches* of every Asiatic bazaar would misconstrue the revival of the Vakíl's office into an evidence of the British Government's preferential good-will towards the party for the time being in possession of Kabul, had desired, if possible, to reserve the imaginary compliment for the benefit of the rightful sovereign. If, as had been hoped, the Balkh campaign had ended in reseating Amír Sher Alí at the Bálá-Hissár, the credentials of the new Vakíl might have been addressed to the prince whose prior claim on our favour every word and deed of the British Government had consistently proclaimed. The result, however, had disappointed our hopes. Sher Alí was further than ever from the recovery of his lost supremacy—the opposition had obtained a new lease of power. In justice to our own interests we could afford no further waiting on the chances of a career that so repeatedly belied the anticipations of its sincerest well-wishers. Sir John Lawrence determined that our Vakíl should at once proceed to Kabul. A condition, however, obviously precedent to the Vakíl's despatch, was that the authority to whom his credentials were addressed should have been acknowledged by his employers. Hence a necessity for recognising Azím Khán as Amír. In this field, etiquette undoubtedly required that Azím Khán himself should have made the first move; he ought to have claimed British recognition by a special letter to the Viceroy, formally announcing his installation. On the other hand, Sir John Lawrence knew for a fact that the submission to Azím Khán had been universal; he saw that the Vakíl could not start until the new Amír had been recognised; he had reason to hope that our policy of moral, though inactive, preference for Sher Alí was too well proved to be lightly called in question; he felt the logical obligation which the previous recognition of Afzal Khán now imposed on him to recognise Afzal Khán's successor; and, finally, he held in the request for condolence, expressed by Azím Khán to the Munshí, sufficient groundwork for taking action, without derogating from the viceregal dignity. These considerations decided him. On the 13th November he issued two simultaneous letters to the address of Azím Khán as Amír of Kabul and Kandahar. The first bears on its face the signs of a studied brevity; in it Azím Khán was offered due condolence for his brother's demise, and also congratulated, in a single frigid sentence, on his own accession to power. The second comprised the credentials which Atá Muhammad Khán was personally to deliver at Kabul. Nothing now remained to prevent our Vakíl's departure, but the obtainment of a proper Afghán escort for his protection on the road from the Pesháwar frontier. This was soon arranged. Atá Muhammad Khán hastened to the scene of his duties, and from the date of his arrival at Kabul the reproach and inconvenience of British India being without a spokesman in Afghánistán ceased to be felt.

So ended the year 1867. Its close left Sher Alí in worse plight than he ever yet had been. All the brave hopes that Balkh had held out to him in the spring were buried in the grave of Faiz Muhammad. His own sway over the Úsbeg population of the province fell far short of the standard requisite to unite their scattered clans in any fresh effort against the victorious arms of Abdul Rahmán. Further stay in Balkh was useless, and might be dangerous; he had no choice but to retire from Takhtapul. In all Afghánistán not a corner was left to Dost Muhammad's heir but Herat. Worn in body and broken in spirit, Amír Sher Alí prepared to fall back on that asylum.

Here my tale of Afghán history must pause. The epoch we have reached marks for Sir John Lawrence's government the culminating point of the policy, which popular criticism, creating a catch-word of definition out of a chance phrase of mine in the *Edinburgh Review*, has quaintly agreed to laud or reprobate under the name of 'Masterly Inactivity.' Half the censure which has been showered on that policy springs from a misconception. Our relations towards the states lying within the limits of the Indian peninsula have been confounded with the fundamentally different relations we hold towards the powers lying beyond those limits. Familiar with the right of intervention which we justly exercise in the affairs of feudatory princes bound to us by ties of subordinate alliance, the Anglo-Indian mind forgets that we are lords-paramount of India only, not of all Asia, and expects us to throw down our truncheon between hostile factions in regions which geography has made independent of our control. Quite as justly might England have been called on to thrust herself, some years ago, between North and South in America, or, more recently, between Monarchists and Republicans in Spain. In the case of Afghánistán the obligation to let foreigners alone, that they might settle the form of their government and the person of their governor as they please, was enforced on the Indian Government, not only by the general spirit of international law, but by the particular provisions of a written treaty. The second article of Lord Dalhousie's Treaty of 1855 with Dost Muhammad bound us 'never to interfere in the territories of Afghánistán.' Dost Muhammad's sons were now fighting among themselves for the sovereignty of Afghánistán, and if to have granted either of them arms or money against the other would not have constituted a breach of treaty, it is difficult to imagine what would. Yet, oddly enough, this very treaty is reprinted at full length by more than one of the many writers who condemn our long-continued refusal of assistance to Sher Alí. What is stranger still, one pamphleteer,[1] by an ingenious perversion more creditable to his own daring than complimentary to the discrimination of his audience, has not shrunk from quoting

[1] 'The Oxus and the Indus.' By Major Evans Bell.

the very clause which lays an embargo on our interference, as a foundation from which to denounce the Indian Government's postponement of a particular act. Surely the force of casuistry can no further go than when inaction and interference are found to be convertible terms. The act referred to, is the original recognition of Sher Alí, as Dost Muhammad's successor, which Lord Elgin's administration delayed to issue till six months after the decease of the old Amír. The delay has been imputed to the Foreign Office of India as a sin, disgraceful in itself, and lamentable in its consequences; disgraceful, because it amounted to a repudiation of the 'perpetual peace and friendship' which Sher Alí, as his father's heir, had a right to demand of us; and lamentable, because it stimulated the insurrectionary designs of his rivals. In point of fact, the apparent dilatoriness of the Government was, to a considerable extent, accidental, caused partly by the length of time that necessarily elapsed before authentic information of the death and dying wishes of Dost-Muhammad could travel from the distant camp of Herat to the viceregal lodge at Simla, and partly by the check which Lord Elgin's mortal illness was then inflicting on every wheel of the State machinery. But extenuation need not be pleaded, when the means of justification are ample. Each of the two charges may be traversed by a direct negatur. In the first place, the nomination of Sher Alí by his father, though binding on the Barukzai family, gave him not a tittle of claim to our recognition; no such being as Dost Muhammad's 'heir' could have any existence for the British Government, until the voice of the chiefs and people should have ratified the deceased Amír's choice; we simply allowed time for that voice to make itself heard, and, as soon as it had spoken, the recognition which then, and not till then, became Sher Alí's due, was granted with prompt cordiality. Secondly, anything that the Indian Government, then or subsequently, did or refrained from doing, had no more effect in rousing or quelling the force of Azím Khán's revolutionary ambition, than it could have upon the motion of the planets in heaven. Sher Alí, very likely makes a secret grievance out of the guarded slowness of our procedure; but if every word an Afghán says in his own cause is to be believed, the faith of some of us will be sorely tried. Sticklers for Sher Alí's 'rights' appear to forget the origin of his title. In comparison with his brothers he may be called the 'rightful sovereign;' but the father was nothing more or less than a usurper. Representatives of the family displaced by Dost Muhammad are still forthcoming, and still cherish expectations of a recall from exile in India to kingly power in Kabul. Among them, if anywhere, is the 'rightful sovereign' to be looked for. The truth, however, is, that the Afghán policy contains no such institution. The only 'rightful sovereign' is he who can take the crown, and keep it. Lord Dalhousie fully admitted the validity of the national custom, when, by the treaty already cited, he recognised Dost Muhammad as founder of a new dynasty in supercession of the house of the Sadyozais, whose more legitimate title Lord Auckland's Government had formerly advocated by force of arms. If Lord Dalhousie's act was justifiable, so, too, must have been Sir John Lawrence's conduct—first, in taking time to recognise Sher Alí as Amír of all Afghánistán, and afterwards in not scrupling to recognize successively Afzal Khán and Azím Khán as Amírs of that portion of Afghánistán which had fallen under their *de facto* authority. The several operations are all parts of one consistent policy—the policy of assenting peaceably to the visible facts, resultant from a neighbour's settlement of his own affairs after his own fashion.

The more the historic facts of the case are sifted the firmer will be the conclusion of every dispassionate inquirer, that the course pursued by the Indian Government up to the end of 1867 did no injustice to Sher Alí, and that any other course would have been unjust to the Afghán nation. Further, it cannot be denied that a system which, by the transparent simplicity of its quietism, lulled the wakeful Anglophobia of Russian generals, and disarmed their inconvenient propensity to meet supposed plots of ours in Afghánistán by counter-plots of their own in the same country was not without positive merit of some kind. Whether, on the whole, it was the best that could be devised for British interests, is a question which the inordinate space already occupied by this paper warns me to defer to another—though, I hope, an early—opportunity. Towards the end of 1868 the Government of India abandoned inactivity for action. Each, therefore, of the rival methods having now had a fair trial, the English people has the means of judging which the more rightly may be entitled the 'masterly' one. The new scheme bore blossom at the Ambálá Darbár in March 1869, but the soundness of its fruit remains to be tested.

NOTE BY THE EDITOR.

MR. WYLLIE has here stated with admirable force, the policy which the Government of India pursued during the unsettled period of Afghán history, while the sons of Dost Muhammad were struggling for the supremacy. On some points he would probably have revised his opinion had he lived to see the period of comparative rest which has supervened since Amír Sher Alí finally obtained the ascendancy in 1868-69, and was definitively recognised by the British Government. Nor do I think he would have expressed himself with so much certainty regarding the very complex question of the military occupation of Quettá. Such an occupation would doubtless have been attended with very great expense and danger at the time when Mr. Wyllie wrote. But with the extension and approaching completion of the Panjáb and Sind Railway System, some of these difficulties disappear. I have had the advantage of going over the proof sheet of the foregoing Essay (pp. 87-92), referring to Quettá, with the General Officer who is now the leading authority on affairs connected with the artillery defences of India. He said—'I look on this subject purely from a military point of view. I do not think General Jacob's plan was practicable 18 years ago; but I object to it being summarised as "a popular error." The truth is, that with the railway system completed to Sakkar, and a short and inexpensive extension across the desert to the foot of the Bolán Pass, I look upon Quettá as one of the great possibilities for the more complete defence of the Frontier, and for the improved health of our English troops. But railway communication is a first necessity. Given a line of railway, and we might have the English troops in perfect health in the English climate of Quettá, instead of dying like sheep in Sind. Moreover, concerning the strategic aspects of Quettá as a great outlying defence, I think these pages do not fairly state the case. If we have ever to fight for the Bolán Pass, we should do it at the Quettá end. We should there have our troops in perfect health, and have the choice of our ground. I do not agree with the small print at the top of page 91, about fighting on the western extremity. If we were to defend the western extremity, our troops would have an open desert behind them, and be encamped in the most deadly spot in India; I know that country well. It is all very well to speak on paper about arraying forces "on any field we might choose between Shikárpur and Dadur." The malaria would render any such field a field of skulls for our army, while we were waiting for the enemy. I look upon Quettá as a question not yet settled. It cannot possibly be settled until the completion of our railway system. Meanwhile, it is not according to knowledge to dismiss it as a "popular error." The question must, some day or other, and probably before long, be considered in the light of the new capabilities of Frontier defence, which the railway system will develop.'(1874) This Quettá question may serve as an example of several other points, regarding which Mr. Wyllie would probably have modified his views. With the rapid development, both moral and material, at present going on in India, there is scarcely a question of Indian policy which can be considered as definitively settled. W. W. H.

MISCHIEVOUS ACTIVITY.

NOTE BY THE EDITOR.

In 1868 Amír Sher Alí finally established his authority in Afghánistán. Lord Lawrence, the then Viceroy, in pursuance of the policy of recognising and befriending the *de facto* ruler, deemed it wise that the British Government should acknowledge, in a public manner, the change which had thus taken place. He therefore intimated that he would grant to the Amír a State interview or Darbár, and that he would befriend him, in the consolidation of his power, with a present of money. Sir John Lawrence quitted the Viceroyalty in January 1869, and it fell to his successor, Lord Mayo, to carry out these promises. This he did at the Ambálá Darbár in March 1869. The effect of that Darbár was to give to our policy of *de facto* dealings with Afghánistán, its legitimate development. So long as the claimants to the Afghán sovereignty were fighting among themselves, that policy debarred us from interfering. But when one of them had finally emerged triumphant, and concentrated the *de facto* authority in his hands, the same policy led Lord Lawrence to strengthen him in that *de facto* authority. The five years which have elapsed since the Ambálá Darbár prove that Lord Lawrence had accurately gauged the situation. The successful claimant, Sher Alí, whom the Ambálá Darbár publicly recognised, has maintained his *de facto* authority ever since, and still reigns as the rightful ruler of Afghánistán (1874).

When Mr. Wyllie wrote the following essay, it was impossible to foresee this. The Darbár was held at the end of March 1869; the latest information which Mr. Wyllie had regarding its results was an Indian newspaper of the 30th November 1869. During the next few months Mr. Wyllie was in bad health; and he died in March 1870. In writing his former essays, he brought to his work special knowledge acquired in the Indian Foreign Office. To this essay he brought no special knowledge of his own, and it was written before the results of the Darbár had had time to develop themselves. At first, indeed, it seemed doubtful to his brother and myself whether this paper should be reprinted. It was not written with Mr. Wyllie's usual knowledge of the facts. Nor have its anticipations and forecasts been realised by subsequent events. On the other hand, it not unfairly represents a view which was at that time shared by many careful thinkers, and which will always have a body of supporters. That view is non-interference, pure and simple, in the countries lying between the Indian frontier and the Asiatic possessions of Russia. Hitherto it has not been found possible either in Persia or in Afghánistán to give political effect to this view. In Persia it has proved expedient to maintain an embassy at the court of the legitimate sovereign. In Afghánistán the policy has been to stand aloof during internal struggles for the throne, and on their termination, to recognise and befriend the *de facto* ruler.

It is right to add that although the calamities which this essay foreboded from the Ambálá Darbár have not happened, yet the absolute tranquillity of Afghánistán has not been secured. The anticipated complications with Russia only required a little time and a little explanation on both sides, to disappear. The Seistán difficulty between Persia and Afghánistán became a subject of peaceful arbitration, instead of a chronic *casus belli* as it had been for many years. And to this end the results of the Ambálá Darbár materially contributed. It would be unwise, however, to assume that such an hereditary source of irritation between two Asiatic powers has been entirely laid at rest by the intervention of a third party. The picture on page 160, of Ishakh Khán overthrowing Afghánistán in 1870, was a purely imaginary one; and had Mr. Wyllie lived a few months longer, he would have been the first to acknowledge its fanciful character. But while the evils which he anticipated have not happened, the Amír Sher Alí has not enjoyed unbroken rest. He reigns *de facto* sovereign, so far as his brothers, the sons of Dost Muhammad, are concerned. Time and death, and Sher Alí's strong arm in the battle-field, have settled their claims. But Sher Alí is himself a father, and the struggle among the sons of his father now threatens to be reproduced among his own sons. Of these sons, Yákub Khán is a man of mature years, personal popularity, and great military talent. Abdullá Ján is a mere boy, but he is the favourite of his father. Sher Alí brought him to the Ambálá Darbár, and has in many other ways put him forward as his heir. This conduct Yákub Khán resents, and he maintains a great party in Herat, of which he is now governor (as lately in Kandahar), ready to assert his claims on the death of his father, or if needful, by rebellion during his father's lifetime. Amír Sher Alí's dearest object was to obtain a recognition at the Ambálá Darbár of his youngest son, Abdullá Ján. In this, notwithstanding his astuteness, he was outwitted, and the subject was not allowed to enter into the discussions. The father has since recognised him, and Yákub is now in arms (Sept. 1874).

While, therefore, the Ambálá Darbár has during the past five years been productive of nothing but good, and has contributed to the consolidation of the *de facto* authority in Afghánistán, it has not removed all the sources of present disquiet and future strife which lurk in that unhappy country. The question of interference with the internal affairs of Afghánistán may arise again on the death of Sher Alí, if not before that event. The following essay will represent the views of an important class of Indian politicians, whenever that question is resuscitated. I have therefore thought it best to include it in this selection of Mr. Wyllie's writings, with omissions and modifications of expression, such as, I believe, he would have himself made had he lived to reprint it at this date (1874). In every point dealt with, from the instability of the Amír's rule and the danger of his administrative reforms, to the Seistán complication and the evil effects of the Ambálá Darbár in Russia and in Persia, the events of the five years since the Essay was written have falsified its predictions. Nevertheless it represented the views of a considerable class both in India and in England at the date when it was written; and it will ever possess this basis of truth that, in its own words, the 'true bulwarks of India are to be found within her own limits.'

W. W. H.

MISCHIEVOUS ACTIVITY.[1]

WHO hath not seen Seville, according to the Spanish proverb, hath not seen a marvel. The same may be said of an Indian Viceroy's Darbár. The scenic splendour of the pageant constitutes its humblest charm. That might be rivalled or surpassed in other lands; but, except perhaps at an imperial coronation in Moscow, nowhere else can be found so harmonious a combination of the distinctive types of Europe and the East, so vivid a revelation of all that can best symbolise the wonders of comprehensive empire. On one side there is the disciplined might of England, represented by a gathering of picked troops—infantry, cavalry, and artillery—capable, as they stand, of making a victorious promenade throughout the length or breadth of India, though half the country should be in arms against them; on the other, the fantastic pomp of Asia, impersonated in an array of luxurious princes, who, by the lustre of their jewels, the bellicose aspect of their motley followers, the bulk of their elephants, and the costly caparisoning of their horses, convert the act of homage to their common master into an occasion of emulous display, each striving to outshine his peer. In some sense, it is an Oriental edition of the Field of the Cloth of Gold. The vast plain all round the city of rendezvous is white with innumerable encampments. Every camp clusters round

[1] 'Fortnightly Review,' March 1, 1870.

the flag-staff of a separate authority, and at every staff, save one, the drooped flag denotes subordination to a superior power in the vicinity. A long, broad street of marquees, tenanted by the various members and attachés of the supreme Government, leads up to the palatial mass of canvas forming the vice-regal pavilion. The feudatory chief whose turn may have come to approach the 'Lord Sáhib's' presence, is greeted at the mouth of the street by a salute of guns in number apportioned to his rank. Up the street his *cortége* slowly moves through lines of British troopers, whose sabres flash welcome in the sunshine. A fanfare of martial music announces his arrival at the entrance of the pavilion; secretaries and aides-de-camp receive him as he alights, and see him doff his shoes; the infantry guard-of-honour presents arms, and so, between two rows of clashing weapons his Highness is conducted to his allotted place in the assembly. The throne under the central canopy is vacant for the Viceroy. Right and left of it, in horseshoe fashion, chairs are arranged; these for the native potentates, and those for British officers. Behind the latter, and drawn aside, as having no proper status in a purely Eastern ceremony, gleams a small and select *parterre* of English ladies. All present are seated, and a growing stillness indicates the hour for the Viceroy's advent. All rise as he appears, heralded by a royal salute, and with a brilliant staff around him. Proceeding to the canopy, he stands motionless below it—the whole conclave also standing in silence—until the last of the twenty-one guns, which recognise the majesty of India's absent empress, has ceased. Then he mounts the throne, and the business of the Darbár begins.

Such was the scene at Ambálá, in Upper India,

under the sun's declining rays, on the 27th March 1869. Yet in some respects the spectacle on that occasion presented a striking contrast to the usual routine. A truthful sketch of it appeared shortly afterwards in the *Illustrated London News.* The central personage is, of course, Lord Mayo, and, not far from him, sits Lord Napier of Magdala, both of them bareheaded ; below the dais the slipperless figures of half-a-dozen Panjáb chieftains, and the bared heads of Sir Donald Macleod, Sir William Mansfield, and Sir Henry Durand are equally familiar to the eye. But who are these, a man and a boy, occupying chairs of equality on the dais with Lord Mayo, their heads covered with the tall black lamb's-wool hat of Persia, and their lower limbs encased in trousers and boots of European pattern ? They must be sovereign lords of foreign territory, owning no allegiance to the British Crown. The boy is Abdullah Ján, a younger son of Sher Alí, of Afghánistán ; the man is Sher Alí himself. Sher Alí's past history is legible in his externals. In his air there is all the dignity which Royal birth, coupled with a long experience of misfortune, seldom fails to confer ; and the habitual melancholy of his passion-ravaged countenance is eloquent with the tale of that domestic grief[1] which four years ago shook his reason with an almost irreparable throe. But the dominant feature is the eye, and its expression sternness—the practised sternness of one never known to spare any adversary that might be wisely struck. But here, five hundred miles within the British frontier, and parading a precedence co-ordinate with the jealously guarded supremacy of the British Viceroy, how comes Sher Alí here ?

[1] His favourite son and his full-brother were both killed in hand-to-hand combat with each other at the battle of Kujhbáz, on June 6, 1865.

Fifteen short months ago he was a helpless fugitive, beaten out of Kabul, beaten out of Kandahar, beaten out of Balkh, and seeking a precarious shelter at Herat. Russia and Persia had alike refused to help him, and the determination of British India to leave him to his fate had been brought home to him by a score of humiliating rebuffs. He appeared sunk in complete and irretrievable ruin. Now his lot is changed indeed. The same English who lately had not an obolus of alms for his destitution, are now receiving him with the honours of a royal guest. From approaching in supplication at their feet he has risen to appear among them as an equal who can name his terms for mutual obligations given and conferred as between friends. He has already accepted ten thousand stand of muskets, and 120,000*l.* in cash. He is to take back with him to Afghánistán a perfectly equipped battery of light guns; and he has a prospect of more supplies of money in the years to come. The gifts merely personal to himself, which in the present Darbár strew the carpet before him in one-and-fifty trays, are valued at 5,000*l.* See, Lord Mayo takes a jewelled sword, and, offering it to him with his own hand, says: 'May you be victorious over your enemies, and with this defend your just rights.' And listen to the Amír's reply: 'I will also use it against the enemies of the Queen of England.' Never was such a metamorphosis. It beats the caprices of a Christmas pantomime in the 'transformation scene.' Spectators may rub their eyes and rack their brains for an explanation. Has the new Governor-General reversed the policy of his predecessor? Is the civil war of Afghánistán at an end? Or has Russian aggression proceeded of late with such intolerable increase of menace as to demand an imposing counter-demonstration in India?

Let us take up these hypotheses separately in their order.

And, first, Lord Mayo's share in the business. As might have been expected, the Russian press has attributed to him alone the responsibility of initiating a new policy towards Afghánistán. Yet, on the face of things, it was unlikely that a steady official, within three months of his assuming the government, should of his own judgment have decided to undo all previous arrangements, and strike out a fresh path for himself. All doubts on either side of the question may be set at rest by reference to the declaration contained in Lord Lawrence's maiden utterance in the House of Peers on the 19th of April last. The words of the late Viceroy are: 'I believe that Lord Mayo has done no more than act on the principles I suggested.' Moreover, another passage in the same speech shows that the subsidy of 120,000*l.*, received by Sher Alí for the maintenance of his army, was in part granted and in part promised by Sir John Lawrence before Lord Mayo's arrival. Clearly, therefore, Sir John Lawrence, and not Lord Mayo, is answerable for our embarkation on a voyage of active alliance with Sher Alí.

This being the case, let us investigate the second theory. Over and over again Sir John Lawrence had announced his solemn determination not to take sides either with Sher Alí or anyone else in the civil war of Afghánistán. When at last he came forward, consenting to interfere in Afghán affairs, there would be a strong presumption that the war must have already terminated. Nevertheless, Lord Lawrence's own description of the circumstances belies this presumption, and proves that his action was taken irrespective of the condition which had been the *sine quâ non* of all his previous declarations. 'Each party,' he says, in the explanatory statement addressed to the Lords, 'was sufficiently strong to maintain itself against the other, but neither party was strong enough to beat down the other and restore order.' And, further on, he expressly affirms that the subsidy was given to the Amír, 'with a view of affording him a chance of recovering his power.' To me it seems from this, as if Sher Alí's rivals were still in the field, and could not be suppressed without extraneous assistance.

Remains the third possibility. Undoubtedly the recent capture and occupation of Samarkand by the Russians, and their reduction of the Amír of Bokhara to a position in which the retention of nominal sovereignty only made him a more pliant vassal of the Czar, were facts [1] of startling sound to many politicians. But they were not so to the Government of India. Sir John Lawrence's scheme of inactivity had been deliberately framed in full view of these very contingencies. It is incredible that their realisation, a few months perhaps sooner than had been anticipated, could have deflected his plans by a hair's breadth.

Thus, one after another, the several explanations, which, from their simplicity, most readily occur to an enquirer, have been weighed in the balance and found wanting. Sher Alí's sudden exaltation to the pinnacle of British favour continues as strange a stroke of fortune as before. A more complex method is needed for the

[1] Samarkand fell, May 2, 1868. General Kaufmann then advanced towards Bokhara, with the intention of capturing that city also, the metropolis of the Khanate; but when he had accomplished half the distance, he was obliged to hurry back to Samarkand, where a formidable insurrection had broken out in his absence.

right reading of the riddle. The best that I have been able to devise is as follows.

I must begin by reverting to the course of events in Afghánistán during the year 1868. At the commencement of that period the government of Azím Khán, the usurping Amír, was acknowledged throughout three-fourths of the kingdom. One province, Balkh, was held for him by his nephew, Abdul Rahmán, with a considerable army; and another, Kandahar, was administered by his son, Surwar Khán; he himself held his court at Kabul. Herat, the remaining territory, alone stood faithful to Sher Alí. The ill fortune, however, of which Sher Alí had experienced so long and severe a run, was now at its turning-point. In the spring his son, Yakub Khán, began the new deal by attacking and taking Kandahar. Sher Alí followed his lead from Herat, and, after a short pause at Kandahar, saw his way to an advance on Kabul. Three previous attempts to recover the capital had been scored against him as ruinous defeats within the last two years; the fourth was launched under better auspices. By this time, in fact, the Afghán people were ripe for a return to their former allegiance. Not that they had forgotten aught of their old dislike to Sher Alí, since he was last at Kabul, but that in the interval they had learned to detest his rival far more; any prince of the Barukzai family, whose accession to power would relieve them from the frightful tyranny of Azím Khán, would be more or less of a godsend; and for this purpose Sher Alí seemed as good as another. So the rightful Amír had really no opposition to contend with. Azím Khán evaded a violent downfall by spontaneously evacuating Kabul, and retiring to Balkh. After an absence of forty months, Sher Alí found himself reseated in his royal citadel, the Bálá Hissár, and repossessed of all his dominions—Balkh only excepted, where Azím Khán and Abdul Rahmán still flew the flag of rebellious defiance. The Amír backed his luck gallantly. Because the Indian Government had hitherto turned a deaf ear to his innumerable entreaties for arms and money, that was no reason why a fresh trial of the Viceroy's temper might not have a happier result now; at any rate, he had naught to lose and much to win by the venture. Accordingly he again wrote to India, urging the old, old request with unabated pertinacity.

This time the application caught the Governor-General in a mood of more than usual anxiety regarding our future relations with Afghánistán. For his own part Sir John Lawrence may have thought the right thing to do was nothing, or next to nothing. Yet on all sides he felt a pressure to do something. He had braved the impatient taunts of the Anglo-Indian press for nearly five years; but now there were signs of a restlessness among his own official advisers. Voices began to be heard in the council-chamber, arguing from the analogy of international custom in Europe that British officers should be deputed as diplomatic agents to the principal cities of Central Asia; a course to which Sir John Lawrence entertained deep-seated objections.[1] He looked to England for guidance, and found cold comfort there.

[1] These objections have been often stated. Firstly, whatever we want in the way of political information from such places is already supplied in sufficiency by natives. Secondly, Europeans, conscious of ability and yearning to prove it, have that dangerous tendency to 'zeal' which Talleyrand deprecated. Thirdly, white faces, the Christian faith, and her Majesty's uniform, are to the unregulated patriotism and burning fanaticism of Central Asiatics what a red rag is to a bull. And, lastly, the person of a British officer embodies so large an emanation of the Government's prestige, that the maintenance or vindication of his dignity and safety may, at any moment, create necessity for war, costly as that of Abyssinia and far more perilous.

He saw that there existed among some portion of his countrymen at home a craving for action and intervention; but from the standpoint of Simla he had no means of gauging the extent or depth of the sentiment, and his apprehensions magnified its proportions out of all semblance to the reality. He was equally in the dark as to the intentions of the India Office. The Secretary of State's trumpet gave an uncertain sound. Perhaps the very plenitude of Sir Stafford Northcote's trust in the Viceroy's competency to deal with the Afghāns as they deserved, made him less communicative and explicit than he otherwise would have been; but, whatever may have been the cause, the instructions sent to India on this topic were unquestionably scanty and timid. And if to this the further fact of significance be added that Sir Henry Rawlinson, the brilliant and powerful champion of all that Sir John Lawrenee most disapproved, had recently joined the Home Council, and was already giving unmistakable proof of his active interest in Central Asian business, it will be apparent that there was cause enough for doubt and perplexity. Nevertheless, all these things combined might not have shaken Sir John from his resolution, had he commanded a prospect of retaining in his own hands the control of India's destinies for a further period. But his tenure of office was close on expiration; and the new Governor-General would be a peer from home, having no personal acquaintance with Asiatics of any shade. There was no knowing to what lengths of *rapprochement* with Afghánistán such a successor might not be borne, especially in the earlier years of his administration, by a natural surrender of his private judgment to the confident clamour of local experience. It was due to Lord Mayo that he should not be left without the stay of a political testament from the outgoing ruler; and the programme that seemed most likely to secure his abstention from the extremity of evil would be one permitting a certain dalliance with milder forms of the popular infatuation. In fine, Sir John Lawrence may have possibly concluded that his policy of quiescence was doomed to modification of some kind, but that he still had it in his power, by a timely concession, to trace beforehand what the modification should be, and so to confine the impending mischief within bounds. Hence, perhaps, it came to pass that he, who had, a score of times, rejected Sher Alí's request for assistance, now inclined to entertaining it. He proposed to his council that the money should be granted. His colleagues accepted the proposal with unanimity. Even at this last moment the Viceroy perhaps saw reason for shrinking from decisive action. What he proposed to do touched English relations with Russia, and he was ignorant in what light it might be viewed by the European Governments. Therefore he telegraphed for orders to the Secretary of State in England. The reply he received from Sir Stafford Northcote, showed insufficient appreciation of the interests at stake, and neatly exemplified that laxity of control which most bewilders conscientious subordinates. Mr. Disraeli's Government told[1] Sir John Lawrence that he 'might pursue his own policy, and that they trusted entirely to his knowledge and judgment.' The sequel may be told in Lord Lawrence's own words:—

'Accordingly, I sent him (Amír Sher Alí) something like 60,000*l.*, and I told him further that, if this money did not suffice,

[1] See the Duke of Argyll's speech in the House of Lords, April 19, 1869.

I would give him a further supply, and would also aid to a certain extent in the maintenance of a standing army. He replied most gratefully, and desired to come down and pay his respects to the British Government, to enter into a treaty with them as his father had done, and to maintain friendly relations with them. It was considered by the Government of India that overtures of this kind ought not to pass unnoticed, and I therefore wrote to the Amír, and told him what were my views—that I was willing to help him still further in a moderate way; that I could not bind myself by any treaty, which would involve obligations on the part of her Majesty's Government to assist him; but that I was willing, from time to time, as circumstances might suggest, and as his own conduct might show that he deserved it, to give him some further assistance hereafter, as I had already done. Things remained in that state until the period of my service as Governor-General came to an end. I then placed on record my reasons for having made this arrangement. I suggested that my successor should act on the same policy; that he should make no treaty or engagement by which we should be bound in any way, directly or indirectly, to interfere in the affairs of Afghánistán; but until the Amír should recover his authority, and consolidate his authority, that we might from time to time assist him.'

Two points in Sir John Lawrence's conduct remain to be noticed, before we pass on to Lord Mayo's proceedings. The first is the question whether help to Sher Alí, while his half-brother and great antagonist, Azím Khán, still survived in arms against him, was compatible with the Indian Government's engagements to abstain from intervention in Afghán affairs. To me it seems incompatible. The circumstances of the case may be arrayed to explain the apparent divergence from Article 2 of the Treaty of 1855, by which England is bound never to interfere in the territories of Afghánistán; but no sophistry can deny or mitigate the outrage done to the pledge, which in Sir John's letter of the 25th of

February 1867, recognising Afzal Khán as Amír of Kabul and Kandahar, had been voluntarily given to the faction whose head was Azím Khán. The expressions the Viceroy had then used were—

> 'Neither men, nor arms, nor money, nor assistance of any kind, have ever been supplied by my Government to Amír Sher Alí Khán. I propose to continue the same policy for the future. If, unhappily, the struggle for supremacy in Afghánistán has not yet been brought to a close, and hostilities are again renewed, I shall still side with neither party.'

Azím Khán and his friends had not forgotten this assurance. Neither is it likely that the Afghán people, against whom collectively we are wont to level the charge of Punic faith, should have omitted to note an instance in which the plighted word of Great Britain does not show to advantage. The second point wears an equally unsatisfactory look. It is the language which, after Sir John Lawrence had committed the Government of India to a policy of activity, he employed to describe what he had done. On two occasions—once at a farewell banquet in the Town-hall of Calcutta, and again in his statement to the House of Lords—he spoke as if he had never made the slightest deviation from his principles of neutrality. In these statements he seems to me to have been unconsciously deceiving himself far more than he misled his audience. His wishes, hopes, and beliefs all lying in one direction, he could not bring himself to realise how fast and far he had gone in an exactly opposite quarter.

But while the inception of the new policy must indisputably be laid to Lord Lawrence's charge, the fashion in which it was carried out is a second question. Lord Mayo seems to me to have erred on the side of complaisance to his guest. The principles which, if our national dignity had been considered, would have given the key-note to the Darbár were, firstly, that our previous refusals to help Sher Alí had been altogether right and just; and, secondly, that the interference which we were at last reluctantly exercising in the domestic dissensions of the Barukzai family, sprang less from any regard for the Amír's individual interests than for the general welfare of the Afghán people. These, in experienced hands, might have been impressed on Sher Alí with a gentle firmness which would have done little violence to his self-love. But, not satisfied with the fortunate recovery of his hereditary possessions, he requested—and Lord Mayo agreed—that we should call Persia to account for alleged encroachments in the debatable land of Seistán. At the close of the conference, when he was privately shown the draft of a letter of good advice which, it was proposed, he should take back with him to Kabul, he entreated that a clause might be inserted, pledging the Indian Government to view with displeasure any infraction of his legitimate authority which his subjects might commit in Afghánistán. And this, too, Lord Mayo conceded.

If Sher Alí, on his return to Kabul, had suddenly been dethroned, slain in battle, assassinated, or poisoned—any of which contingencies were clearly on the cards—Lord Mayo might possibly have been obliged either to take another and a deeper plunge into the whirlpool of Afghán politics, by extorting reparation for the cause with which he had identified the British Government's reputation, or else to endure the dangerous laughter of all Asia, by shrinking from the vindication of an alliance inaugurated at vast expense and with much flourish of trumpets. The predicament, however, did not arise.[1] Sher Alí's enemies were for the time smitten with despondency. Azím Khán and Abdul Rahmán retired through Seistán towards Meshhed, in Persia; and Azím Khán's son, Ishakh Khán, evacuated Balkh, seeking shelter across the Oxus in Bokhara. The Amír, therefore, before the end of last spring (1869), was once more established as lord of all Afghánistán. The task that lay before him was to consolidate his power within the recovered limits. How he fared in the undertaking we will enquire presently.

By many the Darbár was interpreted as a counter move against Russia. The ill-omened phrase of 'the grand game,' which, thirty years before, had been in vogue at Calcutta to describe Lord Auckland's unhappy designs for repelling Russian approach by an English occupation of Afghánistán, was now revived in the Anglo-Indian newspapers. The leading journal of Bengal fanned the professional enthusiasm of 'the services' by assurances that ere long we should have Political Agents in Afghánistán, military officers employed in drilling and organising the Amír's army, and a portion of that army held completely at our disposal as a British contingent: 'the grand game,' it was said, promised well.[2]

In Persia the result was, I think, mischievous. The Sháh's Government, mindful that the Afgháns once over-

[1] The truth is, that the event proved that Lord Lawrence and Lord Mayo, in finally recognising and helping Amír Sher Alí, had rightly estimated his position as the *de facto* ruler of Afghánistán. The five years which have since elapsed confirm this view. W. W. H.

[2] This correctly states the case as regards the party in India who are always crying out for 'the grand game.' But, if Mr. Wyllie had been in India at the time, he would have known that this statement applied only to that party, and was as usual discountenanced by the majority, both among officials and the public. W. W. H.

ran Persia and held it for seven years, has a traditional jealousy of anything approaching to an aggrandisement of the power of these intractable neighbours. Neither can his Majesty forget that from British championing of Afghán grievances he has twice reaped war, defeat, and humiliation; and that the same cause still operates to keep him out of Herat, a city which he considers his own by right, and which he desires for the protection of his border subjects from the raids of the kidnapping Turkomans. Prepared, therefore, under any circumstances to view with suspicion signs of a fresh alliance between England and Afghánistán, the Sháh might see in the Ambálá pageantry special reason for alarm on account of Sher Alí's request that British assistance should procure the expulsion of the Persians from Seistán. It is not easy to understand how Lord Mayo can have been induced to sympathise with this demand; unless, indeed, he was moved by the consideration that British interests would be better served by a transfer of the disputed territory from Persian to Afghán possession.

The Blue Book published by the India Office shows that the Afghán claim rests on little more than an occupation of the province for forty-four years, which terminated in 1793, and that at all other times, except for a short interval of independence under local chiefs, Seistán has formed an integral part of the Persian dominions. Sher Alí's pretensions amount, in fact, to a reclamation of the limits of the Afghán kingdom, as they stood under Ahmad Sháh and Timor Sháh. England cannot enforce that principle against Persia without allowing that it must also hold good against herself, in which case she will have to renounce to Afghánistán all the broad lands of Peshá-war, Multán, Lahor, and Káshmír. This argument, if it had ever been adopted by Lord Mayo, would be thus reduced to an absurdity. No wonder that the Persian Government called on the English Cabinet for an explanation. Our diplomatists promptly furnished the reply, that the arrangements effected with Sher Alí in no way militated against Persian interests, and that our Afghán policy generally was not conceived in a spirit hostile to Persia. At the same time Lord Clarendon satisfied himself of Persia's superior right to Seistán, and refused to act on Lord Mayo's suggestion, that British pressure should be brought to bear on the Sháh in support of the Afghán claims. But both the positive assurance of our friendly feelings and the negative evidence supplied by our abstention from an unjust interference, were powerless to disarm Persian apprehensions. The Sháh determined to send a special envoy to Kabul who should probe this business.[1]

Worse, however, than either the impetus communicated to certain of our countrymen's ambitious longings in India, or the alarm inspired in Persia, was the offence which the Darbár gave to our great rivals at St. Petersburg. The Russian press unanimously denounced the event as 'the first stone of the wall which the Anglo-

[1] The net result was that both Persia and Afghánistán agreed to be bound by England's award regarding the disputed Seistán territory. Such an act of arbitration had been expressly provided for by the Treaty in 1857; since 1863 it had constantly been growing more necessary; in 1870-72 both parties agreed to abide by our decision; in 1872-73 that decision was given and confirmed; and although from its impartiality it was at first pleasing to neither Persia nor Afghánistán, it has been formally accepted by both. So far (1874), a great and bloody conflict has been averted by the very policy which the essayist in 1870 denounced. It would be unwise to vaticinate regarding the future of this question. Seistán forms a permanent and almost inevitable source of complications between Persia and Afghánistán. All that can be said at present is that the policy bequeathed by Lord Lawrence, and accepted by Lord Mayo, has hitherto been productive of only peaceful results as regards these two great states of Central Asia. W. W. H.

Indian Government was hastening to build across the road of the Russians in Central Asia.'[1] The *Moscow Gazette* significantly observed that, since the English had chosen to begin intrigue in Afghánistán, the same game was open to Russia in Bokhara; and that although Russia, if let alone by the English, had no desire to menace their possessions, yet, in the event of an Eastern war, Turkistán would afford her a formidable base of operations against the Indian empire. The *Golos* (*Voice*) breathed open defiance of England.

'The commercial war,' it said, 'already being waged between England and Russia, on the northern frontiers of Afghánistán, is not at all unlikely to give way some day to a combat with more sanguinary weapons than weights and measures. In this case, the rifles presented to the Amír by the Earl of Mayo would stand him in good stead, though, for the matter of that, the Amír, after taking pounds sterling, is quite as likely as not to try roubles for a change.'

Nor was this indignation without some basis of reason. The Darbár, among its other effects, had inflamed the malcontent population of Russia's new conquests in Central Asia with an idea that England might yet be induced to enter the lists and do battle against the oppressor. A more unlucky time for the spread of the belief could not have been chosen, for it happened that the nomad hordes of the Kirghiz steppe, about the northern shores of the Caspian and Aral Seas, were in open rebellion, cutting off the communication between Orenburg and Tashkend, and blockading the numerous isolated forts among which the Russian garrison of that enormous desert is dispersed in weak detachments, averaging not more than fifty Cossacks to each post. The insurgents, and those

[1] 'Exchange Gazette' of St. Petersburg, April 16, 1869.

who, like the Khán of Khivá, were in secret league with them, took heart from the retribution they believed to be in store for their embarrassed enemy; and hence, though undesignedly, the demonstration at Ambálá may have inflicted a real injury on Russia.

In another respect, I think, the Darbár occurred at an awkward time. Negotiations had been begun, and were still pending, in London, between the Russian Ambassador and our Foreign Secretary, for the settlement of the long-standing differences arising out of Central Asia's geographical position, by a mutual agreement to recognise the space then separating Russian Turkistán from our Trans-Indus frontier as a zone of neutral territory, beyond the influence of both Powers alike. Considering the predatory and turbulent disposition of the tribes inhabiting the intermediate region, there must, one would think, always be serious difficulties in the way of either Russia or England binding herself by specific treaty never to stretch a hand in advance of a given line. Wherefore, even if no Darbár had turned up to mar the course of Baron de Brunnow's interviews with Lord Clarendon, little could have been expected from their conferences beyond the exchange of amicable generalities. Yet such generalities are not without a certain value in the maintenance of international amities; and the assurances conveyed to us on this occasion by the Czar's representative would have been all the more acceptable as having originated,[1] not

[1] 'The 'Moscow Gazette' volunteers a disclosure, the accuracy of which it says it can vouch for. . . . 'Not England, we are told, but Russia, proposed the neutralisation of Afghánistán a short time ago—not England asked Russia for a pledge of pacific intentions, but Russia, seeing England uneasy at the turn of affairs, offered of her own accord to vouchsafe such a guarantee.' —'The Times,' September 25, 1869. Berlin Correspondent's letter.

in any nervous questionings on our part, but in a frank move from the opposite side, intended to establish between the two Courts a mutual understanding as to their respective programmes for the disposal of Central Asia. Russia laid her cards on the table, animated, no doubt, to do so by her experience of the absolute and continuous honesty with which the Anglo-Indian Government's declarations of a *laissez-faire* policy had till then been observed. The unexpected intelligence of the meeting at Ambálá fell like a shock on her cordiality. She shrank back into an attitude of reserve, and the conferences ceased, barren of the useful result they might possibly have borne.

There was trouble in Downing Street when the disadvantageous aspects of the business became apparent. Lord Clarendon, I suppose, gave the word that no hasty language could be allowed in Parliament to aggravate the situation, and under his inspiration the Prime Minister, throughout last spring (1869), refused to admit Central Asian affairs to discussion in the House of Commons.[1] On two separate occasions a private Member (Mr. Eastwick), who attempted to ventilate the question of our relations with that part of the world, was forced to withdraw his motion, in deference to a special appeal from Mr. Gladstone, who, while denying that the Indian Government had commenced an annual subsidy to the Amír of Afghánistán, at the same time deprecated a premature debate on the matter, lest it might interfere with the satisfactory progress of the communications then passing

[1] As the Ambálá Darbár did not take place till the close of March, all the papers were not before the Home Government till quite the end of spring. In the summer the question came before the House.

W. W. H.

between the English and Russian Cabinets. When, on the 9th of July, Mr. Eastwick's motion eventually came to a hearing, the tone of the House must have agreeably disappointed Lord Clarendon's misgivings. Not a word was said inimical to Russia, while much was urged for and against our new alliance with the Afghán Amír. The gist of the mover's long speech was, as might have been expected from his previous connection with the British Mission at Teheran, a plea for closer intimacy with Persia, as a preferable investment for our money and our hopes to any that could be found in Afghánistán. The seconder was Sir Charles Wingfield, than whom no more competent authority on Indian topics has ever sat in Parliament. Sir Charles, with evident advertence to Lord Lawrence's speech in the Upper House, which has been above quoted, tore to pieces the flimsy fallacy that asserted the Ambálá Darbár to be no departure from the Indian Government's previous policy: he laid bare the irreconcileable antagonism between the principles pursued up to the year 1868, and those which the Darbár had just inaugurated; and he dwelt with asperity on the suicidal folly of our beginning in Central Asia a course of intrigue against the Russians, which would infallibly elicit from them ceaseless counter-intrigues against ourselves. On behalf of the Ministry the Under-Secretary for India made a strikingly able reply. The felicity of Mr. Grant Duff's diction—spirited, terse, and lucid—gave interest and charm to names which the British public generally hears sounded with alien ears, while the copiousness of his matter satisfied the most exacting critics of the thorough mastery he possessed of his recondite subject. The only blot in an otherwise admirable oration was that the speaker over-stated the case committed to him to defend. The paramount duty of soothing the irritation of Russia fettered his thoughts in one direction, and he was led astray in another as well by the glamour of Lord Lawrence's reputation as by his own generous anxiety to see good in measures for which other men than himself were responsible. Only on this supposition can I understand how a statesman of Mr. Grant Duff's calibre was persuaded to accept, amplify, and reissue in bolder form the fiction which Lord Lawrence's oracular dicta had dimly started, as to the meaningless character of our recent intervention in Afghánistán:—

'The Government,' said the Under-Secretary, 'did not dream of erecting Sher Alí into a bulwark against Russia, or against anybody else. If any bulwark was wanted in that part of the world, nature had planted bulwarks enough in all conscience, as we once found out to our cost, and as anybody else would soon find out to theirs. What was wanted was a quiet Afghánistán, just as they wanted a quiet Burmah. The Government wanted to be able to use every penny they could scrape together in India for the moral and material development of the country. They wished to stimulate commerce round the whole of the land and sea frontier, and it did not at all suit to have one of their trade gates locked up by a burning house, the cellars of which were known to be full of highly explosive compounds. They wanted Sher Alí to be strong for the suppression of lawlessness, and rich, if possible, into the bargain. They wanted him to understand that they did not covet a square inch of his territory, or ask any kind of assistance from him, other than the sort of indirect assistance which a civilised Government must always derive from being known to exercise a pacifying and semi-civilising influence around its own borders. . . . And the fact that Russia had advanced to a point between Samarkand and Bokhara had not induced them to do any one thing which they would not have the strongest motives for doing if she had never passed a verst beyond the Ural or Orenburg line.'

This seems to me a hazardous flight of rhetoric. To test the soundness of its assertions let us glance at the parallel case—so cited by Mr. Grant Duff himself—of our relations with Burmah. Burmah, both in itself and as a stepping-stone to the markets of Western China, is of far more value to our merchants than Afghánistán has ever been, or will be. Insurrections and anarchy may choke the course of trade in Afghánistán, but their counterparts prevail in Burmah, and do much more detriment to our interests. The King of Burmah can point to a clearer title for his authority than Sher Alí possesses, and his past conduct towards his own people and the British Government invests him with an incomparably larger claim upon our regard. If, then, it was for the relief of commerce that we lavished money and arms on Sher Alí, how much greater should be our obligation to supply the Lord of the Golden Foot with the means of enforcing order in Burmah? Yet we have never spared the latter a cowrie, and any proposal to help him would move derision both in England and in India. 'A quiet Burmah,' in fact, is not worth the lifting of a finger; while for 'a quiet Afghánistán' we move heaven and earth. Manifestly it cannot be commerce that lends Afghánistán such signal preponderance in our scales. Trade, no doubt, was spoken of to Sher Alí at Ambálá; but had trade been all we wanted, his cries for help would have gone unnoticed by us to the end of the chapter.[1] What we did for him

[1] Omitting no point of which anything could be made, Mr. Grant Duff also referred to the advantage which a good understanding with the Amír would give us for checking the raids of the independent mountaineers who separate India from Afghánistán. But this is rather an imaginary advantage. The tribes would not like to be caught between two fires, and are on their guard against such a combination; otherwise they care not a straw for the Kabul Government. Sher Alí himself, who, from a matrimonial connection with one tribe (the Momunds, if I remember rightly), exercises among them some small influence of a personal, not a governmental character, paid according to custom, on entering and on leaving India, to the clansmen of the Khaibar Pass the usual black-mail for permission to traverse their defile.

was dictated by a very different motive. That motive, notwithstanding Mr. Grant Duff's inability to believe it, seems to have been 'the dream of erecting Sher Alí into a bulwark against Russia.' By blinking it, we may deceive ourselves; we shall impose on nobody else. The Under-Secretary had been nearer the mark on the previous 9th of March, when he had defined our gifts as 'the expression of a hope that *a strong Government was about to be established* in a long-distracted country.' And the less premeditated definition ought not to pass into oblivion: for there is a distinct note of warning in its sound; it reproduces the identical words commonly used to describe the intention, with which, to our shame and sorrow, we once before undertook to interfere in the domestic dissensions of the Afgháns. It was precisely this idea, the idea of '*establishing* a friendly Power and *a strong Government* in Afghánistán,'[1] that inspired the expedition of 1838; and the phrase into which the member for Elgin so naturally slipped is a distinct memento of that evil time. True, there is a vast difference in the methods by which Lord Auckland thirty years ago, and Lord Mayo in these days, have respectively proceeded; but the fact of their both having sought the same object, throws a startling light on the true bearings and ultimate tendency of the present Viceroy's policy.[2]

However, it must be admitted that the debate of the 9th of July had, on the whole, the effect primarily desired by Mr. Grant Duff and the Ministry. One organ of

[1] Kaye's 'War in Afghánistán,' vol. i. p. 370.

[2] The object of Lord Auckland's policy was to force back on the Afgháns, by means of a British Army, a ruler whom they had ignominiously and finally expelled; the object of Lord Mayo's was to help the ruler whom the Afgháns had themselves finally accepted, to consolidate his power without sending a single English soldier into the country. W. W. H.

public opinion at Moscow (the *Sovremenni Izvesti*) warned its readers not to be diverted from mistrust of our actual deeds in India by our farcical assertions of innocence in the House of Commons; but Russia, at large, was for the time mollified and appeased.

Some approach to a better understanding with the Muscovite Government was day by day growing into a political necessity. For while our diplomatists had been smiling, and our Ministers, like the lady in *Hamlet*, protesting too much, the local politics of Central Asia had kept the bias imparted to their course by British hands in India, and were developing events calculated to re-awaken and intensify any previous suspicion which Russia might have conceived of our designs. The Amír of Bokhara, who in the summer of 1868 had been compelled to accept terms[1] of peace from General Kaufmann, was troubled with a rebellious son, known to the Russians as Katti Tura and in India called Abdul Mallik. This young prince, with the blessing of all the priesthood, had taken the leadership of a quasi-national party in Bokhara, comprising the numerous classes whose patriotism or fanaticism spurned accommodation of any kind with the invading infidel from Russia. The south-eastern provinces adjoining Afghánistán had enthusiastically responded to his war-cry; and with the help of the well-known guerilla chief, Sádik, operating in the north on the new Russian frontier about Samarkand, this modern Absalom had so nearly succeeded in deposing his father that, in November 1868, General Abramoff had felt constrained to rescue and re-establish the Amír by force of arms. Then the prince

[1] The terms were—cession of the conquered territory; payment of 80,000*l.* indemnity; protection and liberty of trade for all Russian subjects throughout Bokhara; and limitation of import duties on Russian goods to 2½ per cent. *ad valorem*.

had fled, first to Khivá and afterwards to Merv, labouring hard, wherever he went, to organise a league of Islam against the renegade Amír and the accursed Russians. His movements up to this point had mattered nothing to British India. But from Merv he came into the Afghán territory of Balkh, and there converted the asylum afforded him by our friend, Sher Alí, into a lever for raising rebellion across the Oxus among his compatriots and former associates in the Bokhariot territories of Shahr-i-sabz, Sherábád, and Hissár. Not this only, but, for the furtherance of his designs, he falsely used the names of Sher Alí and of the British Government as his aiders and abettors. It would be superfluous to observe that the British Government was totally free from any complicity in these intrigues. Whether Sher Alí was equally guiltless is open to doubt. The Amír of Bokhara had done him injury in the late civil war by siding with his rivals, and the present enterprise afforded him a fair chance of repaying the Úsbeg Darbár in its own coin. Also, perhaps, he may have thought that, although no hint regarding the conduct expected of him in this affair had reached him from his patrons, the English, he could not wrongly interpret their unspoken wishes if he fostered a project avowedly intended to hamper the Russian advance. Be this as it may, the refugee pretender to the throne of Bokhara was allowed to have his own way while he stayed in Balkh; and when, towards the close of the summer, he repaired to Kabul, he was received by Sher Alí with every sign of the most distinguished consideration. The menacing shadow thrown by the conjunction of these hostile forces across the southern border of Bokhara filled Amír Muzaffar-ud-dín with disquietude. Looking to his Russian allies again for salvation, the

Úsbeg monarch determined to send an embassy all the way to St. Petersburg. He placed his fourth and favourite son, a boy of twelve years, at the head of the mission; and he officially avowed to the local Russian commandant that his object was to inform the *Ak Pádsháh*, or White Emperor, of the danger in which he stood from the English and the Afghláns. The *Invalide Russe*, a Government organ, made no secret of the Amír's declaration. Its semi-official voice proclaimed to all the world that Bokhara had appeared before the Czar's tribunal to accuse the English of kindling war against herself and her Russian protectors. After such an announcement no one can be surprised to find an impartial witness reporting presently from St. Petersburg[1] that 'the ill-will with which England is regarded in Russia is slowly but steadily increasing,' and that an impression is spreading in the Russian capital 'that the complications in Central Asia must lead to a violent collision with the ruler of India.'[2]

To relieve the morbid state of our relations with the Northern Power, the doctors of diplomacy—a profession as grudgingly honoured by the British public as that of medicine is by healthy youth—again came on the stage. The London conferences between Lord Clarendon and Baron de Brunnow had been adjourned without any definite conclusion; and so when the happy coincidence arose last autumn that Prince Gortschakoff, the Russian Minister for Foreign Affairs, and our own Foreign Secretary were both spending their so-called holidays in Germany, the one at Wiesbaden and the other at Baden-Baden, what more

[1] The St. Petersburg correspondent of the 'Cologne Gazette.'

[2] It is fair to add that the same language had been used by the Continental Press a score of times before. W. W. H.

natural than that the pair should arrange a meeting at an equidistant third point, Heidelberg, and there take up the thread of the unfinished negotiations? In past years it had been England's constant complaint, that while the Czar's Government at St. Petersburg disowned all ideas of further territorial aggrandisement in Central Asia, his Majesty's generals on the spot nevertheless proceeded unchecked to add conquest to conquest, thereby leaving us in helpless perplexity between Russian professions and Russian actions. Now the tables were turned, and the charge of inconsistency pointed against ourselves. Prince Gortschakoff could not get over the wide discrepancy between our pacific sentiments in London and our inimical doings, real or supposed, at Ambálá and at Kabul. Lord Clarendon, however, was ready with a remedy. There happened at the time to be in Europe, on leave, a Bengal civil servant, Mr. T. D. Forsyth, who was understood to possess the confidence of the Indian Viceroy in respect of Central Asian affairs. It was therefore proposed and settled between the two high negotiators that the discussions begun in London and renewed at Heidelberg should be concluded at St. Petersburg, the English side being represented at the Russian capital, not by our ambassador alone, but by Sir Andrew Buchanan, aided by Mr. Forsyth's Indian experience and knowledge of the situation. In the meantime the path for our spokesmen was cleared for them by the despatch of instructions from the Duke of Argyll to Lord Mayo, desiring that efforts should be made to induce Sher Alí to abstain from any such exaggeration of the duties of hospitality as might involve Afghánistán in complicity with Abdul Mallik's scheme against the Governments of Bokhara and Russia.

The St. Petersburg conference came off in October.

Rightly to understand the circumstances which had to be handled, we must remember that the preceding twenty months had wrought a great change in the position not only of Russia and of England towards Bokhara and Afghánistán, but of Bokhara and of Afghánistán towards one another. Formerly Russia had been at war with Bokhara, and Bokhara had been vainly seeking assistance from England against Russia; England had been keeping aloof from any responsibility in Afghánistán; while between the Amír of Bokhara and the faction headed by Azím Khán, then dominant in Afghánistán, a cordial understanding had prevailed. Everything was now reversed. Russia was at peace with Bokhara, and Bokhara was said to be claiming protection from Russia against the supposed hostility of England. England was deemed responsible for the conduct of Afghánistán; while between the Amír of Bokhara and Sher Alí, the restored ruler of Afghánistán, there was hatred, malice, and all uncharitableness. Out of this new combination flowed a clear necessity that Russia, on behalf of her client, Amír Muzaffar-ud-dín, and England, on behalf of her client, Amír Sher Alí, should take steps for ensuring a maintenance of the peace between the neighbouring kingdoms of Bokhara and Afghánistán. And the first step was to separate the antagonists by a definite boundary. What quickened our interest in this point to the highest degree was, that Russia had affirmed, and we had accepted, the axiom, that in regard to all territory within Bokhariot limits she must hold herself unfettered to act as she in the future might think fit. Hence the arguments at St. Petersburg revolved principally about the question whether Balkh, the province intercepted between the river Oxus on the north, and the mountains of Hindu Khúsh on the south, should be assigned to Afghánistán or to Bokhara. Though held for a score of years past by the Afgháns, it has always been a bone of contention between the two states. Russia accepted the principle we advocated of existing possession, recognised the Afghán tenure of Balkh, and contented herself with securing the ferries of the Oxus for Bokhara. With this result the negotiations were brought to a final close; and nothing, I believe, has since occurred to modify the situation. The end obtained by our representatives seems as much as, under the circumstances, they could have hoped for; and it may, therefore, be considered creditable to them and satisfactory to England. But obviously it falls far short, I will not say of a settlement of the Central Asian question, which perhaps lies in the limbo of impossibilities, but of the neutralisation of Afghánistán; which except for the intervention of the Darbár might have been accomplished for us at the beginning of the year. Further, we must note that Russia's concessions, if concessions they can be called, are not guaranteed to us by a single stroke of her pen. The agreement effected was purely conversational. Sir Andrew Buchanan read aloud to Prince Gortschakoff, General Miliutin (Minister for War), and M. Stremöukhoff (Chief of the Asiatic Department), the despatch reporting to his own Government the incidents and issue of the conference, and his audience assented verbally to its general correctness; but this was all. The corresponding despatch which Prince Gortschakoff addressed to the Russian ambassador in London, and of which, it was hoped, a copy would have been furnished to Lord Clarendon, proved, on receipt by Baron de Brunnow, to be of a confidential character, not intended for communication to the English Government. I do not presume—indeed, I have not even the wish—to question the good faith of Russia in this transaction. I merely regret the omission of a formality, without which the pledges she has given are, from a diplomatic point of view, incomplete.

Another consideration not to be overlooked is that Russia, while politely deferring to English views in respect of the northern boundary of Afghánistán, has not carried conciliation to the length of relaxing her aggressive efforts in other parts of Central Asia nearer to her present frontier. As for pausing in her southward march, she is rather striding forward with redoubled speed and energy. Quite recently she has sent an expedition across from the Caucasian to the eastern shore of the Caspian Sea to establish a fort in Krasnovodsk Bay, and from thence to construct a caravan road along the ancient bed of the Oxus to a convenient point on the modern river; and this is but the prelude to a campaign against Khivá in the spring. The anexation of Khivá will lead immediately to absorptions of Bokhariot territory higher up the Oxus, so that really now we are in a fair way to see verified an important event which hasty writers have often already anticipated, namely, a Russian occupation of the *tête-de-pont* at Chárjui. Further eastward, other signs of movement are not wanting. Against the Afghán principality of Badakshán the Khán of Kokand, Khudá Yár Khán, who is a mere Russian cat's-paw, is said to have been making hostile demonstrations at Koláb: and in Eastern Turkistán, unless the Atálik Ghází speedily throws open to Russian trade his own markets and the old commercial communication with China, the independence of his state is threatened with summary extinction. Generally, Russia's policy at the present time appears animated by a resentful determination to meet our recent activity by increased activity of her own. She has entered with a will upon measures of aggression which, except for our step forward, she might have indefinitely postponed. Far from retarding, we have positively accelerated, the appearance of the Cossacks at Chárjui.

Having now tried to show that in India, in Persia, and above all in Europe, the consequences of the change in our Central Asian plans from quiescence to action are evil, my readers might expect to find some compensation for these diplomatic difficulties in an ameliorated condition of Afghánistán. Surely the year cannot have terminated without 'a strong Government,' or at least its stable foundations, having been built among the Afgháns. By this time surely Sher Alí must have done much to consolidate his power; and so the success of our *protégé* shall supply the amends owed us by fate. Yet, what are the facts?[1] All, I fear, in an opposite direction. The official version of late events in Afghánistán is that Sher Alí, penetrated with admiration for the British institutions he saw at work in India, and impelled by a laudable desire to communicate similar benefits to his own countrymen, has been occupied, since his return to Kabul, with introducing reforms in the administration of the kingdom; but to me he seems to have prosecuted this task with rather more vigour than caution. The Anglo-Indian press, committed as it universally is to approval of Lord

[1] Mr. Wyllie unfortunately wrote this, and died, before the 'facts' were known to him. The reforms in the Afghán administration which immediately followed our final recognition of Sher Alí are mentioned on next page; but the five years of comparative rest in Afghánistán which resulted from the Ambálá Darbár could not have been anticipated in December 1869, when this paper was written. W. W. H.

Mayo's Central Asian policy, has gladly endorsed the official story; and through the veil of this consentient approbation the real state of the case has been difficult to discern. To my view there is one point only by which Sher Alí's prospects have been advanced since last spring; and that he has obtained more, as the saying goes, by good luck than good management. Death has done him the inestimable service of taking away the ex-Amír, Azím Khán. Sher Alí's history, whatever may be its future course, will never contain a more conspicuous landmark than that which records the removal from his path of his most formidable rival, Azím Khán. In other respects the Amír has, in my opinion, lost ground. His 'reforms' must be viewed in connection neither with English models nor with any standard of Utopian perfection, but with the customs of the country he practically had in hand. The two branches of administration on which he set to work were the revenue and the army. Hitherto Afghánistán had been parcelled out among governors, each of whom received and used the taxes of his province after his own fashion, and remitted to the central authority only so much balance as he thought it unsafe to withhold. Similarly the army had been nothing more than an assemblage of the contingents which, on sound of war, the heads of the various clans severally brought to the royal camp. These federal and feudal arrangements Sher Alí endeavoured to replace by a system of monarchical centralisation. He wanted a standing army of his own; and, still more, he wanted local treasuries of his own, so that the taxes might reach him entire, and the emoluments of the provincial governors take the form of fixed salaries. In fact he renewed, on a scale amplified in proportion to the increase of strength accruing to him from English money and English weapons, the self-same scheme for exalting the kingly power at the expense of the nobility, his indulgence in which, soon after the commencement of his reign, had been a principal cause of his deposition. Of all the unpopular measures among which his former government had suffered shipwreck, not one had damaged him so much as his attempt to commute the fiefs of the aristocracy into cash allowances. He now recurred to it, having, like the Bourbons of the Restoration, learned nothing by adversity, and forgotten nothing. As a natural result, conspiracies were secretly hatched, or his authority openly defied, all over the kingdom. Two of his nephews, who had been detected in a plot at Kabul, he deported into India, where the British Government obligingly undertook for him the gaoler-like duty of detaining them under surveillance. But the Amír's greatest difficulty lay northwards, in Balkh. His recovery of that unruly province in the spring, when Azím Khán's son, Ishakh Khán, withdrew from it into Bokhara, had never been confirmed by vigorous treatment. Day after day he was said to intend sending troops to restore order, but nothing came of all the talk. His procrastination was intertwined with another folly equally dangerous, of which mention has been already made. He was harbouring and highly honouring a rebellious Úsbeg prince, Abdul Mallik, who aspired to dethrone the Amír of Bokhara, at the very time when a rebellious Barukzai prince, Ishakh Khán, who aspired to do the same by him in Afghánistán, was a refugee at Bokhara, ready and longing to be used by the Bokhariot Darbár as an instrument of reprisal upon the Afghán Darbár. The Amír of Bokhara clutched the opportunity, and put at Ishakh

Khán's disposal every facility for organising a fresh expedition into Afghánistán. It is even alleged that the undertaking was encouraged, if not actively assisted, by the Russian general at Samarkand. This may or may not be true: it is not unlikely; and, if true, it is an immediate realisation of Sir Charles Wingfield's prophecy in the House of Commons that intervention in Afghán affairs would for England be equivalent to entering on a game of intrigue and counter-intrigue with Russia. Ishakh Khán recrossed the Oxus in August last. Cordially welcomed by the local chiefs, and without any opposition from the royal troops, he repossessed himself of Balkh. To this hour he remains in undisputed occupation of the province. Indeed it appears an open question whether, when the disappearance of the winter's snows (1870) renders military operations again practicable, the Amír Sher Alí will win back the lost jewel of Balkh to his crown, or whether Ishakh Khán will add the remainder of Afghánistán to his present conquest. Supposing the latter contingency came really to pass, and that the avenging son of the man whom we helped to destroy in 1868-9 should emerge as ruler of all the Afgháns in 1870, where then would be the English ascendancy in Kabul politics for which we have sacrificed so much? In suggesting this awkward question I may be suspected of prejudice. I anticipate the charge by soliciting reference to the facts confessed by the most able organ of the policy I impugn. A correspondent of the *Friend of India*, vouched for by the editor as 'a careful observer, who knows the country well, and had some conversation with the Amír on his late visit to India,' employed the following language, on the 26th of October last, to describe the condition of Afghánistán:—

'So far as I can judge from the accounts brought me from Kabul, there seems good reason for believing that the Amír is ruining his own cause. He has money, but he does not pay his troops. One of his regiments has been destroyed to a man, and in Balkh, Ishakh Khán, son of Azím Khán, is gaining ground, and is well supplied with money—some say from Samarkand. If so, it tells a tale. At Kandahar there is a rising, and a Sardàr' (chief) 'has collected a lakh' (100,000) 'of well-armed ruffians, who will probably give the Amír much trouble. Already they have taken some guns from him, and disposed of the few troops sent against them. There is a storm brewing, and many respectable natives seem to think it not at all improbable that Sher Alí, if he escapes with his life, will soon seek a refuge in our territory. Uslum Khán is about the only faithful Sardár left him, and he begs the Amír to pay the troops, and send him to the seat of war. It is a pity he has not sense enough to pay his soldiers. Even his friends think his reason is failing, or he would not so foolishly persist in alienating his people. I sincerely hope he will maintain his position, and govern the country wisely; but, if native information is worth anything, misfortune is not far off, and that entirely through his own fault.

The same journal, in its issues of the 2nd and 23rd of November, admits that Ishakh Khán is complete master of Balḳh; that the rebellion at Kandahar, mentioned in the above extract, has spread to the neighbourhood of Ghuznee, where it has been strengthened by defections from the Amír's forces; and that through all Afghánistán a restless and insurrectionary spirit is abroad.[1]

To look at the subject from another point of view. Is the contact of Russia with the north-west frontier of India a thing to be desired or deprecated? If the welfare of Central Asia is to be considered, we cannot deny that Russian order in place of Úsbeg or Afghán anarchy, and that Christian tolerance in place

[1] These conjectures turned out to be without foundation. Sher Alí's power has grown more stable every year since the definitive recognition of him by Lord Mayo in 1869. W. W. H.

of Muslim bigotry, would be supreme benefits to that unhappy region. But what is Central Asia to us, what are we to Central Asia? The general cause of humanity, if I may hazard a guess at 'the painful riddle of this world,' seems to be best served by each nation minding its own business. It is the business of England to civilise India up to a point when the natives can be left to govern themselves. Were we to be interrupted in this mission, and forced to quit the country before our time, the result in India—to say nothing of the shock to England, and, through England, to the inhabited world—would be, under any circumstances, long years of war, confusion, and misery, such as befell the denizens of our own island on the departure of the Romans. We, in our turn, might become recipients of the pathetic appeal, 'The barbarians drive us into the sea, and the sea drives us back on the barbarians.' I believe that we shall be traitors both to ourselves and to the peoples committed to our charge if we regard the progress of Asiatic Russia from any other point of view than the security and benefit of our own empire. In this relation, and in this only, should the 'Central Asian Question,' as it is called, have any meaning for England.[1] So regarded, the advent of a great European Power to our close neighbourhood, occupying the historic path by which all the various conquerors of India, except ourselves, have advanced, and summoning to her standard all the warlike clansmen of

[1] Well said Sir Stafford Northcote, in the House of Commons on July 9:—'When he heard that the House was asked to discuss the policy of England in Central Asia, he was tempted to say that the only answer we could give was, that England had no policy in Central Asia. In point of fact, we ought not to have a Central Asian policy. It ought to be an Indian policy. We had enough on our hands with the management of our own interests.'

or Afghán anarchy, and that Christian tolerance in place of Muslim bigotry, would be supreme benefits to that unhappy region. But what is Central Asia to us, what are we to Central Asia? The general cause of humanity, if I may hazard a guess at 'the painful riddle of this world,' seems to be best served by each nation minding its own business. It is the business of England to civilise India up to a point when the natives can be left to govern themselves. Were we to be interrupted in this mission, and forced to quit the country before our time, the result in India — to say nothing of the shock to England, and, through England, to the inhabited world—would be under any circumstances, long years of war, confusion, and misery, such as befell the denizens of our own island on the departure of the Romans. We, in our turn, might become recipients of the pathetic appeal, 'The barbarians drive us into the sea, and the sea drives us back on the barbarians.' I believe that we shall be traitors both to ourselves and to the peoples committed to our charge if we regard the progress of Asiatic Russia from any other point of view than the security and benefit of our own empire. In this relation, and in this only, should the 'Central Asian Question,' as it is called, have any meaning for England.[1] So regarded, the advent of a great European power to our close neighbourhood, occupying the historic path by which all the various conquerors of India, except ourselves, have advanced, and

[1] Well said Sir Stafford Northcote, in the House of Commons on July 9:—'When he heard that the House was asked to discuss the policy of England in Central Asia, he was tempted to say that the only answer we could give was, that England had no policy in Central Asia. In point of fact, we ought not to have a Central Asian policy. It ought to be an Indian policy. We had enough in our hands with the management of our own interests.'

summoning to her standard all the warlike clansmen of the Afghán hills, who look on Hindustán as their natural prey, must assuredly prove a grave inconvenience. I put aside the contingency of a Russian invasion. The public discussion (thanks to Sir Henry Rawlinson) of our dimly apprehended perils has had the good effect of demonstrating that Russia, neither at present nor for many years to come, can command the means to attempt an open attack. The practical danger consists in the encouragement to insurrection which her proximity will supply to all our discontented subjects in India. These in proportion to the two hundred millions of population are marvellously few, but in proportion to our garrison of sixty thousand soldiers unpleasantly numerous; even while our peace with Russia continues unbroken, they may keep us in perpetual fidget; and in case of war the necessity for watching them may cripple our power for operations in Europe. On the other hand, it is asserted that if we have disaffection in India, Russia has the same in Turkistán; that the nearer she comes to us the greater will be her embarrassments; and that if she foments troubles within our border we can retaliate by doing the like within hers. This no doubt is true; but in such a game we should be risking gold against her copper; we have infinitely more at stake in India than she has in Turkistán, and by the loss of a single trick we should be hit harder than she would be by the loss of a hundred. As for commercial considerations, it is Russia's declared object to secure a monopoly of the Central Asian trade by rigidly excluding the superior and cheaper manufactures of England; markets, therefore, which at present under the indigenous rulers are open to us, will be hopelessly closed as soon as they pass within the Russian pale.

Only in one respect can I conceive any good accruing to us from further enlargements of the Russian boundary: they operate as a heavy blow and great discouragement to the cause of Islam, not only at the scene of their occurrence, but throughout Asia generally; and, as Muhammadan fanaticism is the main source of our intestine dangers in India, they, to some extent, serve to damp the designs of our domestic enemies. But, on the whole, our interests decidedly demand that India should be separated from Russia for as long a time and by as wide a territorial gap as possible.

Now, the question is, What can we do either to prevent the meeting of the two empires, or, if that be impossible, to render their collision innocuous?

Several authorities have proposed that we should lay a plain statement of our difficulties before Russia, and obtain a written guarantee from her never to overstep a certain line of limitation. The distinguished President of the Geographical Society has on more than one occasion announced his confidence in the Czar's intention to leave Afghánistán untouched. But for myself I can give only a qualified adhesion to this belief. Bokhara is intimately connected with Afghánistán; and Russia, who is now virtual mistress of Bokhara, hardly has the power, though she may have the wish, to refrain from contact with men and things south of the Oxus. Omitting, as unproved, the support that Ishakh Khán's invasion of Balkh is said to have obtained from the Russian authorities at Samarkand, we know that General Kaufmann two years ago took into pay a large body of Afghán soldiers, and that their commandant, who is a prince of the royal Barukzai house, now holds an official position at St. Petersburg. These facts are incompatible with utter isolation from Afghán politics. Indeed, I cannot suppress a doubt whether, when Russian troops hold the ferry of the Oxus leading into Balkh, it will be possible for them long to observe the limit which, under Sir A. Buchanan's negotiations, has just been established for parting Bokhara from Afghánistán. A river is notoriously a bad frontier; incursions from Balkh will provoke the Russians to cross in pursuit of the offenders; and ultimately the Úsbeg nationality of the inhabitants will afford an argument for their incorporation into the same empire with Bokhara. The imperial boundary cannot, I believe, stop at the Oxus; there is more likelihood of its pausing at the northern foot of the Hindu Khúsh mountains. Local complications of this kind are almost beyond the Czar's control; and, without a proper allowance for the effect they are certain to exercise, his Majesty's intentions are liable to be misread. Besides, we must bear in mind that diplomacy between the Courts of St. James's and St. Petersburg has been already tried, and has not done much for us. To cap all, it seems unworthy of our ancient nation that Englishmen should cringingly approach any power on earth with a confession of fear and an entreaty for forbearance. Our dignity demands, as our strength warrants, that we should look to ourselves for our own protection.

The independent courses open to our option are of two kinds, those which lie beyond, and those which are contained within the British frontier. Bright with the attractive glitter of foreign enterprise, the former line has always commanded the larger share of popular favour. Its characteristic principle is the interposition between India and Russia of Governments friendly to ourselves and capable of withstanding our northern rivals. Thirty years ago we pursued this idea so far as to enter on a military occupation of Afghánistán, and to assume a large share in its civil administration. Some say that the experiment, though it then ended in ruin, ought to be repeated with the omission of old blunders and the addition of new precautions. My own belief is that, even though the strategic advantages of a renewed march to Kandahar and Herat were clearer than they are, their cost of three and a half millions sterling per annum is more than India can furnish. The scheme, however, is too large for discussion in this place. Moreover, its advocates speak of it rather as a measure of future expediency than of immediate necessity. We may pass on therefore in a practical spirit to the notion now dominant in our national policy, of giving Afghánistán 'a strong Government,' not in our own person, but in the person of a native ruler subsidised by us. That this notion, as set to work by Lords Lawrence and Mayo, has hitherto produced nothing but disappointment, cannot be doubted.

'But,' it may be objected, 'Sher Alí has only had a ten months' trial; he may yet become real master of the country; or, supposing even that he does break down altogether, the failure in this case will be no argument against better luck with the better men who will succeed him on the Kabul throne; one accident ought not to damn a great policy.'

I reply, firstly, that the artificial erection of a 'strong government' on foreign soil must, under the most favourable circumstances, be about as arduous a task as it is possible to conceive any nation undertaking; and secondly, that in the national character and customs of the Afgháns there are inherent defects which reduce our attempt to a complete impossibility. The Afghán nation is an aggregate of separate clans, republican in their internal organisation. Their common saying is that 'all Afgháns are equal.' The authority which the Amír, the head of the principal clan, nominally exercises over them all comprises, at best, little more than a right to levy a fixed proportion of troops and money from each for the common defence. Governments and sovereigns are changed with inconceivable rapidity.[1]

'He who possesses a little money, and can scatter it amongst the crowd, will soon have a sufficient number of partisans to assist in raising him to power; and though this power is hereditary in Afghánistán, the regular succession to the throne is by no means liked, and is the most uncertain thing possible. The legitimate heir is always obliged to submit the question of sovereignty to an election and the chances of war. . . . In Afghánistán everything that succeeds is legitimate, and in this way success favours the greatest rascal; his crimes or his virtues are of little importance to the people: if he pays well he is their idol; but let his purse get empty, let a reverse of fortune overtake him, he at once becomes an object of contempt and aversion, and is obliged either to expatriate himself or retire into a greater obscurity than that from which he sprung.'[2]

The Sardárs, or chiefs of clans, are all sovereigns within their respective domains. Jealous, turbulent, and ambitious, they are always impatient to see their prince replaced by another from whom they expect greater advantages. 'They will sell their services to the highest bidder; it is indifferent to them whether their friend of to-day is their enemy to-morrow, or whether they have to

[1] The Ambálá Darbár took place at the end of March 1869; Mr. Wyllie's latest information when he wrote this was an Indian newspaper dated the 30th November 1869. Had he lived a few years, or even months, longer, he would have seen his apprehensions for the stability of the Amír's power removed.
W. W. H.

[2] Ferrier's 'History of the Afgháns,' p. 304.

take arms against their relations or not.' Anything for money is their maxim. The common people follow the example of their chiefs.

'They will desert one party and attach themselves to another, without feeling any compunction or incurring the least disgrace. They always welcome, and with enthusiasm, the arrival of a new sovereign; but a reign too long, or a peace too prolonged with their neighbours, is to them insupportable; and when no opportunity presents itself of getting rid of their over-excitement on their foes without, they make war upon one another.'

This description is mostly taken from Ferrier; but Mountstuart Elphinstone says much the same thing, and supplies, in addition, the following anecdote:—

'I once,' he states, 'strongly urged to a very intelligent old man of the tribe of Miyánkhail, the superiority of a quiet and secure life, under a powerful monarch, to the discord, the alarms, and the blood, which they owed to their present system. The old man replied with great warmth, and thus concluded an indignant harangue against arbitrary power: 'We are content with discord, we are content with alarms, we are content with blood, but we never will be content with a master.'[1]

What is to be done with a nation of this sort? We cannot make the Ethiopian change his skin or the leopard his spots. A war of succession, such as Sher Alí has just gone through, is not the exception, but the rule, in Afghánistán. His four predecessors spent their lives in making or meeting insurrections. The normal constitution of the country, since it ceased to be a football between the Sháh of Persia and the Great Mughul of Dehli, is not one strong monarchy, but several weak and

[1] Elphinstone's 'Account of the Kingdom of Kabul,' p. 174.

antagonistic principalities. Twice only in Afghán history have the discordant tribes been united under a native king of substantial power. And the two soldiers of fortune who achieved this feat were in their way Napoleons, born rulers of mankind, such as are not found in every generation. If out of the present turmoil a second Ahmad Sháh or a new Dost Muhammad were to come to the surface, and, by establishing his own supremacy, restore comparative order to the land, such a Government, born of indigenous materials and possessing a vital principle of its own, might perhaps be susceptible of some confirmation at our hands. But even then the hold which an outlay of arms and money might procure for us on Afghánistán, would only be co-extensive with the life of the individual monarch; when he died we should again be adrift in the periodically recurring deluge. I will not dwell on the moral aspect of the subsidy system, though whether we are justified in giving any Government the means to coerce its subjects without taking some security that our gifts shall not be abused to purposes of oppression and cruelty, is a question well meriting attention. On strictly political grounds it seems to me that we may, at any rate, wait for the avatár in Afghánistán of a hero equal to the occasion. Until he appears, our most elaborate efforts to keep any ruler going who has not strength within himself to keep his legs, must be, to use Mr. Bright's phrase, 'sheer tinkering.'

Afghánistán, however, is not the only kingdom which has attracted attention as a fit locality beyond the British frontier for our operations in search of a breakwater against the tide of Russian progress. 'Russia,' says Sir Henry Rawlinson, 'could never establish herself at Herat, and keep up her communications with Asterábád.

without the co-operation of Persia; and against that co-operation our efforts should be accordingly directed.' I have dared to differ from Sir Henry on many points of our Central Asian policy, but in regard to the value of cordial relations with the Sháh's Government, I gladly seize an opportunity for expressing humble concurrence with that great master. The administration of Persia is not a model organism; it is inferior to that of Turkey. Still, Persia is a settled, and, so to speak, civilised state, having representatives resident at the Courts of Europe. She presents a tangible and reasonable personality to our approaches; and Mr. Eastwick is amply justified in declaring that time and money spent at Teheran would be much more to our purpose than if sunk in the chaos of Afghánistán. We are too much given, especially in India, to disparaging Persia as 'the mere tool of an aggressive Russia.' The late Lord Strangford—ah, that he were back to guide our counsels! —protested against the 'brutal levity of thought' involved in this assumption.[1] Persia deserves no such reproach. She is keenly alive to the danger of being caught within the snaky folds of her northern neighbour's fascination. Moreover, as she is quite aware of the sympathy with which England views her determination to shun the fatal embrace, English influence might, and ought to be, supreme at Teheran. If this is not the case at present, the fault is our own. There are many ways in which we might show an increased regard for Persia. Foremost stands the retransfer to the India Office of the control over our Mission which is at present exercised by the Foreign Office. Hear the words of one who, being more eminently fitted than any other man alive to repre-

[1] 'Selected writings of Viscount Strangford,' vol. ii. p. 274.

sent British interests at Teheran, resigned the post of Minister as soon as he found himself subordinated to the Foreign Office:—

'Persian diplomacy is essentially an Eastern question, and mainly dependent on considerations of Indian policy. . . . The Indian revenues contribute a sum of 12,000*l.* per annum toward the expenses of the Persian Mission. There is no single element, indeed, of European diplomacy connected with Persia, except the relations of that country with Turkey; and even these relations, referring almost exclusively to frontier grievances, come more naturally under the jurisdiction of Bagdad or of Erzeroum than of Constantinople. It may further be questioned whether the traditions and practice of the Foreign Office, admirably adapted as they are to European diplomacy, are fitted to deal with the peculiarities of Eastern character. . . . It may be doubtful if the duties of the Teheran Mission, reorganised as a powerful machine of Indian defence, could be carried out by an ordinary staff of Foreign Office attachés. At any rate, it would be infinitely better to employ Indian officers, accustomed to the native character, acquainted with the language, and who would look to Persian and Afghán service as their career in life, instead of pining for the luxuries and leisure of Paris and Vienna.'[1]

From my own experience I may add that the information on Persian and Perso-Afghán questions, which, under present arrangements, the Viceroy of India derives from our Minister at Teheran, is not what it ought to be. Imperfect information leads to rash and headstrong measures; and until Lord Mayo is put in communication with an Indian officer at Teheran—one of that military-political school of which Sir Henry Durand and Colonel Meade are shining examples—his Excellency will be in a false position. I believe that Mr. Gladstone's speech of the 9th July, ill reported in next morning's papers,

[1] 'Memorandum on the Central Asian Question,' by Major-General Sir H. C. Rawlinson, K.C.B., dated July 20, 1868.

contained some assurance that the proposed retransfer of the mission was open to consideration. All who have at heart our preservation from Central Asian difficulties must hope that the ministerial capacity to be convinced will, in the coming session, be developed into positive acceptance of this urgently needed reform (1869–70).

Now, withdrawing our gaze from outside movements, we have, in conclusion, to see what can be done in the way of defence within our own border. All parties, including the Government, are agreed that our system of railways leading to, and skirting along, the north-west frontier of India must be completed with all speed. Nor will any one deny that, as the contentment of the people is the cheap defence of nations, we should put forth all our industry and ingenuity in order to reconcile the natives, as far as possible, to our alien yoke by mild, firm, and sympathetic administration. These should be the objects with highest claim on our attention. Of subordinate, yet very real, desirability is the proposal that when the long-impending redistribution of Indian governments and provinces takes place, Sind should be detached from the Presidency of Bombay and fused into the Lieutenant-Governorship of the Panjáb. As Sir Henry Durand has pithily said :—

'It is anomalous that on so important a frontier we should be liable to have a different policy advocated in Sind from that pursued at Pesháwar; still more anomalous that the military force on the Lower Indus should be under the Commander-in-Chief at Bombay, whilst the troops on the Upper Indus and its affluents are under the Commander-in-Chief in Bengal. One Government, one policy, and one command should watch over the frontier, from the sea-board to Pesháwar.'[1]

[1] Minute in the Viceroy's Council, dated October 5, 1867.

I believe that the only true bulwarks for India are to be found within her own limits. By reconstructing the Teheran mission we may create a useful outwork in Persia; but the firmest of alliances with a foreign Government can never be of equal value to us with the triple line of internal ramparts which we may raise in frontier railways, popular contentment, and uniformity of border organisation. To take a stirring part in Central Asian politics may tickle our national love of adventure, but it fills Russia with increased jealousy of our trade, and with a lively alarm for the political security of Turkistán; that is, it incites the Czar's generals to accelerated aggression, and so precipitates the very collision we most wish to postpone. If meddling could bring us any gain, we might chance the inconvenience of irritating a great military power; but when the only gain is a distinct loss, why should busybodies in India be allowed to compromise England's position in the great comity of European nations? Indian interests themselves demand a system of abstention. Russia in Turkistán is still a weakly exotic. She has entered on a task which Mons. Grigorieff,[1] one of her highest Asiatic authorities, rightly describes as novel to her experience; governing Úsbeg Muhammadans is decidedly 'a big job,' and what she will make of it remains to be seen. Dangers anticipated do not always come to pass; and time, if we will but let it work, may spontaneously relieve us of the Cossack cloud that now overhangs the Indian horizon. Though the worst should happen that can happen, our capacity for meeting it is not bettered by close intimacy with Afghánistán. The dreadful day may come for another European war, in which England and Russia shall be ranged on

[1] Letter to the Editor of the 'Moskva,' January 28 (February 9), 1867.

opposite sides, and then we may find the savage independence of the Afgháns a weapon of deadly utility ready to our hands. But meanwhile,

> Non tali auxilio nec defensoribus istis
> Tempus eget.

We lose nothing by waiting. The Afgháns, when wanted, are much more likely to answer our call if, as a rule, we keep aloof from their internal dissensions, and at the right moment appear to pay all parties handsomely, than if we identify ourselves with a particular faction, and in the end approach them with a largesse diminished in proportion to our premature disbursements. I trust that Sir Charles Wingfield and Mr. Eastwick will not allow the next session of parliament to pass without obtaining from the Government a stoppage of Sher Ali's allowance. It is irritating to think that at a time when the Indian exchequer seems to show a chronic deficit[1] of two millions, and when reduction of public expenditure combined with the prospect of increased taxation is spreading discomfort throughout the empire, we should be spending 120,000*l.* on what appears to many a chimera. The capital of which this sum represents the annual interest is three millions sterling; it would defray two-thirds of the entire amount required for the construction of the Pesháwar railway; and so appropriated it might do real, instead of imaginary, service for our defence. What I pray is that England may yet withdraw her hand from Central Asia.

[1] Had Mr. Wyllie lived another month he would have substituted the word surplus for deficit—a surplus which till this Famine Year (1874) may be rightly described as a chronic one. W. W. H.

WESTERN CHINA.[1]

Our principal information regarding China is derived from the commercial ports on the eastern sea-board, but secondary approaches to the Flowery Kingdom also exist through India and Siberia; and the latter routes, though little regarded in modern England, deserve some attention, for they are the only channels of intelligence with reference to the western boundaries of the Empire. These Indian lines of communication are to be looked for not in the direction of Assam, where the advantages of geographical propinquity to the Chinese frontier are neutralised by the barbarism of interjacent tribes and the barrier of impassable mountains, but towards Burmah in the far south, where the absence of the Himálayan range reduces physical obstacles to a minimum, and towards Káshmír, in the extreme north, where the presence of a Mahárájá, holding his principality in declared dependence from the British Crown, affords facilities for political correspondence. Hence the tidings that reach India over-

[1] 'Edinburgh Review,' April 1868.

I. 'Rising of the Dungens or Musalmán Population in Western China.' By O. K. Heins. Translated from the Russian Military Journal for August 1866.

II. 'Journal of the Royal Geographical Society.' Volume the Thirty-second. Articles I. and II., Notes on the Yang-tsze-Kiang, from Han-kow to Ping-shan. By Lieutenant-Colonel Henry Andrew Sarel, F.R.G.S., 17th Lancers, and Dr. Alfred Barton, F.R.G.S. London: 1862.

III. 'Cathay and the Way Thither.' By Colonel Henry Yule, C.B. London: Printed for the Hakluyt Society: 1866.

IV. 'The Middle Kingdom.' By S. Wells Williams. New York and London: 1857.

land from China relate almost exclusively to the two provinces of Yunnan and Eastern Turkistán; though at rare intervals something is heard also of Thibet and Szechuen *viâ* Nepál.

Now the recent intelligence (1868) received through Káshmír from Eastern Turkistán is but an echo of the rumours which for some time have been current in the bazaars of Burmah respecting the political condition of Yunnan. Both in Eastern Turkistán and in Yunnan the yoke of the Pekin Government has been thrown off by the native population, and the insurgents in both cases are Muhammadans. The first impulse on hearing of these simultaneous outbreaks, the one apparently the counterpart of the other, is to wonder whether, in spite of the 1,500 miles of Thibet, by which they are separated, they may, by any possibility, be connected parts of a single organised movement. Scarcely has the conjecture been started before we receive accounts from St. Petersburg, indicating that the insurrection in Eastern Turkistán is not confined to that locality, but extends over the provinces of Kansu and Shensi and all the intermediate country. And next we are told that, in the Szechuen districts bordering on Thibet, midway between Kansu and Yunnan, there has for some years been prevalent just such a rebellion as might establish continuity of action over the whole of the immense area stretching from the Pamír Steppe to the Hoang Ho, from the Great Wall to the borders of Annam. So, in the end, we really have before us grounds to surmise that this remote part of the world may at present be the scene of a great Muslim revival, and that under the proselytism of scattered knots of enthusiastic Mullahs, millions of Chinese and Tartars, recoiling from the cold nihilism of

Buddha to the vivid faith that is in Muhammad, must have flown to arms in a spirit of fiery fanaticism, directed primarily against their own Government, but ready to blaze out in any direction where infidels are to be exterminated. If facts could be found to verify such a theory, it would be impossible to assign any limits to the grave political consequences that might be apprehended for Asia generally and China in particular. It therefore becomes a matter of some importance to ascertain what the condition of Western China actually is; and with this view we now propose to lay before the public such information on the subject as we have with difficulty succeeded in collecting.

Of the eighteen provinces into which China Proper is divided, Yunnan lies farthest to the south-west. It is a mountainous country, rich in mineral products, and, up to the date of the recent outbreak, it formed the channel for an overland traffic with Burmah of considerable value. From very early times there has been a large Muhammadan element in the population. Marco Polo, whose book was written in 1295, describes the inhabitants of the principal city as a mixed assemblage of 'idolaters, Nestorian Christians, and Saracens or Mahometans.' And Rashid-ud-dín, who was Vazír of the Persian Empire at the beginning of the fourteenth century, says roundly, in his Historical Encyclopedia, that 'all the inhabitants are Muhammadans.' Now to what source can this ancient leaven of Islam be traced? Are we to look eastwards to the sea, by which the Arabs first entered China on mercantile ventures? Or in a north-westerly direction to the sandy Desert of Gobi, across which numbers of roving Muhammadans, beginning from the eighth century, have found their way into the upper provinces of Shensi and Kansu from Khorasan, Transoxiana, and Eastern Turkistán?

Questioned as to their own origin, the Musalmáns of Yunnan give rather a fanciful account of themselves. Once upon a time, they say, there came a plague of evil spirits on China. The sun waxed dim, and the fruits of the earth ceased. Then the Emperor dreamed a dream, and, behold, there appeared unto him a man, clothed as an Arab, but friendly withal and of a cheerful countenance. And the Emperor told his dream to the magicians, and they said: It is a sign unto thee to seek salvation from Arabia, that our land may be quit of the evil spirits that plague it. And the Emperor hearkened unto the word of the magicians, and sent forth messengers to the Prophet Muhammad, saying, Grant me, I pray thee, some of thy followers. And Muhammad granted unto him three hundred and three score men. And it came to pass that the evil spirits fled away before the face of the three hundred and three score Arabs, and the land had rest. Then the Emperor honoured these holy men, and gave them ground close to his royal city, whereon to dwell; and they grew and multiplied exceedingly. But it came to pass that the Emperor died, and another Emperor arose, who knew them not. And he feared lest, when war might fall out, they should join his enemies. Wherefore, having taken counsel with himself, he broke up their dwelling-places near his royal city, scattered their families, and sent them, in separate bands, to dwell on the utmost confines of his empire.

Divested of its mythical trappings, this story does not essentially differ from the more sober narrative supplied by the orthodox Chinese. According to the latter version, a great rebellion broke out in China about a thousand years ago. The Emperor, being reduced to great straits, sought assistance from 'a[1] certain king named Rází or Khází, who ruled over the countries to the west of China.' He thus obtained the services of a Muhammadan contingent, 10,000 strong; and, with its aid, he succeeded in quelling the rebellion. Then arose the difficulty how to dispose of auxiliaries whose military prowess was no longer necessary to the empire, and who, for their part, had lost all desire to return to their own country, in consequence of their reputation among the true believers at home having become compromised by their long contact with the swine's flesh and other abominations of remote paganism. In the end, the Emperor despatched them to colonise the frontier province of Yunnan, as permanent subjects of China.

The general coincidence of these two accounts affords a presumption that they rest on some basis of substantial truth. Moreover, they harmonise with the Chinese custom of deporting a suspected tribe *en masse* from one end of the empire to another, and also with the historical fact that applications for military assistance actually were made to the Abbaside Khalifás by two successive Emperors of China, Sutsung in 757 and Tetsung in 787. Indeed, it is worth while to compare the passage which, in Colonel Yule's learned work on 'Cathay,' is devoted to the incident of 757. Colonel Yule says (p. lxxxi.): 'When the Emperor Sutsung was hard pressed by a powerful rebel, he received an embassy from the Khalifá Abu Jafar ul Mansur accompanied by auxiliary troops. . . . Ouïgour and other western troops also joined the

[1] This quotation, as indeed most of our information regarding the Yunnan rebellion, is taken from a memorandum by the Chief Commissioner of British Burmah, the materials for which were supplied by Captain Sladen, the British agent accredited to the Court of the King of Ava at Mandalay.

Emperor's standard, and the rebel was completely defeated in the immediate neighbourhood of Singanfu. These auxiliaries seem to have been found very unmanageable: the eastern capital, Loyang, was pillaged by them; and, as we have seen,[1] one account ascribes to them, on their way to embark for the west, the sack of Canton which occurred at this time.'

May it not then be possible that the modern Muhammadans of Yunnan are in truth descendants of some remnant of the contingent supplied to Sutsung by the founder of Bagdad—some band so warworn that they had no heart to accompany the bulk of their comrades through the perils of the return voyage from Canton to the Persian Gulf, and preferred to remain in peace on the alien shore? However this may be, the general drift of both the accounts above given indicates the eastern sea instead of the northern desert as the door by which the Muhammadans of Yunnan entered China. Another circumstance testifying to the same effect is that they pride themselves on their *Arab* origin, and that the more learned among them cultivate Arabic not merely as the language of their formal prayers, but as a medium of polite communication. Now the most eastern point which the tide of Saracen invasion ever reached was Kashgar in Eastern Turkistán, and the Muhammadans of Northern China are not of Arab, but of Túrki descent. Therefore, supposing the Yunnan Musalmáns to be justified in their boast, the hypothesis that they reached their present seats by percolation from the north

[1] The previous passage to which Colonel Yule refers will be found at page lxxx. of his 'Cathay.' 'The Arabs at an early date of Islam, if not before, had established a factory at Canton, and their numbers at that port were so great by the middle of the eighth century that in 758 they were strong enough to attack and pillage the city, to which they set fire and then fled to their ships.'

through the intermediate province of Szechuen, ceases to be tenable,[1] and, as a further consequence, it must be admitted that the tie, if there be any, connecting the insurgents in Yunnan with their co-religionists, who have also taken up arms in Eastern Turkistán, cannot be one of a common nationality.

The Musalmáns of Yunnan, though they speak of themselves simply as Muslims, are known by a different designation to both the Chinese and the Burmese. The latter called them *Panthays;* the former are said to call them *Quayz.* The word 'Panthay' is merely a corruption of 'Páthi,' by which name all followers of the Prophet are distinguished in Burmah; and 'Quays' may possibly be identical with 'Hoai-Hoai,' the generic title applied to all Muhammadans in China; for such a distortion is not greater than might be expected from the phonetic spelling by which an Anglo-Indian officer would endeavour to reproduce on paper Chinese syllables reaching his ear from Burman lips.[2]

The Panthays belong to the Sunni sect of the Muhammadans. In physical aspect they are fair, tall, and strongly built. The fashion for their dress is, for the most part, Chinese, 'though many of them cut their hair to a certain length, and allow it to fall back on the nape of the neck; they also wear in many instances a distinctive turban, of more ample form than in use among the

[1] Not less untenable appears to be the theory that they may have filtered into China from Bengal through Burmah. The Muhammadan conquest of Bengal took place in 1203, and the interval of seventy or eighty years from that date up to the time when Yunnan fell under Marco Polo's observation cannot, in the absence of any special explanation, be accepted as sufficient to account for a large Muhammadan colony having taken firm root in lands so far removed from the supposed mother-country.

[2] There are more Chinese Muhammadans than is commonly supposed. Thus, the butchers in Pekin are said to be all Muslims, though their orthodoxy may have suffered by long residence amongst a pork-eating people.

Chinese.' In character they are described as industrious and enterprising. Their annals, during the thousand years of their subjection to Chinese authority, seem a perfect blank; it may be inferred therefore that they enjoyed a fair measure of tranquillity and material comfort. They certainly managed to preserve their own social usages intact; nor was any obstacle offered to the erection of mosques and the public practice of their religious observances; even their political status appears to have been little, if at all, inferior to that of the autocthonous population. The cause of the disaffection which latterly spread among them was, so far as can be ascertained, nothing more complex than the extortion and oppression of the individual officers entrusted by the Pekin Government with the administration of the province. It is possible that the foreign extraction and peculiar religion of the Panthays may have attracted towards them the jealousy and cruelty of the local Government in an extraordinary degree; or it may be that men with Arab blood in their veins were not to be trampled on with the same impunity as Chinese, to the manner born. The paralysis of the central power induced by the Taeping rebellion in Eastern China, offered the Panthays just such an opportunity as is of itself a motive to action; and in 1855 their pent up indignation at last exploded, with a vehemence which carried everything before it. Colonel Fytche describes the occurrence as follows :—

'The Lusunphu silver mines of Yunnan were worked by Panthays under the superintendence of Chinese officers. On a certain day a dispute arose at the mines, and the miners, exasperated by unjust treatment, had recourse to force, and murdered every Chinese officer they could find. The revolt of the miners was at once followed by a general armed rising of the Panthays throughout Yunnan. Being inferior in number to the Chinese, they at first took to the woods and mountain fastnesses, from whence they carried on a fierce guerilla warfare. Meeting everywhere with success, they were soon joined by large numbers of the neighbouring semi-independent hill-tribes of Shans, Kakhyens, and others, whereupon they extended their operations to the plains, and laid siege to large towns. The local Government, receiving no assistance from Pekin, finally succumbed; the insurgents became supreme, and a separate Panthay Government was established with its head-quarters at Tali or Talifu, then only a city of secondary importance, but where the Muhammadan element had always been very strong. Feeble attempts have since been made, from time to time, to recover the lost province by the despatch of imperial troops from the capital; but the Chinese Government has never been able to make head against the Panthays; and the troops sent have generally been repulsed, before they could even penetrate within the Yunnan frontier.' . . . . 'Panthay traders' (residing at Mandalay) 'state that, during the past year, an embassy was received from the Emperor of China by which the Imperial Government sued for a cessation of hostilities, and volunteered to cede Yunnan to the Panthays, provided they would come to terms and commit no further acts of aggression on neighbouring provinces. The offer, it is said, was indignantly refused, and the embassy was obliged to return to Pekin, without accomplishing its object.'

In fact Yunnan is now in the twelfth year of its independence, and seems likely to maintain that position. The head of the new Muhammadan Government is a chief known to the Panthays as Sulaimán, and to the Chinese as Tuwintsen. He has had himself formally installed on a divan, wears the imperial yellow,[1] and in

[1] A proclamation from the new Sultán of Yunnan (too long to be offered to our readers in translation), has recently been circulated at Lhassa, with a view of attracting to his camp Muhammadan recruits from Thibet. Prefaced by a quotation from the Kurán, it announces, in tones of Oriental hyperbole, the overthrow of the polytheistic Chinese, and the triumphant erection of a kingdom of true believers, under a Sultán wise, just, and generous, whose ministers and chiefs are 'as single-hearted as Abu Bakr,' and as 'bold as Alí.' It is pervaded throughout by a cant of religious motives and divine

all other respects displays the insignia of supreme power. He is assisted by four military and four civil ministers, of whom the one highest in rank is stationed at Momein, a large town close to the Shan frontier, west of Yunnan. The form of administration, except that it partakes of a more military character, is the same as previously obtained under the Chinese. Taxation is extremely light, being restricted apparently to a moderate assessment on land.

Among the immediate results of this revolution the one that chiefly concerns British interests is the extinction of the overland trade between Burmah and China. The value of this traffic stood in 1854 at half a million sterling; and, as an indication of the distant sources from which the Chinese imports into Burmah were gathered, it may be mentioned that Russian broad cloth used to be procurable at Mandalay, which had found its way through Siberia and Pekin. Caravans of enterprising Chinese, among whom the Panthays were always conspicuous, came, in those days, to Bhamo on the Irrawaddy river, bringing silk and bullion to barter with the Burmese for cotton, jade, and amber. But all this abruptly ceased with the secession of Yunnan from the Chinese Empire. The province that so long had vibrated with the flow and reflux of a lively commerce at once became a non-conductor; the trader found his short-cut closed. At present such small interchange of commodities as still survives between Talifu and Bhamo merely represents the produce and requirements of Yunnan alone, isolated from the rest of China. This is a fact

favour, such as could not be surpassed even in a despatch from the Wahábi Court of Nejed. This very curious document is written in remarkably good Arabic. For the copy in our possession we are indebted to Colonel G. Ramsay, the British Resident in Nepál, who obtained it from the Nepálese Envoy, stationed at Lhassa.

which might be commended to the notice of the merchants of Manchester and Rangoon, who clamour for a railway from the latter place to the Yunnan frontier. Hitherto they have made light of every obstacle to the project. The sparseness of the population in British Burmah, which would necessitate the importation of foreign labour, and consequently cause not only enormous expense to the State, but serious mortality amongst the labourers; the distracted condition of Ava, passing from one insurrection into another, and infested by gangs of organised banditti; the mountainous nature of the country between Ava and Yunnan, and the lawless character of the Shan tribes that inhabit it—all these are regarded by the agitators in question as matters of detail which Anglo-Saxon perseverance would readily dispose of. But they seem totally ignorant that even if the impossibility for which they cry were granted them, and they were actually landed on the platform of a terminus at Talifu, they would still be as far removed as ever from the coveted prize of a trade with China direct from the Bay of Bengal. Their only customers would be our interesting, but impecunious and hot-headed, friends, the Panthays.[1]

[1] Two separate projects have been started for establishing a mercantile connexion with Yunnan: one, that referred to in the text, for a railway direct from Rangoon eastwards to the nearest point in China; the other, for water-carriage up the Irrawaddy northwards to Bhamo, combined with a revival of the old caravan traffic on by land from that point. Of these two schemes the *first* has now been definitely abandoned, though not before the Indian Government was constrained to go through the farce of a 'preliminary survey' of the route. The discontinuance of the survey has been regretted by one officer of great local experience, on the ground that it might have furnished a useful pretext for ascertaining what, if any, has been the political action among the Shan tribes of the party of French explorers, who last year (1867) made their way from Saigon up the Cambodia river as far as 21° N. lat.; but, with all deference to the eminent authority in question, we hesitate to believe that English interests in that direction can have aught to apprehend from the excursions, however adventurous, which may be made in their

From Yunnan we now pass northwards to the large and well-watered province of Szechuen, which has Thibet for its western boundary. The inhabitants of Szechuen are a mixed community; the Chinese of the plains and along the banks of that 'silent highway,' the Yang-tsze-Kiang, being peaceable, inoffensive, and loyal, while the Maoutse towards the south are wild mountaineers, who have never been under any effectual control from the Government. Even at the best of times Szechuen used to suffer from constant commotions and rebellions, which the Chinese authorities, while their power lasted, were wont to quell, in their own peculiar way, partly by force, but chiefly by bribes and concessions.

The high road from Lhassa to Pekin traverses Szechuen through Ta-tsin-deo, a frontier town, and Ching-tu-fu, the capital. Messieurs Huc and Gabet, the well-known missionaries, used this route in returning from their adventurous sojourn among the Lamas of Thibet; and it is periodically followed by the embassy which the Mahárájá of Nepál ought every five years to despatch to the Emperor of China. This also was the way by which a party of English officers, under the leadership of Colonel Sarel, endeavoured, in 1861, to make an overland journey from Shanghai across the Himálayas into India. From M. Huc's silence as to any disturbances in Szechuen, it may be inferred that in

vicinity by the colony of Cochin China, which, notwithstanding the recent extension of its territorial limits, still bears the reputation of an administrative failure, unremunerative to the French empire, and unpopular with the French nation. With regard to the *second*, and far more reasonable project, we believe that the sanction of the King of Ava has been obtained for a survey by British officers of the country beyond Bhamo towards Talifu. Probably the greatest difficulties we shall encounter in this work will arise from the jealousy of the Chinese traders at Mandalay and Bhamo, who are strongly opposed to the apparition of Europeans directly competing for a share in their market.

1846 the province was comparatively quiescent. But at the time of Colonel Sarel's expedition, affairs bore a very different aspect. In fact, the cause which compelled that officer to abandon his project, after he had penetrated within 150 miles of Ching-tu-fu, was simply that he had reached a country weltering in rebellion and anarchy, through which no guides would venture to accompany him.

The originators of the movement appear to have been a set of hereditary and professional robbers called Tufeh. Four different bands of these people, encouraged by the success of the Taepings in Eastern China, and by the helpless attitude of the central Government, united their forces in 1859, and began to plunder on a grand scale. Every day brought an addition to their strength; for wherever they turned, the Mandarins fled in terror, the soldiery fraternised with them, and even of the unhappy people, who had begun by resisting them desperately, many afterwards joined them, not from any natural proclivity towards a bandit's life, but simply because homes gutted and burning left no other escape from starvation. In two years' time the rebel force had swollen to 300,000 men, who had carried fire and sword through the greater part of Szechuen, and were then besieging the capital. Numbers of headless bodies floating past Colonel Sarel's boats on the Yang-tsze-Kiang attested the proximity of the ruffians; and at last, on the night of the 29th May, the expedition came into actual contact with them at a place called Pingshan. The meeting and its consequences have been vividly portrayed by a member of the party, Dr. Barton, as follows:—

'All preparations having been made for leaving our boats the following morning, we sat down to our dinner, when suddenly a noise like the shouts of a legion of maniacs rent the air, and we instantly armed ourselves, thinking the people were making a rush at the boats; but we found the rebels were pouring down the hill at the back of the city and attacking it. The whole hill-side was lighted up with hundreds of lanterns, and the city walls also suddenly became illuminated with torches at each of the embrasures. The yells and cries from the combatants and the explosion of gingalls and cannon were so great that we could scarcely hear each other speak. I had only just time to jump into my boat when our crew cut us adrift: from the darkness of the night and the din of the battle we could neither see nor hear each other, and consequently our boats became separated, myself and one Sikh only occupying the smaller.

It was an anxious night for all; for wherever we attempted to make fast to either bank, an explosion of gingalls drove us away. During the night, however, we effected a mooring on the Yunnan side, and I and my Sikh were standing on the house, watching the battle, when several men rushed at our boat, and, after firing three heavy gingalls within fifteen yards, obtained a footing on our junk, but we soon cleared the deck and got away with the loss of only one of our crew. The next morning we picked him up on the opposite bank, he having taken to the water for safety. At daybreak, seeing no trace of the other boat, I slowly dropped down the stream to search for it, when a few miles below the town, to my great joy, I discovered it safely at anchor under a beetling cliff.

Thus, after ascending 1,800 miles of this river, exploring and surveying 900 miles beyond any other European, save the Jesuits in Chinese costume, and penetrating to the western borders of the Empire—for we were only a few miles from the country of the independent tribes, the Maoutse—we had now to abandon all hope of carrying out our original plan of reaching India *viâ* Thibet, and returned to Shanghai after an absence of five months.'

The conclusion at which our travellers arrived was that Western China had slipped altogether 'out of the hands of the Government.' Bands of robbers and rebels were devastating the country in all directions.

'In the eastern provinces were the Taepings; in the south-west the formidable band of Musalmáns; and in Szechuen the Tufeh: how many others we could not tell, but many no doubt; and these have no connexion with each other. We also found that the followers of the Prophet were very numerous, and Roman Catholics were everywhere to be met, ready, at all times, and at their own risk, to assist Europeans.'

This latter extract indicates that the rebels of Szechuen have a character of their own, distinct equally from the Taepings of Nankin and from the Muhammadans of Yunnan. As observed by Dr. Barton, every province of modern China contains a certain number of Muhammadans; indeed, there is one city in Szechuen which alone contains 1,000 Musalmán families; and therefore it is not improbable that several of this sect may be found in the ranks of the Tufeh insurgents. But, if so, they must be an inappreciable portion of the whole force; and, even in their case, the Kurán is not the spring of action. In the mass the rebels are Buddhists, and the motives by which one and all of them are animated, are not religious, but secular. They care little for Fo, and next to nothing for Muhammad; all they seek is plunder.

Not much has been heard of Szechuen since Colonel Sarel visited it. The latest information that has reached India is connected with the quinquennial embassy from the Nepálese Darbár to the Emperor of China, which started from Kátmandu in August 1866, and ought to have reached Pekin in the following March. Quite recently Jang Bahádur (the 'Mayor of the Palace' who rules Nepál) received through Lhassa despatches from his envoy, dated from Ta-tsin-deo, the first town within the limits of Szechuen, reporting that the party, after suffering considerable hardship in the snowy passes through which their route had lain, had succeeded in passing the Chinese frontier, but could get no farther in consequence of the country being overrun with rebels; orders, it was added, had been received from the Emperor that the letter and tribute destined for himself should be delivered up to his representatives at Ta-tsin-deo, and that the usual return-presents should be issued to the Nepálese at the same place, for any advance towards Pekin was out of the question; accordingly the envoy contemplated an immediate return from Ta-tsin-deo to Kátmandu. The following is a translated extract from the despatch:—

> 'In our journey onwards from the city of Batang, every city we passed through had been destroyed by fire, and deserted by the inhabitants; habitations were rarely met with. As far as Lithang the country is in the same bad state, and everything is dear. Lithang is inhabited, but the governor's palace there has been pulled down by the enemy, and the governor is living in a thatched tenement. The war has now lasted nine years, and the country is in a miserable condition. Some wounded men and deserters have come here (Ta-tsin-deo) from the seat of war, which is only four or five days' journey distant.'

Thus it is clear that the Szechuen insurrection has not in the least degree been suppressed, but that the Emperor's authority nevertheless survives at some points, and that communication with Pekin, though difficult and hazardous, is still kept up by some circuitous route (1868).

In speculating on the present condition of Szechuen, special interest attaches to the fate which may have befallen the city of Chung-king-fu, an important trading port at the junction of the river Hotow with the Yang-tsze-Kiang. Chung-king, whatever may be its present aspect, not only used to be the largest and most flourishing city in the west of China, being of greater extent and population than the provincial capital, Chingtu, but it also formed the head-quarters of a small band of those heroic men whose toils and sufferings have for centuries illumined the dull obscurity of Chinese annals—we allude, as hardly needs to be explained, to the Catholic missionaries. The head of the mission establishment at Chungking in 1861 was Monsignor Desflèches, bearing the title of Vicar Apostolic of Eastern Szechuen, and his flock numbered over 2,000 souls. It is devoutly to be hoped that this notable outpost of Christianity has escaped falling into the hands of the rebels. And there is reason, we rejoice to observe, for believing this to be the case. For, among the despatches received from Ta-tsin-deo by Jang Bahádur, was a very interesting communication to the address of the British Resident in Nepál from certain French missionaries, who, being stationed at a town near Ta-tsin-deo through which the Nepálese envoy had passed, had taken this opportunity to inform the Indian Government of their position and prospects.[1]

[1] There is a pathetic simplicity in the narrative. The original seat of the Mission was a valley called Bonga on the Lon-tsa-Kiang river in the south-east corner of Thibet, close to the western frontier of Szechuen, and the northern border of Yunnan. Here in 1854, MM. Renon and Fage took some land on lease, and soon afterwards converted to Christianity the inhabitants of a neighbouring village, within the limits of Yunnan, called Kion-na-tong. In 1858, the landlord forcibly ousted them from Bonga and destroyed the house they had built. In 1861, upon the strength of the new treaty between France and China, several recruits from Europe joined the Thibetan Mission, and, in the beginning of the following year, the intercession of the French envoy at Pekin procured the restoration of the Bonga valley to its rightful tenants. In May 1863, M. Renon left Bonga for Kiangka, the chief town of the district, and established there a new centre of missionary labour. He died at Kiangka about September of the same year, 'some days after a nightly attack of paid rascals;' his place being taken by MM. Fage and Goutelle. Meanwhile five Thibetan villages in the neighbourhood of Bonga had embraced Christianity. Enraged at this encroachment on their influence,

This letter contained no mention of Chung-King, and though the writers appear to have no closer connexion with the establishment at that place than as pioneers thrown out in advance, yet, if aught untoward had befallen their base of operations, it is not likely they would have omitted to notice so important an occurrence.

The political relations of Thibet with China, and of Nepál with both those countries, are curious. There is a native government in Thibet, as we all know, of a sacerdotal character; or it might even be called theocratic, for the Grand Lama at the head of the administration is

the Lama priests caused three out of the five villages to be simultaneously attacked in June 1864; the inhabitants were beaten and carried away captive, and the resident pastors were obliged to retreat to Bonga. The station at Kiangka came in for similar treatment on June 7, 1865, and MM. Fage and Dubernard fled for their lives out of Thibet into Szechuen. The next that suffered was the village of Kion-na-tong; M. Durand was murdered there on September 28; but his colleague, M. A. Biet, and the bulk of the native converts, made good their escape to found a Christian colony at the town of Tsekou on the Kincha-Kiang river in Yunnan. Bonga was the last to fall: towards the close of the year MM. Desgodins and F. Biet were deported with their flock, after much ill-treatment and some murder, out of Thibet to Tsaka in Szechuen. Thus the missionaries lost at last all foothold in Thibet; and at present the only stations left to them are Tsaka near Ta-tsin-deo in the Batang district of Szechuen and Tsekou in the extreme north of Yunnan; at the former are MM. Desgodins, Goutelle, and Fage, the writers of the letter to Colonel Ramsay; at the latter is M. A. Biet. They ascribe their persecutions entirely to the religious jealousy of the Lama priesthood as a body, and the political ill-will of one or two individuals among the Chinese bureaucracy at Lhassa. Their words are:—'Though people helped in expelling us, it was certainly against his own will. People of Thibet is so slave of powerful men that his deeds are to be counted for nothing; but we know his good feeling for religion as well as for Europeans. We know very well that he would feel very glad if he become freed from the heavy yoke of the Lamas.' The Indian newspapers, from which the above account is taken, seem to have been unaware that this is not the first occasion on which the Catholic missionaries in Thibet have succeeded in sending a letter overland into British limits. On August 9, 1859, they despatched a geographical description of the country about Bonga to Bishop Bigandet, the Vicar Apostolic at Rangoon, which travelling *viâ* Yunnan and Bhamo, reached its destination in about ten months' time. The letter was communicated by the Bishop to Sir Arthur Phayre, and was subsequently published in the Proceedings of the Asiatic Society at Calcutta.

venerated throughout the Buddhist world as an incarnation of the Deity. But side by side with the native government stands the Chinese power, in the person of a diplomatic agent, bearing the title of Amban, who occupies at Lhassa towards the Grand Lama a position analogous to that which, before the Italian war of 1859, the Austrian Ambassador used to hold at Rome towards the Pope. How completely the Amban was master of the situation at the time of M. Huc's visit to Lhassa, may be inferred from the circumstance that, when it became a trial of strength between the Amban and the native government whether the French missionaries should be allowed to remain at Lhassa, the Amban carried his point and caused them to be deported back to China. The Chinese military force at that time quartered in Thibet, appears to have been inconsiderable, comprising, besides a guard of honour for the Amban at the capital, only a few scattered garrisons, employed in guarding the frontier towards Nepál, and keeping open communications with Szechuen. But in truth the Amban's influence has always rested less upon the strength visibly at his command, than upon his supposed power of summoning at any time unlimited reinforcements from the province of Szechuen. With the people of Lhassa, the Chinese element in their government is by no means popular: on this point M. Huc has testified that 'the Thibetans fear the Chinese, the Katchi[1] despise them, and the Pebouns laugh at them.' Similar evidence occurs in a despatch dated July 1854, from Sir John Bowring, to Lord

[1] The Katchi and the Pebouns are the principal foreign settlers at Lhassa,—the latter being emigrants from Bhután, chiefly of the artisan class, and the former a colony of wealthy Múhammadan merchants from Káshmír, who have a monopoly of the trade through Nepál with British India.

Dalhousie, in which a good authority (M. Gabet apparently) is represented to have said 'that the Chinese yoke was oppressive to the Thibetans, and that they would avail themselves of any favourable occasion to revolt against their masters.' Therefore it certainly might have been expected that now, when the Chinese Government is threatened with total collapse at home, and the Amban has been cut off from his communications with Szechuen, the Thibetans would at once have recognised their opportunity, expelled the Chinese, and established their own independence. Facts, however, in the field of Asiatic politics, invariably belie the best-grounded anticipations. Thibet at the present time is perfectly tranquil, and the Amban, though backed by only 500 Chinese soldiers at Lhassa and not more, say, than 1,500 in the provinces, still continues the virtual master of the kingdom. It remains to be seen how long, by dint of incredible brag, he may succeed in retaining this position.

As regards Nepál, the quinquennial embassy above mentioned, which the Mahárájá is bound to despatch to Pekin, had its origin in events which occurred at the close of the last century. The Gorkhás, a Hinduised race, had barely completed the conquest of Nepál from an aboriginal tribe of Mongols called Niwárs before they turned their arms in the direction of Thibet; and, in 1790, they penetrated as far as Digurche, ravaging the country and pillaging the sacred temples. The Lamas had recourse for aid to the Emperor of China, who despatched an army of 70,000 men to avenge the outrage. The Chinese drove the Gorkhás back into Nepál, and compelled them, within a few miles of their capital, to accept an ignominious peace. The precise terms of the treaty have never come to light; but it is certain that the Gorkhás had not only to acknowledge the supremacy of China, but also to undertake the despatch of tribute every five years to Pekin. Matters continued on this footing until the year 1854, when the Crimean war in one direction, and the Taeping insurrection in another, presented to the scheming brain of Jang Bahádur (not then a Knight Grand Cross of the Bath) simultaneous and irresistible temptations to military action. He collected a considerably army, and then deliberated on what errand it should be launched. Should he march into China and aid his feudal sovereign against the rebels? Or could he make a better bargain by helping the Lamas to extrude the Chinese from Thibet? Or—and here he wondered whether the prodigious tales of Russian victories and English defeats in Europe were altogether to be trusted—might he venture to make a sudden pounce on those rich plains in Bengal and in Behar north of the Ganges, the financial heart of the Anglo-Indian Empire, which, save at the one point of Calcutta, he saw ungarrisoned by a single sepoy? He concluded to take none of these courses, but to pick a quarrel with Thibet on the ground that insults and ill-usage had been inflicted in that country on the members of the Nepálese embassy, just then returned from Pekin. In December 1854 a formal declaration of war was despatched to the native rulers and to the Chinese Amban at Lhassa; and at the same time the Emperor of China was informed, in very humble terms, of the injuries which had constrained Nepál to take up arms against a fellow-tributary of the empire. In the following spring the expeditionary force started in three columns, intended to operate by separate routes; altogether, it included 30,000 regular fighting men, an equal number of armed followers, 36 guns and 8 mortars. But Jang Báhadur soon found that he had under-rated the difficulties of providing food for so large a body of men, and of forcing snowy passes, defended by hardy mountaineers; so, after one or two positions in Thibet had been occupied by his troops, he was not sorry to receive overtures of peace. In the course of the negotiations that ensued, the Chinese Amban wrote to the Mahárájá of Nepál in the following arrogant strain:—

> 'If you choose to consent to these proposals, do so. If you will not consent to them, we shall address a petition to the Emperor of China, and call from the city of Sutyang an army of Chinese soldiers, and of Gyamis,[1] besides some Kumba[2] soldiers, and some Thibetans, and some Khambaliks,[3]—we will assemble them all, and take them with us in person. We have taken an oath seven times repeated to this effect! We will do this, and will entirely destroy your capital, and seize the ruler, and will deliver him to the Emperor at a time when his Majesty is possessed with extreme anger.'

This intemperate effusion did not tend to smooth the course of the negotiations, and during the last weeks of 1855 some severe fighting ensued. At length, in March 1856, a treaty was concluded between Nepál and Thibet, to which the Amban condescended to give a haughty assent. It was agreed that the Gorkhás should evacuate the positions occupied within the Thibetan border, and that the Thibetans should pay Nepál an annual tribute of the value of 1,000*l*. But the most remarkable part

[1] Said to be a Chinese military tribe.
[2] Tartar cavalry from the Kokonor country, probably.
[3] Can this word have any connexion with the name Cambalu or Khanbalic, by which Pekin was known to European travellers of the middle ages?

of the engagement was the insertion in two places of an acknowledgment that the Emperor of China was the common lord and master of both the contracting parties. It speaks well for the diplomatic audacity of the Amban that he should have successfully insisted on this recognition of his master's supreme authority, at a time when either state might have laughed his pretentions to scorn with impunity. The Nepálese Darbár, however, was only complaisant, not imposed upon. Jang Bahádur accepted the two clauses as being, in respect of his own country at least, a meaningless formality; and, as soon as peace had been fully re-established, he declared a determination to make open disavowal of Nepál's nominal allegiance to the Emperor by discontinuing the despatch of the quinquennial tribute. He adhered to this resolution in the year 1857, when the next embassy should have started, and again in 1862. However, in 1866, cupidity induced a change of purpose. The Chinese Government, at all times in its history, has loved to make a parade before the citizens at Pekin of ambassadors humbly bringing tribute from the most distant potentates to the Emperor's feet; and, as the power of the empire has gradually waned, the only means of persuading states that have acquired a practical independence to keep up a custom no longer extorted from their fears, has lain in so augmenting the value of the presents issued by the Emperor, in return for the so-called tribute, as to make the embassy positively a profitable speculation to the prince from whom it emanates. This was the bait which tempted Jang Bahádur. He had but to get together a pedlar's pack of trumpery and send it off to Pekin with a deferential address to the Emperor, and in return he would secure a re-appearance of those costly gifts, which had not been seen at Kátmandu since 1854—bales of silk and satin, embroidered cloaks, ornaments of porcelain, ivory, jade, and tortoise-shell, pictures, and all sorts of artificial curiosities. Enormous profit was also to be reaped by making the embassy an instrument for smuggling opium and other merchandise into China. With a cynical appreciation of such solid advantages, Jang Bahádur put the national pride in his pocket, and decided to do homage anew to the Emperor. Accordingly a Nepálese embassy was despatched from Kátmandu in August 1866. What its fate has been we have already stated, namely, that it advanced as far as the border of Szechuen, and has been obliged to retrace its steps from that point back towards Nepál, in consequence of the road to Pekin being blocked up by rebels. Jang Bahádur is naturally much disappointed at this result, and the native *quidnuncs* of Kátmandu discuss the probability of a fresh war with Thibet, in case the returning party should meet with any ill-treatment in that territory. There is no real ground, however, for anticipating such a result. All that is at present clear is, that the last links are broken between Nepál and China, and that the former power is therefore drawn into somewhat closer union with the British Empire of India. This, from a national point of view, matters little to England; for, except as regards the mutual extradition of fugitive criminals from either jurisdiction, and the superb field which Nepál opens for recruiting the Bengal regiments of Native Infantry, the Gorkhás are of little interest in British eyes, and our relations with their Darbár have, for several years past, been so frank and cordial, that no better understanding is left to be wished for. But to China it is different.

The final loss of all connexion with Nepál distinctly marks a further stage in the decadence of the Empire; and this specially is the point to which, on the present occasion, we desire to draw attention. It is one more instance of that general mortification in the extremities of the body politic, which forms the subject of our review.

North of Nepál and Thibet lies a vast expanse of territory, throughout which the present insurrections against the Chinese power offer some appearance of continuous and systematic action. Speaking roughly, we may take for the boundaries of this area the parallels of 35° and 45° north latitude, and of 72° and 110° east longitude; and we may divide it from west to east into three zones, of which the first shall include Eastern Turkistán and Dzungaria, the second the Desert of Gobi, and the third the Chinese provinces of Kansu and Shensi. The events that have recently occurred within these limits were carefully investigated in 1865 by a Russian officer, Monsieur Heins who, in the following April, communicated to the Imperial Geographical Society of St. Petersburg the paper mentioned at the beginning of this article. Monsieur Heins, entitles his contribution 'The Rising of the Dungens;' and, considering that little has hitherto been heard in Europe of any such people, it appears advisable that we should begin by explaining who the Dungens are.

At the beginning of the Christian era, the inhabitants of Eastern Turkistán were a branch of the great Ouïgour horde of Túrks,[1] who, from their geographical

[1] Túrks, Mughuls, and Manchus are the three great species into which that most indefinite entity, the genus Tartar, may be divided. Mountstuart Elphinstone gives their geographical distribution as follows:—'The Usbegs who now possess Transoxiana, the Turkmans both on the Oxus and in Asia Minor, the wandering tribes of the north of Persia, and the Ottomans

proximity to China, and the fact of their having, for long intervals, been subject to Chinese dominion, had acquired both in physical characteristics and in language, a closer resemblance to the Chinese than was to be found in any other Turkish tribe. In China their name assumed the forms of Hoeike, Oihor, and Hoai-Hoai. Towards the close of the eighth century the Emperors of the Tang dynasty took strong measures for their coercion by deporting, it is said, as many as a million families from the neighbourhood of Kashgar, and settling them in Kansu and Shensi. Buddhists by original profession, the Kashgari-Ouïgours, about the year 966, followed the example of their famous Prince, Satúk Búkrá Khán, and embraced the Muhammadan religion. Led by the same chief, they conquered Transoxiana, and carried away captive an immense number of the inhabitants, who were Turks of the Tárghi tribe. In 972 the majority of these prisoners were allowed to return to their homes about Samarkand, but many stayed where they were, and the latter came consequently to be known by their own countrymen as Turghánis, or Tungánis, a name signifying *remnant.* The conquests of Chinghiz Khán and of his successor, Okkodai Khán, in the first half of the thirteenth century, brought a fresh influx of population from Eastern Turkistán into China, the immigrants this time being mingled Ouïgours and Tungánis. These new comers were Muhammadans; their religion spread, and by the end of the fourteenth century it had been universally adopted throughout the Tur-

or Turks of Constantinople are all *Túrks*, as was the greater part of the army of Tamerlane. The ruling tribe and the greater part of the army of Chinghiz Khán was *Mughul.* The Tartar dynasty that now reigns in China and the adjoining part of Tartary is *Manchu.*'

kish colonies in Kansu and Shensi. And so it came to pass that the bond of a common faith was added as a new link between the exiles in China and their western mother-country. Another circumstance which must have had considerable influence in preserving them isolated from the Chinese, and united in sympathy with their own race, was the facility of communication they had with the latter from their geographical position in the track of the great commercial highway between Europe and Pekin; for the caravans across the Desert of Gobi kept a perennial stream of Turkish Muhammadans passing to and fro between Kashgar and the western termination of the Great Wall. Meanwhile in Eastern Turkistán the fusion of the Tungánis with the native Ouïgours became so complete that the distinction between the two nationalities ceased to exist, and a single designation sufficed to cover both. The name, however, which was taken up in Transoxiana differed from that current in China. In the former the Tungánis were regarded as having absorbed the Kashgári-Ouïgours, in the latter the Ouïgours were remembered to the exclusion of the Tungánis; and hence the same people came to be spoken of in one direction as Tungánis or Dungens, and in another as Ouïgours or Hoai-Hoai. The idea equally comprehended in either title was that of a community, Chinese in type of features, fashion of dress and language, but of Turkish lineage, and by religion Muhammadan. The early habitat of the people so defined was, as we have seen, the belt of country between the Thian-Shan and Kuen-Lún Mountains, extending eastward as far as the Yellow River; but in modern times they are also found to muster strongly in Dzungaria, as far north as the Tarbagatai range, where their presence may be accounted for partly by the spread of Muhammadan doctrine among the aboriginal Ouïgours of the north, and partly by the fact that, when the Chinese, in 1757, conquered Dzungaria and exterminated the resident Kálmaks, they re-peopled the province by drafts from Kansu and from Eastern Turkistán, having a large Musalmán element in their constitution. The result is that the whole north-western border of the Chinese Empire is thickly sown with Musalmáns who, in spite of some local distinctions among themselves, have enough of a common history to be regarded for political purposes as a tolerably homogeneous body. The generic appellation which we shall prefer applying to this community is *Tungáni*—a word differing in form only from M. Heins's *Dungen*. As for *Hoai-Hoai*, the name in China has quite lost its proper signification; for, from the Musalmán Ouïgours, to whom alone it originally applied, it has been transferred by the Chinese to all Muhammadans of every description resident in any part of the empire, and even to Jews as well.[1]

Like the Panthays, the Tungánis belong to the Sunní sect of Islam, and, like all followers of the Prophet in every part of the world, they are capable of outbursts of splendid fanaticism. In so godless a country as China, a character for devoutness is perhaps more easily obtainable than elsewhere; and we must also remember that in the mere principle of dissent from the religion of the masses, there is an inherent vitality which tends to band the non-conforming minority in closer

[1] 'Les Chinois appellent les Juifs qui demeurent parmi eux Hoai-Hoai. Ce nom leur est commun avec les Mahométans.' ('Lettres Edifiantes et Curieuses,' tome xxiv. p. 50.)

adhesion to their peculiar tenets. But, however it is to be explained, the Tungánis certainly have the reputation of exceptionally rigid compliance with the requirements of their faith, and of extraordinary subservience, even in secular affairs, to the summons of their spiritual leaders, the Imáms and Akhúnds. They abstain from wine and spirits, and smoke neither opium nor tobacco, so that in outward appearance they are easily distinguishable from the drug-stupified Manchus and Chinese, by a more robust physique and a more intelligent expression of countenance. Their temper, according to M. Heins, is passionate and overbearing; and they are too apt to settle quarrels by the knife, which they invariably wear about their persons. Less questionable characteristics are their love of trade, and the honesty which pervades all their dealings, especially those of a commercial character. The latter quality recommended individual members of their body for employment in the Imperial service, and numbers of them held office in the department of police. But, as a whole, the Tungánis were viewed by the Manchu Government with marked jealousy and disfavour. Not only were they made to pay for the luxury of retaining a separate nationality by being subjected to exceptionally severe taxation, but, from time to time, they fell under the weight of special ordinances designed to obliterate their guild and fuse them into the mass of the population. Thus, about the beginning of the present century, an Imperial decree was issued requiring the men to wear pigtails, and the women to compress their feet to the standard of Chinese deformity; attempts were also made to prevent the marriage of their daughters to any Muhammadans but those of purely Chinese blood. These measures, however, so far from producing the desired effect, served only to weld the Tungánis into a political unit, animated throughout with strong antagonism to the ruling power.

In China Proper the Tungáni community was nowhere stronger than at a certain city in Kansu, on one of the right affluents of the Yellow River, which M. Heins denominates Salar, but of which the Chinese name is apparently Hochow. This place has been the scene of frequent insurrections against the present dynasty, and M. Heins regards it as the centre from which a politico-religious propaganda for the subversion of the government has for a long time been carried on. A native of Salar, named Sawun, is said to have been the head of the movement; he died several years ago, and his memory is still cherished by the Tungánis.

It was at Singan-fu, however, the large and well-known capital of the neighbouring province, Shensi, that the present rebellion first broke out. The spark that kindled the flame there in 1862, appears to have been a squabble between two merchants, a Tungáni and a Manchu, in which the latter was stabbed; hence arose a municipal tumult which speedily assumed the proportions of a political revolution: the Manchus were cut to pieces, and the Tungánis remained masters of the city. When the news of this success reached Salar, Sawun's youthful son, Sukhan Ján, set out for Singan-fu and assumed command of the insurgents. The first force despatched from Pekin for the restitution of order numbered only 1,000 soldiery, and, of course, could effect nothing; a second corps, 10,000 strong, was utterly defeated; and a like fate befell the army of 40,000 men, which represented the third effort put forth by the Government.

From Singan-fu the insurrection spread in a north-westerly direction. Sometimes after a struggle with the local garrison, and sometimes without any opposition, the Tungánis soon obtained possession of several towns: at places where they were numerically inferior to the Manchus, they slew their own wives and children and fled unencumbered to join the cause in a more favourable quarter. At Salar a Holy War was proclaimed; and preachers were sent forth in every direction to rouse all true believers against the infidel. These emissaries went to work with a will, and ere long, there was not a town in the two provinces, containing any considerable number of Tungánis, where the mosques had not rung with their passionate exhortations. They announced the arrival of the long-looked-for hour when the Manchus must be either converted or exterminated, and they summoned every male Muslim to join in the good work. Their audience responded enthusiastically to the call, and the crowds that then flocked to Sukhan Ján's banner enabled him, in a very short time, to take the field with vigour, and maintain himself against the enemy with persistent success.

For the internal government of his people, Sukhan Ján took the most experienced and influential of the priests into his counsels, and the institutions he established owe their peculiar form largely to the influence of that hierarchy. The right of private property was abolished until the termination of the war, and, as in the early Christian Church, a community of goods was ordained. Every person, however wealthy, brought the whole of his worldly possessions to the local mosque, and delivered them to the Imám; thenceforward he became, equally with the meanest of his fellow-citizens, dependent for clothes, weapons, food, and the subsistence of his family on such supplies as might be issued to him from the mosque. That establishment was made the pivot on which social life revolved: from the cobbling of a shoe to medical aid for the wounded, whatever any one wanted could only be obtained from the mosque. Disobedience to the Elders was punishable by death. Severe penalties also were prescribed for robbery; and, as all spoil taken in war had to be transferred entire to the common stock, any imitator of the sin of Achan was liable to instant execution. Buddhist temples, wherever found, were plundered and destroyed. Adult Chinese[1] were compelled to adopt Islam, or become hewers of wood and drawers of water; and their children were all placed in mosques to be nurtured and educated as Musalmáns. Lastly, that no outward sign, however trivial, might be wanting to mark the dawn of a new era, the Tungánis discarded the Chinese garb, and assumed one of the fashion prevalent in Turkistán.

The most striking feature in such an organisation as that we have just described is undoubtedly its religious tincture. M. Heins, who is our authority on the point, has been charged by persons well versed in Chinese affairs with giving an undue prominence to the antagonism of Islam against Buddhism; but we are not sure that the charge is just. The principles of the Kurán generally,

[1] The relations of the Tungánis towards the Manchu Tartars, and towards the native Chinese, appear to have been very different. With the former war to the knife was their watchword; but with the latter they had no particular quarrel; on the contrary, they had intermarried with them for centuries, and, but for the stumbling-block of a different religion, they were even inclined to sympathise with them as fellow-sufferers under a dynasty equally alien and inimical to both. M. Heins cites this feeling in explanation of what otherwise would be inexplicable, the 'certain degree of intimacy' which arose between the fanatical Tungánis and the heterodox Taepings.

and above all the text which declares death in battle against the infidel to be the surest passport to the arms of the expectant Houris in Paradise, have established in every Musalmán's breast so intimate a connexion between his spiritual aspirations and his political convictions, that it is only consonant with experience to believe that the Tungánis, in entering on their desperate struggle for civil liberty, should have vociferously appealed to Allah to aid the cause of his chosen people. The war-cry that rang through Musalmán India in 1857 was, 'Dín! Dín!' (for the faith! for the faith!); and it is the same spirit that for the last two years has kept the heterogeneous rabble of Bokhara in arms against the disciplined might of the Russian Empire. Or a yet nearer example is to be found in the tone of the manifesto issued by the Yunnan Muhammadans, which we have above noted.

Respecting recent events in Kansu and Shensi, our information is singularly defective. M. Heins says briefly that 'the Musalmán insurgents in that quarter appear to have sustained a check.' How and when this check was brought about, we have failed to discover; but there is reason for believing it to be a fact; and therefore, although the success of the Imperialist troops is perhaps temporary only, and their snake scotched rather than killed, we may for the present withdraw our attention from China Proper, and concentrate it on the territory west of the Desert of Gobi.

A traveller, taking the great caravan route, which for ages has maintained commercial communication between China and the regions around the basin of the Caspian Sea, would start from the western extremity of the Great Wall, with his face set to the north-west, and, after traversing the Kiayu Pass, would find before him five hundred miles of desolate sand to be traversed ere he could reach the city of Khamil. At Khamil the road strikes the eastern spurs of the Tian-Shan Mountains, and bifurcates along the northern and southern slopes of that range—the upper branch leading through Barkul, Uramchi, and Kurkara-usu into Dzungaria, and the lower through Pijan, Turfan, Karashar, and Kucha, to Aksu in Eastern Turkistán. While the Chinese rule continued, Dzungaria and Eastern Turkistán formed respectively the northern and southern circuits of a single province, which, under the designation of Ili, was administered by a governor-general having his head-quarters at Kulja, in the northern circuit. This administration differed considerably in form and principles from the organisation of the home provinces of China; it was necessarily of a more military character, as having to deal with subjugated foreigners; and at Pekin, it ranged departmentally under the control of the Colonial Office. In short, it was of the type which, if we may be permitted to borrow a comparison from Anglo-Indian institutions, we should denominate 'non-regulation.'

Into this territory of Ili, in the summer of 1864, came fanatical emissaries from Salar, and fugitives from those parts of Kansu where the Tungáni cause had failed. Their path was traceable by the furious insurrections which broke out in city after city as they spread westwards. The Tungánis of Khamil and Uramchi were among the earliest to rise. The latter city is large and densely populated, and from a distant date it had been the emporium on which the whole of Central Asia depended for its supply of tea. Here, as indeed throughout Ili generally, the revolt assumed the form of a military mutiny.

For the soldierly qualities of the Tungánis had blinded the authorities to the danger of employing aliens in the ranks of the Imperial army, and, at the time we speak of, the Tungánis formed the very flower of the 60,000 troops distributed under the command of the Manchu governor-general. The Tungáni soldiery at Uramchi, led by their own officers, seized the city, compelled their co-religionists, the native Sarts,[1] to join their enterprise, and put all the Manchus to the sword. In the course of the struggle a fire broke out, and the flames were not extinguished before many streets of houses and vast stores of tea had been destroyed.

From Uramchi the insurgents advanced westwards in two bands, one making for the northern, and the other for the southern circuit of Ili.

Those composing the force destined for Dzungaria effected an important capture of artillery at Manasy, and, after occupying that town, proceeded to Kur-kara-usu. On the way they met and routed an army sent out to oppose them from Kulja, and their victory was the signal for a general rising of all the Muhammadans in Dzungaria against the Chinese rule. The insurrection at Kulja was at first a failure; the Tungánis were badly armed, and, after a bloody struggle of twelve days' duration, they had to fly for refuge to Old Kulja.[2] Encouraged

[1] Dr. Vambéry identifies the *Sarts* with the people who, in Bokhara and Kokand, go by the name of *Tajiks*. According to the same authority they are of Persian blood, and have for ages been settled throughout the tract which has Siberia and India, Persia and China, for its several borders. In the present narrative all that need be noted about them is, that they represent an urban and quasi-aboriginal population; owning no connexion with the Tungánis, except that of a common religion.

[2] Colonel Yule believes that Old Kulja may mark the site of Almalig, a city which was renowned in the middle ages as the capital of the Chagatai Khánate. In 1339 there was a Catholic bishop of Almalig, who, with six other minor friars, suffered martyrdom there. John de Marignolli, however,

by this result, the Manchu governor-general again gave them battle; but fortune no longer favoured him—he was utterly defeated, and all his artillery captured. He then evacuated the city of Kulja, and fled into the fort, where the victors immediately subjected him to a strict blockade. Elsewhere in Dzungaria the Tungánis and Manchus were in constant collision throughout the year 1865, but step by step the former steadily prevailed. The whole country was full of exiles, who hailed the Tungánis as their deliverers; for Dzungaria, during the century since its acquisition by the Imperial Government, had been the general place of transportation, not only for individual convicts from interior China, but for entire families suspected of political disaffection from Eastern Turkistán. Even the Manchu tribes of Sibo and Solon, who had been brought from the banks of the Amur, on the footing of military colonists, to act as a check on the exiles, proved faithless to their trust, and compounded for peace with the Tungánis by engaging to adopt the Musalmán religion. One after another, the minor forts and towns of Dzungaria fell into the hands of the revolutionary party; and, when autumn came, four points alone remained with the Imperialists, two of which were the citadels of Kulja and Chuguchak. The struggle which occurred at the last-named place is noteworthy as having caught up in its eddy the nomad Kirghizes and Kálmaks, who pasture

who visited Almalig, the following year, on his way to the Court of the Great Khán of Cathay, testifies to the prevalence of a very tolerant spirit in the city. 'There,' he says, 'we built a church, bought a piece of ground, sang masses and baptized several; preaching freely and openly.' It is curious to note these old-world glimpses of a country which, having since been buried for centuries in the thickest darkness, is now inevitably marked out for speedy restoration to the gaze of Europe by absorption within the light of the Russian Empire.

their flocks in the vicinity. No sooner had the Kirghizes shown signs of siding with their co-religionists, the Tungánis, than their ancient foes, the Kálmaks, declared for the Chinese. Nor was the declaration an idle one. On the night of the 4th November, a large body of Kálmaks, joined by a sallying party of Chinese from the beleaguered citadel of Chuguchak, crossed the Russian border, and, *within Russian limits*, fell suddenly with fire and sword on an encampment of the Kirghizes. The work of massacre and plunder continued for two days. The Kálmaks then withdrew to Chuguchak, taking with them 100,000 sheep, 6,000 horned cattle, 1,300 horses, and 600 camels; they left on the field 300 human corpses, 200 sheep killed out of mere wantonness, and 1,500 masterless dogs.[1] This, for the time at any rate, was a crushing blow to the Muhammadan cause in the north of Dzungaria. The Kirghizes no longer dared to lift their heads, and the Tungánis were obliged to raise the siege of Chuguchak. But the single check in this direction was more than compensated to the Tungánis in other quarters. Early in 1866 they carried the citadel of Kulja by storm, and butchered the gallant garrison to a man. And though no detailed accounts of subsequent events have yet reached us, the general tenor of our information inclines us to believe that, at the present time, the Tungánis are masters of all Dzungaria south of the Tarbogatai mountains.

Whether their power promises to be permanent is another thing. From China probably they have little to

[1] These dogs, after devouring the flesh, and gnawing the bones of their slain masters, soon became ravenous and desperate. Scouring the country in packs between Urdjar and Chuguchak, they were so numerous and audacious that the pass of Khatyn-Su was officially reported by the Russian superintendent of the district to be dangerous for a single horseman.

fear. An army of retribution has, it is true, recently recaptured Khamil, thereby cutting off the Tungánis in both circuits of Ili from those provinces of interior China where the rebellion was hatched; but we doubt the competency[1] of the Pekin Government to follow up its first success; and to the Tungánis the loss of Khamil is merely one city the less in their possession; it is not as though they had any base of operations in Kansu. The chief danger to the victorious insurgents in Dzungaria comes from their own disunion and barbarism. Under all circumstances, it is much easier to upset a government, especially an alien one, than to organise a fresh government in its stead. And in Dzungaria we doubt whether the Tungáni, or any other section of the heterogeneous population is capable of producing a dynasty which shall reunite the several townships and encampments under a single sceptre, or even consolidate a strong administration in any one district. Each township aspires to a separate autonomy, and every camp has its own chief: all these endeavour to work out their own ideas of right and order, and as aggressive war upon their next neighbour usually stands high in the programme, the general result is not far off utter anarchy. Now anarchy just beyond a border implies raids within that border. We have already had

[1] Recent accounts from China report the occupation of the eastern districts of Shantung by a body of rebels, called Nien-fei, who are carrying rapine and murder up to the walls of Pekin. 'The *élite* of the Tartar army' (we quote from the 'North China Herald') 'is gathered around the capital, and it is only the terror of this arm of the service which keeps the rebel hordes from the City of Nine Gates.' This is probably an exaggerated estimate of the importance attaching to the Nien-fei movement. And it must also be conceded that the Taepings have disappeared from the scene. But still the Government, which can permit the former to go unchecked, and all but succumbed to the latter, cannot be expected to show more vigour against rebels in a remote and impracticable country like Ili.

an example of this truth in the incursion of the Kálmaks from Chuguchak into the Russian province of Semipolatinsk. And it is as impossible for Russia to let such injuries pass unnoticed as it would be for the Anglo-Indian Government to submit to corresponding insults from the Wazíri or Marri tribes on the Peshâwar or Shikárpur frontier. The press of St. Petersburg already speaks of the Tungáni insurrection in Dzungaria as 'the Dungen question (1868);' and the recent measure of administrative reconstruction, by which the southern portion of Semipolatinsk has been severed from the Government of Western Siberia, and constituted, together with Russia's recent conquests on the Sir-Dariá river, into a new 'Government of Turkistán,' is avowedly adopted with a view to watching, and, if necessary, controlling the affairs of Dzungaria. Had China retained her grasp on the two circuits of Ili, the Czar would have had no reason, and possibly little inclination, to transgress the bounds of empire laid down by recent treaties with the Court of Pekin; but, now that the power to which he was pledged has finally disappeared from the scene, and that its successor is found to be a disorderly neighbour, objectionable in many ways, and specially so for interrupting the course of Russian trade towards the east, we imagine that it cannot be long before the troops at present[1] concentrated about Fort Vernöe have their headquarters transferred across the frontier to Kulja. In short, we look forward to an early extinction of the Tungáni revolution, with all its attendant troubles in Dzungaria, by means of a Russian occupation of the country (1868).

[1] East of Lake Issyk-Kúl, the Russians have five battalions of infantry, ten 'sotnias' (each one hundred strong) of Cossacks, and sixteen guns; and, west of the same point, there are eleven battalions, twenty sotnias, and forty guns; the whole under the command of General Kaufmann, the new Governor-General of Turkistán.

But it is time that we should turn to a field of greater attraction for British interests. We have already intimated that, while one band of Tungánis issued from Uramchi, in June 1864, for operations in Dzungaria, another band, by a more southerly route, advanced into Eastern Turkistán. Before proceeding, however, to follow the fortunes of the latter force, it appears desirable to say a few words as to the physical appearance and past history of the territory forming the new scene of action.

Other names for this territory are Little Bokhara, which is simply unmeaning, and Chinese Tartary, which conveys an incorrect impression; Eastern Turkistán, on the contrary, as the correlative of that Western Turkistán which is to be looked for on the other side of the Bolor mountains, rightly indicates a geographical division of the region which has Túrks for the bulk of its population. Eastern Turkistán then forms a great depressed valley, shut in on three sides by mountains of great height; on the north it is separated from Dzungaria by the Tian-Shan range; on the west from Transoxiana by the Bolor; and on the south by the Kárákoram and Kuen Lún from India and Thibet. Hence its configuration somewhat resembles a blunt-headed cone, except that, towards the east, where the base-line ought to be, there are only barren sands, which merge imperceptibly into the great Desert of Gobi. Sand throughout the interior of the cone, and a clayey soil and stony surface along the edge of the mountain lines, are too largely the characteristics of the country. Morever, the air is of exceeding dryness, and rain is rare. But, on the other hand, the volume of water which flows down from the snowy mountains on three sides of the valley, is considerable, and the rivers which carry this, all of them converging into the central channel of the Ergol or Tarym, afford ample means of irrigation: while the tracts under the shadow of the three ranges, arid as they generally are, nevertheless contain patches of more or less fertile land. The climate is temperate and eminently salubrious. The mineral resources have been very imperfectly explored by the ignorant natives; but there can be no doubt of their abundance. They include gold, copper, sulphur, salt, and especially the jade-stone, on which the Chinese place so high a value. The real importance, however, of Eastern Turkistán lies not in its indigenous productions, but in its geographical advantages as a commercial thoroughfare. It forms an important stage in the ancient line of communication by land between Europe and Asia. This famous route, which we have above traced from the Great Wall as far as Khamil, passes on, along the southern slope of the Tian Shan, through Karashar, Kucha, and Aksu to Kashgar; from thence over the commodious Terektin Pass to Andijan and Kokand; and finally it crosses the Russian border to Orenburg. The distance from Pekin to Aksu is said to be 2,550 miles, and caravans take nearly five months to traverse it, though special couriers accomplish the journey in one month. From Aksu on to Kokand may be reckoned other 800 miles.

As for the history of Eastern Turkistán, the Chinese appear to have been masters of the country from the beginning of the Christian era up to the days of Chinghiz Khán, though their rule during that interval was subject to considerable fluctuations, at one time extending beyond the Bolor mountains as far as the shores of the Caspian Sea, at another receding within the territory of Khamil. On the partition of Chinghiz Khán's mighty empire, Eastern Turkistán became a part of the Chagatai Khanate, and even after the bulk of that Khanate had been overrun by the Kálmaks, a descendant of Chagatai continued in power at Yárkand up to the middle of the seventeenth century. Some insight into the mediæval condition of Yárkand, Kashgar, and Khoten is obtainable from the travels of Marco Polo, and of the pious Jesuit, Benedict Göes. In both narratives the point which most strikingly contrasts with the circumstances of our own day is the religious toleration displayed by the native authorities. Marco Polo testifies to the existence of a large number of Nestorian Christians among the inhabitants; indeed, in his time, Kashgar was the seat of a Nestorian archbishopric; and Göes, whose journey dates 1664, or three centuries after the Venetian, was admitted, in the presence of the Prince of Yárkand, to a religious discussion with the principal Mullahs of the country, who actually came to the conclusion that 'our law also might have some good in it.' Yet Eastern Turkistán, since its first conversion from Buddhism, has always been intensely Muhammadan; and its political fortunes, particularly in the western portion of the province, have received a very strong bias from the national creed. This western portion is known as Altishahr, or the *Six Cities*, and comprises Yárkand, Kashgar, Koten, Aksu, Yanghisar, and Ush-turfan, with the territories subordinate to each. Altishahr, perhaps from its proximity to those centres of Muhammadan theology, Bokhara and Samarkand, has never had any lack of holy men to guide its concerns; and, as the Chagatai dynasty neared its close, the priestly element began to play an important part in public affairs. No better summary of the events of this period can be given than the one supplied by Colonel Yule:—

'Saintly teachers and workers of miracles, claiming descent from Muhammad, and known as Khwájás or Hojás, acquired great influence, and the sectaries attached to the chief of these divided the people into rival factions, whose mutual hostility eventually led to the subjugation of the whole country. For, late in the seventeenth century, Hojá Appak, the leader of one of those parties called the White Mountain, having been expelled from Kashgar by Ismail Khán, the chief of that state, who was a zealous supporter of the opposite party, or Black Mountain, sought the aid of Galdan Khán, sovereign of the Eleuths or Kálmaks of Dzungaria. Taking the occasion offered, that chief in 1678 invaded the states south of the Thian Shan, carried off the Khán of Kashgar and his family, and established the Hojás of the White Mountain over the country in authority subordinate to his own. Great discords for many years succeeded, sometimes one faction and sometimes another being uppermost, but some supremacy always continuing to be exercised by the Kháns of Dzungaria. In 1757, the latter country was conquered by the Chinese, who, in the following year, making a tool of the White party, which was then in opposition, succeeded in bringing the states of Turkistán also under their rule.'

Such were the successive steps by which the Chinese power was at length re-established in Eastern Turkistán. The Khwájás of the White Mountain, however, who, after their expulsion by the Chinese, had found refuge in Kokand, made more than one bold endeavour to recover what they regarded as their patrimony. In 1827, Jahángír Khán Khwájá invaded Altishahr with a large rabble of armed fanatics, and captured Yárkand and Kashgar; but after an eight months' occupation of those cities, he was defeated by the Chinese, and obliged again to fly across the Bolor. The Khán of Kokand surrendered him to the Chinese; he was conveyed to Pekin and executed there in 1828, his fate making a profound sensation throughout Central Asia and even in China also: to this day there is no more popular ballad among the Kirghizes and Usbegs than that which tells the tale of Jahángír Khán's betrayal. In 1852 the Kokand Darbár connived at a fresh expedition against Altishahr, headed by seven Khwájás of the same family, who, after a transient success, were similarly repulsed by the Chinese. One of the seven, Wali Khán Tarrá, renewed the attempt in 1857, and, though he too, in the end, had to retire, his temporary occupation of Kashgar is memorable for a display of cruelty, such as staggered even the unsusceptible Túrks. 'His mania was a thirst for blood, and not a day passed without several men being slaughtered in cold blood, either by himself or in his presence. On the banks of the Kizil he erected a pyramid of human skulls, and anxiously watched the gradual rise of a monument so worthy of him. The heads of fallen Chinese and Musalmáns were collected from all parts and added to the pyramid.' Some of the bravest and best of his own adherents were made to contribute their skulls to this ghastly trophy; and it was crowned by the head of a European traveller, the lamented Adolphe Schlagentweit. He struck a paralysis of terror into the people, and, to be rid of him, even the return of the Chinese was for a time welcomed by all classes. The Chinese, however, were not conciliatory masters, and a national party soon rose into sturdy life again. Still fondly looking in the direction of the saintly family from which they had suffered so much, the Túrks fastened on Buzurg Khán, son of the martyr Jahángír, as their destined deliverer. Their watchword was, 'When Buzurg Khán mounts his steed, Altishahr shall be free.' All that remains to be noted is that, while contact with the fanaticism of Transoxiana had thus kept Altishahr seething in perpetual war and anarchy, proximity to the civilisation of China had saved the eastern towns from participation in the same miseries. East of Aksu the influence of the Khwájás diminished, and east of Kucha it ceased entirely, so that not the Tungánis only but the Muhammadans generally of Karashar, Turfan, and Khamil served actively with the Imperial troops engaged in the pacification of the Six Cities.

This imperfect sketch of previous events in Eastern Turkistán will perhaps suffice to give the reader some idea of the relative position of parties in the province, about the middle of 1864, when the wave of Tungáni insurrection swept in from the Desert of Gobi. There were the Chinese in military possession, with a force of about 14,000 men; there were the Tungánis, forming a large and hitherto staunch portion of the Chinese garrison; and there were the native non-Tungáni Muhammadans (Usbegs, Sarts, Kirghizes, and others), who in the eastern districts identified their interests with the Tungánis, but who in Altishahr held Chinese and Tungánis in equal abomination, and sighed for a return of the Khwájás from their exile in Kokand.

On the arrival at Kucha of the Tungánis, who had been despatched from Uramchi to raise Eastern Turkistán, their clansmen of the Chinese garrison at once fraternised with them and mutinied. The other Muhammadan residents joined the Tungánis; and the Chinese, powerless to resist the combination, all had their throats cut. The triumphant Muslims then elected a Khwájá, named Rashud-ud-dín, of great local sanctity, to be their ruler; and under his direction they rapidly obtained possession of Aksu, Ush-turfan, and Lai Masjid. Rashud-ud-dín's next blow was to have fallen on Yárkand, the seat of the local government of the southern circuit of Ili. The Manchu governor, however, precipitated events at that place by the very measures he took to counteract the move. By largesses and yet more liberal promises he induced his Tungáni soldiers, through their priests the Imáms, to swear solemnly on the Kurán that they would stand by their colours to the death. They observed the oath for three whole days; but, on the 24th July, 1864, they mutinied, broke open the jail, released the prisoners, and plundered all the dwellings of the Chinese civil population. Next day they proclaimed a Holy War against the infidel; a device which secured them the co-operation of every Muslim in Yárkand. The Chinese troops had now to retire within their fortifications and submit to a siege. Scarcely had this result been attained at Yárkand, before the same antagonistic elements came into collision at Kashgar. Here too the Chinese took the initiative, though by a sterner process than that which had failed so signally at the capital. The Manchu commandant of Kashgar invited the Tungánis to a feast in his fort; they came, and as they unsuspectingly sat at meat, a volley of musketry was poured into them from all sides; of the seven hundred men who were in this doomed assembly, fifty only are said to have made good their escape. Instantly the Musalmáns of the city flew to arms, with a cry for vengeance; and the Chinese, like their compatriots at Yárkand, found themselves beleaguered within their own citadel. Almost at the same time a similar tragedy was enacted at Khoten; the Chinese began by massacring a number of Tungánis, and the Muhammadan citizens retaliated with vigour; but in this instance no fortifications availed to save the

Chinese from immediate ruin; they were blotted out of Khoten, and a native priest, named Hájí Habíbullá, was elected to rule in their stead. Soon afterwards Rashud-ud-dín's preparations at Kucha for an advance on Yárkand were complete; and on the 30th September he despatched a force of 7,000 horse and foot and 250 camel-guns to aid the revolted Yárkandis in pressing the siege of the fort. The Chinese defended themselves with the courage of despair; but famine and undermined ramparts soon rendered further resistance hopeless; then they fired their magazine, and anticipated in flames of their own creation the certain death which awaited them from the foe.

The fort of Kashgar was now the last place in which a vestige of the Chinese power remained. While its fate still hung in the balance, Buzurg Khán Khwájá from Kokand rode into the streets of the city with a following of 500 men, chiefly Kirghizes and Kipchaks. At last the Túrks had got their long-looked-for deliverer among them, and they hailed him as their rightful prince with acclamations. But, alas for the misdirection of popular regard, not Charles Stuart nor Louis *le Desiré* ever so disappointed the hopes of their enthusiastic partisans! Buzurg Khán proved a worthless debauchee, who, before many weeks were over, was content that the burden of princely duties should be transferred to an officer of his own staff, Yakub Beg. Of a very different stamp was this new ruler of Kashgar. By birth a Tajik, and a subject of Kokand, he had for many years played a conspicuous part in the stormy politics of his native Khanate. The deed for which he hitherto had been best known, would in Europe have covered his name with hopeless dishonour, but the moral sense of Central

Asia is less nice, and he, who in 1847, as commandant of Ak Masjid, had accepted Russian gold in exchange for a portion of the territory committed to his charge, still retained among his countrymen a reputation for exceptionally fair dealing. Brave, energetic, and open-handed, he was popular with his brother-chieftains, and beloved by his own retainers. At the time to which our story relates he held the rank of Kúshbegi, or commander-in-chief of the Kokand forces; but, as Kokand existed only on the sufferance of Russian generals, his instincts had rightly taught him that even a subordinate share in Buzurg Khán's venture across the Bolor offered a finer field for his ability and ambition than any that was open to him at home.

Meanwhile famine was effectually doing its work within the fort of Kashgar. By March 1865 two thousand Chinese had died of starvation. The remainder of the garrison then for the most part committed suicide, and Yakub Kúshbegi became master of the fort with little difficulty. So fell, after a century of continuous dominion, the Chinese power in Eastern Turkistán.

But the Musalmáns who, in one form or another, had now succeeded to the supremacy, were far from being a united or harmonious body. Rashud-ud-dín in the east, Habíbullá in the south, and Yakub Kúshbegi in the west, each represented a separate faction. At Kucha, Aksu, and Yárkand the prevailing influence was Tungáni. At Khoten, Habíbullá, as the weakest of the parties, sincerely desired, but was not likely to enjoy, a life of quiet isolation; already he had been obliged to fight a pitched battle in defence of his territory against a wanton invasion of Tungánis from

Yárkand. And lastly, Yakub Kúshbegi at Kashgar, though constantly threatened with destruction from the local intrigues of rival competitors for power, was not the man to be content with the possession of a single township. Thus the conclusion to which events manifestly tended was a struggle for mastery between the Tungánis of Rashud-ud-dín and the Kokandi adventurers under Yakub Kúshbegi; Khoten meanwhile endeavouring to keep aloof from either side, but destined to be absorbed by whichever should prove the winner.

The contest that ensued was sharply fought out, but we spare our readers a recital of the varying fortunes of the combatants. The issue was still doubtful, and Habíbullá was consequently still unmolested, when, in 1865, Khoten was visited by a European traveller, the first (excepting Adolphe Schlagentweit, who never lived to tell the tale) that had been seen there for centuries. We allude, of course, to Mr. Johnson, of the Indian Trigonometrical Survey. An account of Mr. Johnson's journey, and of the incidents that followed it, has been already given in a previous page of this volume (51); how, while in the execution of his professional duties on the Káshmír border, he received, and upon his own responsibility accepted, an invitation from Khán Habíbullá of Khoten; how the Khán entertained him with sufficient hospitality, but was strongly inclined to keep him as a hostage for the extraction of money and munitions of war from the Indian Government; how, in the end, he let him go, and endeavoured to obtain what he wanted by the more civilised method of a formal embassy to the English Viceroy at Calcutta; and how his hopes were blasted by Sir John Lawrence civilly refusing to have anything to do with him.

At length victory inclined decidedly to Yakub Kúshbegi; for in April 1866 he captured Yárkand from the Tungánis. He followed up his advantage with ardour, and his career eastward was an unbroken success, so that by autumn of the following year Khoten, Ushturfan, Aksu, and Kucha had surrendered to his arms. In fact Yakub Kúshbegi is at the present time (1868) undisputed master of the whole of Altishahr. [He has since then consolidated his power as Ruler of Eastern Turkistán.]

What bearing this result may have on British interests in India, we shall presently inquire; but, in the meantime, we may with advantage cast a glance at the circumstances connected with the Kúshbegi's capture of Khoten. For there have not been wanting writers in the public journals to sneer at Sir John Lawrence's pusillanimity in declining to enter into close relations with this particular chiefship; and even a responsible and undoubtedly most able Minister like Lord Cranborne was at one time disposed to look with favour on the proposal of a Panjáb official, who volunteered to visit Khoten in search of that brilliant Will-o'-the-wisp, the trade of Central Asia. Statesmen can seldom hope to obtain so immediate and signal a justification of their prudence, as Sir John Lawrence has found in the narrative of Habíbullá's fall, as given by the British Agent at Leh, in a despatch dated September 3, 1867, which has been published in the Indian newspapers. We prefer therefore to give the actual text of the despatch without attempting an abridgment.

'At the end of last year Yakub Kúshbegi of Yárkand, having first imprisoned the Agent from Khoten, to prevent his sending any intelligence, commenced preparations for an advance on Khoten. The Agent, however, managed to send off a letter by two of his servants to give warning to the Khán, but the messengers were stopped, and the letter found sewn up in a shoe. The men were brought back and shot by the Kúshbegi's orders. The Agent was then very closely confined and guarded; and threatened with a like fate, if he did not give full information regarding the strength of Khoten, the number of troops, &c.; and, to save his life, he disclosed everything. The Kúshbegi then, at the beginning of this year, sent a strong force against Khoten, and himself joined it within a march or two of the town. From this point he sent off a letter to the ruler, Habíbullá Khán, expressive of his friendly feelings, and his desire to establish amicable relations between the two countries, as they were neighbours and of the same faith, and begging the Khán to come out and meet him that he might enter into an alliance. Habíbullá at first refused, but, after much pressing, and receiving many assurances of friendship and esteem, he assented and went out to the Yárkand camp with one of his sons and a few followers. He was received with every mark of friendship and honour, and well feasted and entertained, but in the night he and all his followers were made prisoners, and his signet-ring removed; and the next day a letter was sent to Khoten, signed with the Khán's seal, directing all the chief officers and other men of influence to come out and pay their respects to the Yárkand ruler, with whom a friendly alliance had just been formed. Many of the officers and others obeyed the summons, and, as they left Khoten by one road, a large force was sent against it by another. And, there being no one to take the command and give orders, the place was quickly taken and a large number of the garrison slain. The Kúshbegi then entered, and secured a very large treasure in gold and silver; and, after appointing one of his own officers governor, he returned to Yárkand. When leaving, he gave all the women of the Khán's harem to his chief officers and followers: but these women, having formed a plot among themselves, and seizing the opportunity when their new husbands were unarmed and unprepared, attacked and killed many of them. When the Kúshbegi heard of this, he at once ordered Habíbullá Khán, an old man of more than eighty years, and his son to be shot.'

Now, supposing that Sir John Lawrence, in deference to the popular cry for the extension of Indian trade in

Central Asia, should have allowed the English officer above mentioned to proceed on his volunteer journey to Khoten, what, it may be asked, would have been that officer's fate? We think we may reply that, even if he had not been cut off before reaching Khoten at all, he must, upon arriving there, either have perished in that city amid the tumult of Habíbullá's downfall, or have been carried off captive to Yárkand, where England, for all her length of arm, would have then been powerless either to rescue or to avenge him. With this difference, and it is one that would have been most damaging to the national prestige, we should have had a second Abyssinia in Eastern Turkistán, another Theodore in Yakub Kúshbegi. Taught this by lesson, we trust that for some time to come the British public may hear no more of that premature agitation, which, in pursuit of doubtful advantages, clamours for the despatch of English officers among the untried and ill-consolidated states of Central Asia. Were England at war with Russia, and were it necessary for the prosecution of the war that English gold and English lives should be staked in organising hordes of Usbegs and Tungánís for guerilla warfare against the enemy, our money and our lives might doubtless be lavished in the country; but he who, as matters now stand (1867), talks of English embassies to Yárkand or to Khoten, is an enemy to his country.[1] This is strong language, we admit, but it cannot be wholly uncalled for, when a recent writer in a well-informed English journal charges the Indian Government with 'inexcusable apathy' in neglecting to

[1] This was written in 1867, and was at that time true. Since then the Kúshbegi has firmly consolidated his power. The expediency of holding diplomatic intercourse with him has been reconsidered, and has been decided in the affirmative.—W. W. H.

establish consuls in the cities of Eastern Turkistán.[1] Apathy there certainly is not, either for commercial and political purposes, or towards purely scientific ends. Sir John Lawrence refuses to send English officers where their mere appearance might be a signal for their detention (1867); but he obtains all the intelligence he requires by the systematic despatch into the same countries of natives of India, specially trained for inquiry, and handsomely remunerated for their pains. And, if proof were wanted of the efficiency of this agency, we might point to the valuable geographical information acquired by a Pandit who, under Captain Montgomerie's instructions, recently journeyed from India *viâ* the Mánsarowar Lake to Lhassa.

Reverting now to the actual position of affairs in Altishahr, and the extent to which British interests may be affected by the succession of a wild captain of free-lances to the dominion of the Chinese, we can only say that the Kúshbegi's rule is of altogether too recent a growth to admit of any opinion being formed as to the qualities it will display (1867). Hitherto he has had work enough to win his kingdom at the point of the sword; and now that it is fully won, whether he will succeed in keeping it, and, if so, how he will govern it, remain to be seen. Upon these doubts hangs the future as well of Russian policy as of British trade.

[1] This writer in the same sentence denounces the Indian Government for similar neglect at Leh, and also for permitting the Rájá of Káshmír to block the course of trade by monstrous exactions at the frontier; whereas the fact is that so far back as in 1864 the Mahárájá was constrained to make large reductions in his customs duties, and that there already is a consul at Leh, sent there for the special purpose of seeing that the terms of the reduced tariff of 1864 are strictly adhered to by the Mahárájá's officials. The true cause of the depressed state of trade at Leh is the disturbed condition of the country on the other side of the Kárákoram range (1867).

If the Kúshbegi be, as we are disposed to believe, not a mere soldier of fortune, but something of a statesman also, the first use he will make of the consolidation of his conquests will be to resuscitate the trade which recent wars and tumults have all but extinguished in Eastern Turkistán. Most probably it will be beyond his power to reopen commerce with China through the country occupied by the revolted Tungánís; but China's difficulty ought, in this instance, to be India's opportunity. With the Kúshbegi's leave, India should be able to supply most of the articles for which Tartary has hitherto depended on the Chinese, and other goods besides. Already there is one Indian staple which is in urgent demand throughout all the Turkistáns, Eastern, Western, and Russian; and that is tea. The Túrks cannot live without tea; not only do they use it as a beverage at meals, but one person may not receive a private visit from another, nor a chief give audience to his retainers in public darbár, without tea being offered to the guests and freely consumed by all present. Thus if our planters of the Himálayas would only take the trouble to ascertain and imitate the particular appearance, whether brick-shaped or blue-glazed, which Chinese tea has hitherto borne in the Turkish bazaars, they ought to find at Leh a splendid market for the commodity which has caused so much disappointment to Indian speculators (1867). Recently we heard of a single tea-district in the North-west Provinces exporting tea into Central Asia to the value of 15,000*l.* It will easily therefore be understood that the Indian Government scans the prospects of a revival of the caravan trade across the Kárákoram Pass with considerable solicitude.

Still more narrowly are the Russians on the Sir-

Daria watching the movements of the Kúshbegi in respect to the re-opening of traffic over the Terektin Pass. Their frontier at Namangam is only about 160 miles from the foot of the pass; they are indignant at the loss of their ancient commerce with China by this route; and, though they cannot but admit that the more distant Tungánís on the borders of Kansu, or within that province, are the principal cause of the misfortune, they are not likely to overlook any obstructions to their mercantile enterprise which Yákub Kúshbegi may offer in Altishahr, close to their own outposts. If the Kúshbegi is a wise man, he will do his utmost to conciliate Russian sentiments on this score. But there are rumours afloat that he is differently inclined (1867). It is said that he has sent emissaries to the courts of Kokand and Bokhara and to the Tungánís at Kulja, in view to the formation of a league hostile to Russia. This is very likely false. The substratum of truth, however, appears to be that in Altishahr, as in every other part of Central Asia, including Afghánistán, a general feeling has arisen, and day by day gains ground, of antagonism to Russia, as an aggressor from whom much is to be feared, and of inclination towards England, as a power content to remain within her own limits. The time may come when this feeling will be of incalculable value to us; and we owe its existence to that determined policy of non-intervention which among certain critics of Sir John Lawrence's policy is his capital offence. Meantime, if Yákub Kúshbegi should be imprudent enough to give umbrage to General Kaufmann, the newly-appointed Governor-General of Russian Turkistán (1867), events may be precipitated which, upon present chances, are not immediately to be expected. In the end no doubt Altishahr will be absorbed into the

Northern Empire, and it probably will be the fortune of the Kárákoram mountains to form the first common boundary the world may ever see between the dominions of Old England and Holy Russia. But on the whole, we doubt whether the next move of the Russian forces in this quarter will be across the Terektin Pass. An advance from Fort Vernöe for the suppression of the Tungánís about Kulja appears a much nearer contingency; and, since the command of Dzungaria would enable the Russians to reach Khamil and the trade beyond, almost as effectually as they could from Eastern Turkistán, it is possible that, with the accomplishment of that object, they might cease to take all the interest they at present certainly do in the affairs of the Six Cities. But, whatever may be the course of events, whether to accelerate or to retard the southward progress of the Russians, we look forward to their ultimate occupation of Eastern Turkistán without any apprehension. Our trade cannot suffer, for it is impossible that the system of protective duties should be much longer maintained at St. Petersburg, and as for the security of the Indian Empire, even the wildest of Russophobists has not yet conceived the possibility of an invasion by way of the Kárákoram.

Our task is done. We have endeavoured, so far as our fragmentary materials permit, to throw light upon a part of the world regarding which Europe possesses very scanty information, and to trace over an enormous extent of frontier the progress of a famous empire's decline. What effect the events we have reviewed may produce on the central fabric of Manchu power we leave to others to delineate. The result perhaps will be small, for the morbid condition of the extremities is, in this case, less a potential cause of future disaster than a mere symptom of deep-seated evils that have their origin elsewhere. It betokens an organisation sapped at its vital sources by an atrophy, which, sooner or later, must terminate in utter collapse and dissolution.

NOTE BY THE EDITOR.

An able article in the last *Edinburgh Review* (April, 1874), brings down the history of Eastern Turkistán from the point at which Mr. Wyllie's article in the same journal left it in April, 1868. It is, therefore, needful here to say only a very few words regarding this interval. Partly by dissimulation and treachery, partly by a skilful use of the fanatical aspects of Islám, but chiefly by valour and policy, Yákub Kúshbegi has established himself as the *de facto* ruler of Eastern Turkistán, and now firmly governs it. As he strengthened himself in this position, he extended his relations alike towards Russia and India. At first the Russian Government held, that though 'he might have established a Government *de facto*, Russia had treaties with China, and could not enter into diplomatic relations with a successful insurgent against the Chinese Emperor.' The Chinese Government, however, took no steps to recover the revolted province. Various high officers enjoy titles connected with its civil and military administration; but (with the exception of an occasional agitation such as is said to have taken place this spring, 1874) they live calmly at the courts of Pekin or Sze Chuen, and continue to hold their nominal offices as if Eastern Turkistán still formed an integral part of the Chinese Empire. As the ruler of Eastern Turkistán consolidated his power, Russia recognised him.

A Russian envoy was sent to Eastern Turkistán in the spring of 1872 to complete a commercial treaty, and since then an embassy under Baron Kaulbars to the Amír has removed former causes of suspicion, and established friendly relations. In the same year, the Atálik Ghází, or ruler of Eastern Turkistán, despatched an envoy to India. He reached there in 1873. His first object was to obtain the Viceroy's consent to a British envoy returning with him to Turkistán, with a view to forming a commercial treaty. His second object was to visit Constantinople and to obtain from the Sultán a recognition of his master as Defender of the Faith. He succeeded in both his objects. It is now understood that the Atálik Ghází is *de jure* as well as *de facto* the great Muhummadan Chief of Central Asia. In the summer of 1873 the Atálik Ghází's envoy returned to India from Constantinople, and was accompanied to Eastern Turkistán by a British envoy, Mr. Douglas Forsyth, C.B., of the India Civil Service. Mr. Forsyth, now Sir Douglas Forsyth, was peculiarly welcome to the Atálik Ghází, as he had already visited Turkistán in 1870. He has been received with the utmost cordiality, and has now brought his mission to a successful close.

While these sheets were passing through the press (March, 1874) the treaty framed by Mr. Forsyth and the Atálik Ghází arrived in India. As it forms the final result of the series of events described in the above essay, I reproduce it in full at the end of this Note. But, before doing so, it may be well to explain the actual position of the Atálik Ghází in his own dominions, and to state the evidence showing that he is, in reality, the *de facto* ruler. I shall quote first a short passage which the Edinburgh Reviewer cites from the Russian envoy, Captain Reinthal.

To this will be added the description of the present state of affairs in Turkistán, which the writer in the April number (1874) of the *Edinburgh Review* gives. Extracts from a recent letter of Mr. Forsyth, the British envoy, now on his way back from Turkistán, will conclude the series of quotations.

Captain Reinthal, the Russian envoy, writes thus:—

'To all appearance, Yákub Beg wields an unlimited power in his dominions. He enters into every detail of administration and sits all day receiving reports, issuing orders, and confirming sentences of death. There is not the least form of trial. Theft is punishable by hanging; even a simple accusation securing the sentence of death. The nooses never swing idly on the gallows. Information against individuals is the great feature in the administration of Kashgaria. All creatures living in Jetishahr, as well as all private property, are the belongings of Yákub Beg, who disposes of them as he pleases for his own personal benefit or for the good of the state.'

The Edinburgh Reviewer, in April, 1874, thus summarises the evidence which he has collected from English and Russian sources:—

'Eastern Turkistán is now ruled by the Atálik Ghází in an austere manner, which befits his title as Protector and Champion of the Faith. Islám is enforced with a strict adherence to orthodox Sunni observances, contrasting forcibly with the laxness that prevailed during the tolerant rule of the Chinese. At the hours of morning and evening prayer, functionaries duly armed with sticks, as in Bokhárá, now sweep the laggards into the mosques. Idolaters are not allowed to ride or to wear turbans, those privileges being reserved for the faithful; and the Atálik Ghází has prohibited, as contrary to Sunni law, a practice prevalent in and before the days of Marco Polo—that of temporary marriages between visitors and the women of the country, lasting only so long as the visit lasts. He is, himself, completely uneducated—a mere trooper, as he often styles himself, but knows the spell which religious teachers can exercise, and assigns a great part of the revenue of the country for their maintenance.

He keeps them, however, in their place, no less than his other subjects, and permits on their part no interference with his worldly policy. Indeed, he seldom resorts to anyone for counsel, with the exception—and that only an occasional exception—of old Kokandí friends—Muhammad Sunnus, the Governor of Yárkand, and Sayyid Yákub, the late Envoy to India and Constantinople. Almost every offence of any gravity—and even a light offence, if repeated—is punished by death, and, during the early days of his rule, the gallows were rarely empty. It is needless to add that the anarchy which preceded his rise to power has entirely disappeared; and Mr. Shaw has told us that a man who saw a bag of silver ingots lying on the roadside would immediately run over to the other side, for fear of being supposed to have designs upon it. The administration appears to be as impartially just as it is Draconic, and the people do not suffer from what they would regard as oppression. The taxes do not differ materially from what they were in Chinese times; a tenth of the produce of the land being taken partly in kind, partly in cash, while herdsmen contribute each year a fortieth of their stock, and merchants a fortieth on their sales. The officials are not paid in cash, but by the assignment of the revenue from a village, a group of villages, or even a fractional share in a village; and from this they support both themselves and their following. Thus, a tenth share of the produce from the district of Kargalik (on the way to Yárkand from the south) is devoted to the support of the Governor of Yárkand, who, with it, maintains a mighty table, whereat each day, in true Spartan fashion, he sits down to meat with all but the menial employés of the administration. It is true that, besides these regular taxes, the people have to make presents of horses and various articles that are needed by the officials; that the bales of merchants are examined, and any article which pleases the Atálik Ghází or the officials is taken from them at a price which, though not unfair, is fixed arbitrarily; and that no man physically capable is held exempt from service in the field. But none of these demands are repugnant to the notions of a primitive Asiatic people; and as the eye of the master is everywhere, and extortion on the part of an official is mercilessly punished, that class is not able to abuse its powers. There is, again, little freedom of action; and the people are all kept in a state of profound awe, no man venturing to discuss any matter in the most distant way connected with the Government, for fear of his words being reported to the official spies, and his life being taken in consequence; but that, again, is quite in accordance with the Asiatic idea of a strict and even of a just administration. Such administrations have, in fact, not been unfrequent in Oriental history, and have, while they lasted, formed bright exceptions to the monotonous story of misrule; but, as was to be expected, no sooner was the master, whose vigilance had kept the whole artificial structure in proper order, succeeded by another, who preferred ease to toil, than the instruments of order became only engines of organised oppression. As yet, however, the only part of the Atálik Gházi's policy which stirs up actual complaint is the extent to which all offices of trust are given to Kokandís, and that must be viewed as a natural precaution. Kokandís, too, form the most valued constituent of his army, the total strength of which was, four years ago, estimated at 20,000 men, with 70 pieces of ordnance, cast, some by immigrants from the Muhammadan portions of Asiatic Russia, some by Hindustánís. Since then, the necessities of his war with the Tungánís of the north-east have doubtless caused a considerable increase in his force. A large portion of it, even now, consists of Tungánís, whom he has lately begun to pay in money, as they were paid in Chinese times, while the others are paid in kind, as in Kokand. Their drill is still very rude; and, as is usual in Asiatic armies, the object mainly held in view is to produce as noisy a fire as possible, without much regard to aim.'

Mr. Forsyth, the British envoy to Eastern Turkistán, writes on the 2nd February, 1874, from Kashgar:—

'In forwarding the Treaty of Commerce just concluded with His Highness the Amír of Kashgar and Yárkand, I wish to offer some remarks on the prospects of trade between India and Eastern Turkistán, regarding which very widely divergent opinions are held; one class holding the belief that the people of this country are much below the ordinary Hindu in the scale of civilisation, and that the difficulties of the Himálayan route must ever prove a barrier to extensive trade; the other class going to the opposite extreme, and encouraging the British manufacturers to believe that the conclusion of a treaty is only necessary to enable them to ship loads of bales consigned to the Yárkand and Kashgar markets.

'The truth lies in the mean between these two extremes; and whilst those who depreciate the importance of the trade are probably not thoroughly acquainted with the subject; on the other hand, it would certainly save the more sanguine class from disappointment if, before despatching their goods, they weighed well the following facts:—

'What strikes every Englishman who has visited the Amír's dominions is the very comfortable condition of the people, and the degree of civilisation they have attained, considering their entire want of contact hitherto with European nations. They are industrious, peaceful, and, as a rule, remarkably intelligent and very energetic, and would be quick to appreciate and adopt all the advantages offered by European science.

'Russian and English goods are eagerly sought, and though there are certain prejudices of religion against clothes figured with the resemblances of animal life, there are no such caste difficulties to be overcome as are to this day to be met with in India.

'The population is much scantier than we had been led to expect, and there is much more land available for cultivation and capable of irrigation by the numerous canals and streams than there are hands for: in fact, the prolific crops now raised would feed many more mouths than there are at present. Sheep and fowls are abundant, cows are not quite so plentiful. The disturbances of late years have, of course, much to do with the scantiness of the population, as may be seen in the undue proportion of females to males. This would prove an obstacle to a speedy development of trade on a large scale; but it is an evil which a few years of peace and good-will will soon remedy. Already the population in the cities of Yárkand and Kashgar is on the increase, and everywhere that we have travelled there is the appearance of a thriving people. The bazaars are well filled, trade is brisk, houses are springing up on all sides, and poverty is said to be on the decrease, so that on this head I can speak confidently. Time and peace only are necessary for the production of a large demand for necessaries and luxuries.

'The next great drawback is the want of proper currency, in consequence of which all commercial transactions have to be carried on more or less by barter. It is the intention of the

Amír to introduce a silver coinage, until which has been fully established, merchants must content themselves with taking gold-dust, felts, shawls, wool, charas, carpets, &c., in exchange for their European goods. If very large consignments of British manufactures came over, the importer would perhaps find the market swamped by consignments from the Russian side, and they might have difficulty in getting loads in exchange which would fetch any fair price in the Indian markets.

'The next obstacle is the road over the Himálayas. At present mules and ponies are the only beasts of burden employed; and though the road by Kulu and the Bara Láchá has been rendered practicable for camels, it is exceedingly doubtful if Indian camels could stand the great cold of the higher Himálayas north of Ladákh. For mules and ponies, the road between Leh and Yárkand passes for days over an inhospitable tract, where grass and grain are not to be found, and it would be necessary for traders to carry supplies with them, or to lay them out at convenient distances. From the Yárkand side the difficulty of carriage can be met with more successfully, the double-humped Bactrian camel is to be had in any numbers, and is bred in the Kogyar district. These animals are well adapted for crossing the high desert plains of the Kárákoram, and if Mr. Johnson has been successful in finding a road down the Shyok practicable all the year round, there is no reason why camels should not go with their loads to Leh. They have already gone there with ease by the more circuitous Chángchenmu route.

'The Yárkandi ponies far surpass all other animals of their kind as beasts of burden, and, for all animals, the difficulties of the mountain route will be immediately reduced by the opening out of the Kogyar line, by which one low easy pass is substituted for the high and troublesome Suget and Sanju passes, and the journey will be shortened by three days. The question of the best line throughout to be adopted must be reserved for discussion when all the information requisite for forming an opinion has been collected. But it may be assumed at once that the Kogyar route between Aktagh and Yárkand will certainly be adopted, and if so, then mules from the plains of the Panjáb can, without any great risk, make the journey to Yárkand. Last year they came across the Suget pass as far as Sháhidullá, or close to that place, so that they could certainly have crossed the easier pass to Kogyar, and then would have reached the plains of Yárkand. As regards the Ladákh and Káshmír ponies as a means of carriage, the stock is not nearly sufficient for the requirements of the trade as it is at present; and it is not likely that they will increase to any extent, and I look to Yárkand for the supply of carriage.

'Another supposed obstacle to our trade is the competition of Russia. Undoubtedly Russian goods have obtained the chief place in the bazaars of Eastern Turkistán, and the road between Kashgar and Russian territories offers none of the great difficulties to be met with on the Ladákh route. But it is, I believe, a fact that English goods can be conveyed at a cheaper rate through India and over the Kárákoram than through Russia to Kashgar. English goods under Russian covers are sold here, which shows that our manufactures do somehow or other find their way into this country. Russian chintzes have a large sale here; but comparing prices, I find that superior English chintzes could be sold at a much lower figure, and still leave the importer a handsome margin of profit. At present, the few Indian traders who come over with ventures consider they have not done well if they do not clear 75 or 80 per cent. profit. Unless, then, the Russian merchants make the same rate of profit, it is clear that English goods ought to hold their own, to say the least, against all others.

'It may perhaps appear at first sight that I have little faith in the elasticity of the trade which I am specially empowered to foster by treaties and other facilities. But this is very far from the fact, though I believe I am consulting the real interests of our British merchants and of Eastern Turkistán in putting all the circumstances of the case in a clear light.

'That the trade is capable of expansion experience has proved. When the subject was first brought to Lord Lawrence's notice in 1866, the total amount of annual exports and imports at Leh did not exceed one lákh (10,000*l.*), and Wazír Gosháon, whose opinion was sought by the then Viceroy, was considered to have overshot the mark when he suggested a possible increase to ten lákhs (100,000*l.*) per annum. From the returns published by the Supreme Government, we find that within five years fifteen lákhs (150,000*l.*) have been passed; and as the obstacles to which I have alluded to are gradually removed, the expansion of commerce in this direction may spread to a very large extent. But if British merchants try to act in defiance of all prudence, and without proper arrangements, they are sure to meet with disappointment, and will cause discouragement to others.

'I am led to offer these remarks by the receipt of a letter from a gentleman who signs himself 'Director of a Company for Trading with Eastern Turkistán,' in which he informs me that he purposes leaving the Panjáb on the 20th of May next with 600 loads of merchandise, valued at three lákhs of rupees, and he requests me to order supplies for his animals to be laid out on the road between Leh and Yárkand.

'It is not for me to offer him advice, and the idea of laying out supplies for him alone is of course not to be entertained; but as other merchants may be disposed to follow his example, I think they would do well to ponder over the facts I have put forth in this letter. There is wisdom in proceeding by degrees, and not putting too great a strain on a growing structure.

'Experience tells me that to convey 300 loads from the Panjáb to Yárkand requires an immense amount of forethought and arrangement, as well as a considerable expenditure, without which disaster would have been inevitable in crossing from Leh to Yárkand.

'Up to Leh the difficulties of supplies are far less, and each year will decrease. In course of time I hope the Mahárájá on his side, and the Amír on the other, may be induced to arrange for supply houses at convenient distances; and, possibly, by judicious planting, grass and wood may be reared on some parts of the road; but till some such facilities are afforded, I should think small consignments would be more likely to be successful, and the establishment of a market at Leh will give probably a good impetus to the completion of the desired arrangements.

'A mule or pony ought not to be compelled to carry more than 225 lbs., or 2 cwt., and spare animals in the proportion of 5 per cent. should be taken. The hire of a pony or mule from the Panjáb to Yárkand is Rs. 70, or 7*l.* The number of stages is 75.

'Goods consigned from England for the Yárkand market should be packed in bales of 1 cwt. each, wrapped in skins or other stout material to resist damp, as well as the thorny bushes in the valleys, which are very destructive. Spare pony or mule shoes at the rate of three sets per animal should be taken, and it is advisable to have amongst one's followers one or more men who can do farrier's work.

'In selecting goods for the Yárkand market, patterns with figures of birds or animals should be eschewed; stripes find more favour than checks; high colours are much preferred by the people here; black is not at all approved; tweeds are not appreciated. Bright chintzes, and all kinds of cotton goods are in great demand, though a common kind of cotton cloth is largely manufactured at Khoten, and is even exported to Kokand. All goods should be of the best quality, good prices being readily paid for fine cloth, whereas inferior cloths and sized piece goods, though even low priced, are not in favour.

'Having alluded to the fairs in Asia, I may give facts as the result of my observation which appear to account for their extensive use, and afford at the same time an insight into the character of the people. There are not many large towns in Eastern Turkistán, or villages of any size, such as are to be found in India; but the cultivated portion of the country is studded with separate farms and homesteads, many hundreds forming a kind of circle, or what in India would be called parganá.

'As there is no village bazaar, such as we understand in India, in order to supply their wants, a custom has grown up of holding weekly markets at different spots in the parganá. Thus, as we passed along from Sanju to Kashgar, we came across many places called Ekshumbá, or Doshumbá Bazaar, *i.e.*, held on Sunday or Monday, and so on. Here, for instance, within a radius of twenty-five miles, there is a bazaar held at one place or another every day in the week except Friday, to which the peasantry flock with their sheep, fowls, cotton clothes, boots, and other articles of daily consumption or requirement. Even in the large cities one day in the week is devoted to the bazaar, when the chief business seems to be transacted. Frequently, when I have had occasion to send to the city of Kashgar for an article, I have been told that it will not be procurable till Thursday, the market day.

'It is hardly necessary for me to do more than point to the peace and security to property which all this betokens; when a peasantry can live thus unprotected in solitary farms or in small hamlets, there must be little fear of robbers or of violent crime. No need here evidently for enclosing themselves within walled towns, or for the erection of forts, for protection from internal commotions. Though there is no Arms' Act in the country, weapons are never carried by the people, and the appearance of arms is a sign that the wearer is employed on duty for the Government.

'Violent crime is almost unknown, and thefts are rare. The Amír has acquired a character for excessive severity because he punished theft with death. He is undoubtedly a terror to evil-doers, but is acknowledged to be just in his punishments, and the result is a complete stoppage of crime. The peasantry are unmolested, and when peaceful industry is thus allowed to thrive, we may with justice form high expectations of the advancement of the people, and be encouraged to aid in the work of improvements.

'The country is said to be rich in mines of copper, iron, lead, and coal, so that by the aid of European science and skill, machinery of all kinds may be introduced, and would be quickly appreciated where the hands are so scarce. The habits of the people, too, are all favourable to industry. Instead of each man cooking his own food, and thus spending a valuable part of the day in culinary occupation, as is the case in India, there are innumerable restaurants and bakeries, and bread and meat pies are hawked about the streets, and a very cheap dinner is thus provided for the masses.

'In conclusion, there is one point on which any British trader or traveller purposing to visit this country ought to be informed, and which he would do well to bear in mind. The people of Eastern Turkistán, though good-natured, friendly, and hospitable to Europeans, own to no inferiority of race, and will not submit to be roughly treated. They meet Europeans with perfect politeness, but on terms of equality, and any attempt at hauteur or domineering will be quickly and fiercely resented.'

Treaty between the British Government and His Highness the Amír Muhammad Yákub Khán, Ruler of Kashgar and Yárkand; signed at Kashgar on the 2nd February, 1874, by Mr. T. Douglas Forsyth, C.B., on behalf of the Viceroy, and by Sayyid Muhammad Khán Turá on behalf of the Amír.

ART. I. 'The high contracting parties engage that the subjects of each shall be at liberty to enter, reside in, trade with, and pass with their merchandize and property into and through all parts of the dominions of the other, and shall enjoy in such dominions all the privileges and advantages with respect to commerce, protection, or otherwise, which are or may be accorded to the subjects of such dominions, or to the subjects or citizens of the most favoured nation.

ART. II. 'Merchants of whatever nationality shall be at liberty to pass from the territories of the one contracting party to the territories of the other with their merchandize and property at all times and by any route they please; no restriction shall be placed by either contracting party upon such freedom of transit, unless for urgent political reasons to be previously communicated to the other; and such restriction shall be withdrawn as soon as the necessity for it is over.

ART. III. 'European British subjects entering the dominions of His Highness the Amír, for purposes of trade or otherwise, must be provided with passports certifying to their nationality. Unless provided with such passports, they shall not be deemed entitled to the benefit of this Treaty.

ART. IV. 'On goods imported into British India from territories of His Highness the Amír, by any route over the Himálayan passes which lie to the south of His Highness' dominions, the British Government engages to levy no import duties. On goods imported from India into the territories of His Highness the Amír, no import duty exceeding 2½ per cent. *ad valorem*, shall be levied. Goods imported as above into the dominions of the contracting parties may, subject only to such excise regulations and duties, and to such municipal or town regulations and duties as may be applicable to such classes of goods generally, be freely sold by wholesale or retail, and transported from one place to another within British India and within the dominions of His Highness the Amír respectively.

ART. V. 'Merchandize imported from India into the territories of His Highness the Amír will not be opened for examination till arrival at the place of consignment. If any disputes should arise as to the value of such goods, the Customs officer, or other officer acting on the part of His Highness the Amír, shall be entitled to demand part of the goods at the rate of one in forty in lieu of the payment of duty. If the aforesaid officer should object to levy the duty by taking a portion of the goods, or if the goods should not admit of being so divided, then the point in dispute shall be referred to two competent persons, one chosen by the aforesaid officer and the other by the importer, and a valuation of the goods shall be made; and if the referees shall differ in opinion, they shall appoint an arbitrator whose decision shall be final, and the duty shall be levied according to the value thus established.

ART. VI. 'The British Government shall be at liberty to appoint a representative at the court of His Highness the Amír, and to appoint commercial agents subordinate to him in any towns or places considered suitable within His Highness' territories. His Highness the Amír shall be at liberty to appoint a representative with the Viceroy and Governor-General of India, and to station commercial agents at any places in British India considered suitable. Such representatives shall be entitled to the rank and privileges accorded to ambassadors by the law of nations, and the agents shall be entitled to the privileges of consuls of the most favoured nation.

ART. VII. 'British subjects shall be at liberty to purchase, sell, or hire land, or houses, or depôts for merchandize in the dominions of His Highness the Amír, and the houses, depôts, or other premises of British subjects shall not be forcibly entered or searched without the consent of the occupier, unless with the cognizance of the British representative or agent, and in presence of a person deputed by him.

ART. VIII. 'The following arrangements are agreed to for the decision of civil suits and criminal cases within the territories of His Highness the Amír in which British subjects are concerned:—

(*a*.) 'Civil suits in which both plaintiff and defendant are British subjects, and criminal cases in which both prosecutor and accused are British subjects, or in which the accused is a European British subject mentioned in the 3rd Article of this Treaty, shall be tried by the British representative or one of his agents, in the presence of an agent appointed by His Highness the Amír.

(*b*.) 'Civil suits in which one party is a subject of His Highness the Amír, and the other party a British subject, shall be tried by the Courts of His Highness in the presence of the British representative or one of his agents, or of a person appointed in that behalf by such representative or agent.

(*c*.) 'Criminal cases, in which either prosecutor or accused is a subject of His Highness the Amír, shall, except as above otherwise provided, be tried by the courts of His Highness in presence of the British representative or of one of his agents, or of a person deputed by the British representative, or by one of his agents.

(*d.*) 'Except as above otherwise provided, civil and criminal cases, in which one party is a British subject and the other the subject of a foreign power, shall, if either of the parties is a Muhammadan, be tried in the courts of His Highness; if neither party is a Muhammadan, the case may, with consent of the parties, be tried by the British representative or one of his agents; in the absence of such consent, by the courts of His Highness.

(*e.*) 'In any case disposed of by the courts of His Highness the Amír, to which a British subject is party, it shall be competent to the British representative, if he considers that justice has not been done, to represent the matter to His Highness the Amír, who may cause the case to be retried in some other court in the presence of the British representative or of one of his agents, or of a person appointed in that behalf by such representative or agent.

ART. IX. 'The rights and privileges enjoyed within the dominions of His Highness the Amír, by British subjects under this Treaty, shall extend to the subjects of all Princes and States in India in alliance with Her Majesty the Queen; and if, with respect to any such Prince or State, any other provisions relating to this Treaty or to other matters should be considered desirable, they shall be negotiated through the British Government.

ART. X. 'Every affidavit and other legal document filed or deposited in any court established in the respective dominions of the high contracting parties, or in the Court of the Joint Commissioners in Ladákh, may be proved by an authenticated copy, purporting either to be sealed with the seal of the Court to which the original document belongs, or in the event of such court having no seal, to be signed by the judge, or by one of the judges of the said court.

ART. XI. 'When a British subject dies in the territory of His Highness the Amír, his movable and immovable property situate therein shall be vested in his heir, executor, administrator, or other representative in interest, or (in the absence of such representative) in the representative of the British Government in the aforesaid territory. The person in whom such charge shall be so vested shall satisfy the claims outstanding against the deceased, and shall hold the surplus (if any) for distribution among those interested. The above provisions, *mutatis mutandis*, shall apply to the subjects of His Highness the Amír who may die in British India.

ART. XII. 'If a British subject residing in the territories of His Highness the Amír becomes unable to pay his debts, or fails to pay any debt within a reasonable time after being ordered to do so by any Court of Justice, the creditors of such insolvent shall be paid out of his goods and effects; but the British representative shall not refuse his good offices, if needs be, to ascertain if the insolvent has not left in India disposable property which might serve to satisfy the said creditors. The friendly stipulations in the present Article shall be reciprocally observed with regard to His Highness' subjects who trade in India under the protection of the laws.'

It will be observed that the above Treaty not only provides for the opening up of commercial relations between India and Yárkand, but also for the maintenance of ambassadors on the part of the two Governments. This is, perhaps, the most important clause (No. VI) in the whole Treaty. The status assigned is exceptionally high, being 'the rank and privileges accorded to *ambassadors* by the law of nations.' Hitherto the traditions of the India Foreign Office have been averse to any title higher than that of Envoy, Political Agent, or Resident.

W. W. H.

THE RAO OF KUTCH AND HIS BHAYAD (KINDRED).[1]

PROPERLY to appreciate the peculiar character of our treaty-relations with Kutch (Kachh), a glance at the condition of the country, as it stood before we came in contact with it, appears necessary.

The Járejá Rájputs immigrated into Kutch from Sind about the beginning of the fifteenth century A.D. Over the Chaurá Rájputs, who up to that time had been dominant in the West, they established a speedy mastery; and their sway soon afterwards included the Káthis in the central Districts, and (though with a slighter hold) the Waghelá Rájputs in the eastern portion called Wághar. The title borne by the Chief of the Járejás was originally *Jám*, but since the time of Khengar, who reigned in 1580 A.D., it has been *Ráo*.

Before proceeding further, it appears desirable to define the word *Bháyád*. Etymologically it means *Brotherhood*. The institution which it indicates obtains, more or less, among all Rájput States, and may best be described by the following extracts from Tod's 'Rájasthán,' vol. i., pp. 173–4:—

'In all the large estates the Chief must provide for his sons

[1] The following is a Foreign Office note written by Mr. Wyllie when Under-Secretary in 1867. It forms one of several papers which Mr. Aitchison, C.S.I., the Foreign Secretary, has kindly rendered available to me. I select it for publication, as the subject with which it deals has an interest to those who wish to really understand the policy of the Indian Government towards an important class of its feudatories—a class, moreover, with regard to whose ancient system of *frerage* little has hitherto been placed before the English reader.—W. W. H.

or brothers, according to his means, and the number of immediate descendants. In an estate of sixty to eighty thousand rupees of annual rent, the second brother might have a village of three to five thousand of rent. This is his patrimony (*bápotá*): he besides pushes his fortune at the Court of his Sovereign or abroad. Juniors share in proportion. These again subdivide and have their little circle of dependants. . . The extent to which the sub-division before mentioned is carried in some of the Rájput States is ruinous to the protection and general welfare of the country. It is pursued in some parts until there is actually nothing left sufficiently large to share, or to furnish subsistence for one individual; consequently a great deprivation of services to the State ensues. But this does not prevail so much in the larger principalities as in the isolated tributary *thákuráts* or lordships scattered over the country; as amongst the Járejás of Kutch, the tribes in Káthiáwár, and the small independencies of Gujarát bordering on the great Western Rájput States. . . The system in these countries of minute sub-division of fiefs is termed *Bháyád*, or brotherhood, synonymous to the tenure by *frerage* of France. . . . "Give me my *bat* (share)," says the Rájput, when he attains to man's estate, "the bat of the bháyád," the portion of the frerage; and thus they go on clipping and paring till all are impoverished. . . The divisability of the Kutch and Káthiáwár frerage, carried to the most destructive extent, is productive of litigation, crime, and misery. . In this custom and the difficulty of finding *daijás*, or dowers, for their daughters, we have the two chief causes of infanticide amongst the Rájputs, which horrible practice was not always confined to the female.'

One point among others which this quotation makes clear is, that all the members of the Bháyád are necessarily of the same stock as the Chief himself. The Ráo of Kutch being a Járejá, his Bháyád must also be all Járejás. And it is of some importance to bear in mind that, although the Járejá Bháyád constitutes the great majority of the Ráo's feudatories, he has other vassals besides, such as Waghelá Rájputs, &c., representing families settled in Kutch from a date anterior to the immigration of the Járejás.

The reign of Ráo Desal, who was eighth in succession after Ráo Khengar above-mentioned, is described in Captain Walter's sketch of the History of Kutch as comprising the palmy days of the Province, when 'the scenes of cruelty and oppression which accompanied the introduction of the state and pomp of a Darbár' were yet unknown. The sketch, therefore, which this writer gives of Ráo Desal's relations with his Bháyád is of some interest, although allowance, apparently, must be made for its tendency towards rose-colour. 'The Ráo himself,' says Captain Walter,[1]

> 'does not appear to have claimed among his brotherhood any greater supremacy than what he derived from his title and his superior resources. Ingress and egress were freely admitted to his presence without the intervention of attendants, and his habits were as frugal and free from ostentation as his private life was simple. Confiding in the fidelity and attachment of his Bháyád and hereditary servants, all of whom were of the military tribe, no regular force or foreign Sibandí had as yet been introduced into Kutch. The principal Járejás had all recently received their possessions, and as up to this period (A. D. 1716) the ties of relationship had scarcely been severed, they were inclined both by habit and duty to obey their common Chief. A custom of friendly intercourse and mutual support existed between the Ráo and his nominal feudatories, forming an union of interests among them, and presenting a striking contrast to more modern times (A.D. 1827), when each considers his neighbour as an enemy.'

Of the general administration of Kutch from the first Ráo to the tenth, who died in 1778, it may be said that 'the different reigning princes appear to have retained their supremacy over the whole Province, some laxly,

[1] Page 103 of the Selections Volume on Kutch.

others with a vigorous hand,'[1] according to the bent of their several dispositions towards sensual pleasure or public power.

Ráo Ráidhan ascended the throne of Kutch in 1778. The country had been much weakened in the preceding reign by a war with Sind, and the new ruler was foolish and vicious beyond the worst of his predecessors. 'With so much laxity was the administration conducted that some of the Chiefs, and others holding estates, were only nominally subject to the Darbár authority, while security of person and property was at an end.'[2]

Insanity developed itself in Ráo Raídhan, and in 1786 he was placed under confinement. Two usurpers then divided the power in the country between them; the one, a Musalmán soldier of fortune, Jamádár Fathi Muhammad, and the other a Hindu politician, named Hansráj. The head-quarters of the former were at the capital, Bhúj, and of the latter at the sea-port, Mándaví. Standing aloof from the struggles[3] of this pair, and watching their opportunity, the feudal nobles of Kutch, each on his own estate, consolidated an independent authority, which they exercised in any lawless fashion that for the time pleased them. Thus in 1809, when our political relations with Kutch commenced, there was utter chaos throughout the Province.

[1] Memoir on Kutch by Lieutenant S. N. Raikes, page 13 of the Selections Volume.

[2] Raikes' Memoir, page 14 of the Selections Volume.

[3] Fathi Muhammad and Hansráj were supported by 'mercenary troops, Arabs, Sindis, and Musalmáns of Kutch. The Járejás appear to have possessed but little weight, and to have taken little interest in the struggle. Some remained at their forts entirely neutral, others served the contending parties for pay; and although the Ráo's person was in the hands of Fathi Muhammad, and Hansráj had not even the shadow of legitimate authority, the greater part of the Bháyád were entertained in his' (Hansráj's) 'service, or attached to his party.' F. O. Blue Book, page 81.

Several applications for our assistance from the contending factions had been already received, and refused; but about this time the piracies organised from Mándaví, and the raids of freebooters from Wághar into the north-western districts of newly-settled Káthiáwár, had become so intolerable that intervention of some kind could be no longer postponed. Accordingly, in October 1809, separate engagements were obtained from Jamádár Fathi Muhammad and from Díwán Hansráj, by which either leader, on behalf of his puppet master, engaged to eradicate piracy and to stop incursions across the Răn into Káthiáwár.

These engagements failed altogether of their object. Piracy by sea and depredations from Wághar went on as before. The British Government remonstrated again and again, but its representations fell unheeded equally at Mándaví and at Bhúj.

In October 1813 Jamádár Fathi Muhammad died, leaving two sons, Husain Miyán and Ibrahim Miyán. The following month, the mad Ráo Ráidhan died also. The succession to the principality then lay between two children, one the illegitimate son, and the other the legitimate nephew of the late Ráo. By the influence of the Muhammadan party the former obtained the preference, and in January 1814 he was installed upon the *gadí* under the title of Ráo Bharmaljí. Still, the actual administration of affairs lay with the brethren Husain Miyán and Ibrahim Miyán, and in their hands the young Ráo and his cousin, Ladobá, were prisoners of State and nothing more.

In April 1814 Captain McMurdo was deputed from Káthiáwár to visit Jamádár Husain Miyán for the purpose of inducing him to coerce the marauders in Wághar. Captain McMurdo reported, as the result of this visit, his conviction that the control of Wághar was beyond the power of the Kutch Government. His notice of the Járejá vassals on this occasion is significant. 'The feudatories,'[1] he wrote, 'which compose the general force of the State, cannot be induced to act for a length of time sufficient to reduce the petty Chieftains; and it is averse to the principle, as also to the supposed interest of these feudatories, to aid the Government in subverting or limiting the power of Girásiás similarly situated to themselves.'

In September 1814 Ibrahim Miyán was murdered, and in the following January his brother, Husain Miyán, fell from power. The men who succeeded to the chief place in the young Ráo's councils were inimical to British interests. One of their first acts was unceremoniously to dismiss from the capital the native representative of the British Government. Shortly afterwards the Wághar[2] banditti, becoming more insolent than ever, attacked and plundered Captain McMurdo's camp in Káthiáwár. The British Government, provoked at last beyond endurance, addressed an ultimatum to Ráo Bharmaljí in November 1815, giving him 24 hours to comply with its demands for satisfaction. At the same time, in order to conciliate the Járejá feudatories of the Province, a proclamation was circulated, assuring them that, so long as they refrained from interference with the operations about to be undertaken against the Ráo, their rights and privileges would be respected by the British Government. It is worthy of remark that the letter, by which the Resi-

[1] Page 8 of Major Shortt's Blue Book. Para. 10 of the letter to Resident at Barodá.

[2] These are not to be confounded with the outlaws, of whom so much has been lately heard in Káthiáwár. The latter are Wághars by *tribal* designation, are subjects of the Gáikwár, and reside in the Káthiáwár District of Okhámandal; whereas the people mentioned in the text (being chiefly Waghelá Rájputs) are from the *locality* Wághar, and subjects of Kutch.

dent at Barodá forwarded this proclamation for the approval of the Bombay Government, appears to be the origin of the phrase 'constitutional,' as applied to the position of the Járejá feudatories in the Government of Kutch; the Resident described them as 'respectable Chieftains who form a constitutional branch of the State.'[1]

The British force entered Kutch on the 14th December and soon captured Anjár. It then moved on towards the capital Bhúj, where no resistance was offered. Captain McMurdo, the Political Officer accompanying the troops, was at first in some doubts whether to treat with Bharmaljí, or with his cousin Ladobá, as legitimate Ráo of Kutch. He therefore assembled fifteen of the principal Járejá Chieftains in his tent, and explained to them that the British Government 'wished to understand whether the accession of Bharmaljí to the *gadí* was acceptable to their body, or whether, with the aid of our Government to effect it, they would prefer the establishment of Ladobá.' They unanimously gave their voice in favour of Bharmaljí; and thereupon Captain McMurdo proceeded to execute a treaty with Ráo Bharmaljí. By this instrument, dated 14th January 1816 His Highness made full reparation for the depredations of his subjects in Káthiáwár, pledged himself to put a stop to such raids and also to piracy for the future, and ceded to the British Government the town of Anjár with its dependent lands. But for the purposes of the present note, the most remarkable features in the arrangement are those contained in Articles VIII. and XIII. By Article VIII. 'the British Government, in consideration of the distracted

[1] Page 12 of Major Shortt's Blue Book. Letter from Resident to Bombay Government, dated 7th August, 1815.

state of the Government of Ráo Bharmaljí, and its inability to fulfil the above obligations without aid,' engaged 'to cause such possessions as' had 'been alienated by the treachery of his servants to be restored to His Highness' authority.' Article XIII., which is of still greater importance, runs as follows :—

'A representative of the Honourable Company's Government shall reside with the Ráo in the capital, in order that all questions which may arise between the contracting Governments be discussed in a friendly manner, and the engagement of both parties be watched over and preserved inviolate. *This Vakíl shall not listen to any complaints, either from the Ráo's Bhâyád or his Minister;* at the Ráo's request, however, the Sarkár will afford him its best advice.'

Immediately after the conclusion of the Treaty, the British force was marched into Wághar, in fulfilment of the pledge given in Article VIII.; and by the end of February this turbulent District was completely subjugated for the Ráo.[1]

'His Highness, Ráo Bharmaljí, was now for the first time in undisputed possession of the Sovereignty of Kutch (with the exception of the Anjár Parganá ;[2] and thus, after nearly twenty years of turmoil, a descendant of the former Ráos again ruled the destinies of the Province.'

Captain McMurdo now became the first British Resident in Kutch.

Ráo Bharmalji's reign was short and bad. He chose his public ministers and private associates from men of low rank and bad character: gave himself up to drunkenness and every kind of debauchery; murdered his cousin Ladobá; insulted the British Government; and finally evinced unmistakable signs of the insanity which

[1] Raikes' Memo., page 30 of the Selections Volume.
[2] Ceded to the British Government under the Treaty.

he had inherited from his father. As for the feudatory Chiefs of the Province, he made it his settled object to sap their power in all ways, and especially 'by kindling disputes in families, and espousing the cause of that branch which was willing to lose its independence by applying for his aid.'[1] He was much strengthened in this undertaking by the prestige derived from his alliance with the British Government. On the other hand, there is good authority for believing that the Bháyád were bent on insubordination. Writing to the Bombay Government on the state of the Wághar District in June 1816, Captain McMurdo said[2]:—

> 'The Girásiás have a dire aversion to acknowledge the supremacy of the Chief of their Bháyád,[3] although they would not hesitate to accept a foreign yoke. In this state of mind, the smallest relaxation on the part of the Kutch Government would instantly be followed by the overthrow of the Ráo's power in the District.'

Nevertheless Captain McMurdo's sympathies were all on the side of these stiff-necked vassals. He was of opinion that 'on the strict preservation of the feudal system of government, and the privileges of the Járejás, depended everything that could render Kutch at all serviceable to our Government;'[4] and it is probable that he acted on this principle quite as far as, with reference to our treaty-pledge not to interfere between the Ráo and his Bháyád, could be considered justifiable.

With the increase of the Ráo's misconduct, it began

[1] Page 14 of Major Shortt's Blue Book. Captain McMurdo's letter of 30th January 1818.

[2] Page 13 of Major Shortt's Blue Book.

[3] Greater condemnation than this it seems difficult to conceive, considering that the condition of this tenure was military service against all invaders.

[4] Page 15 of Major Shortt's Blue Book. Captain McMurdo's letter of 11th September 1818, para. 3.

to be perceived by the Bháyád that their Chief's alliance with the British Government was sensibly cooling. They, therefore, took heart of grace, and in September 1818 presented to Captain McMurdo a memorial, protesting against the pressure put on them by the Ráo, and begging that the British Government would intervene for the reformation of the affairs of the Province.[1]

'This application, however, was negatived, and it is impossible to surmise what might have been the result had not the Ráo placed himself in the light of an enemy by directly molesting our villages in the Anjár Parganá, and by attacking the town of Arisir in Wághar, at a time when its Chief was, in conformity with the first Treaty, in attendance on Captain McMurdo for the settlement of his differences with the Darbár.'

In November 1818 Captain McMurdo was authorised to 'open a communication with the principal Chiefs, and to declare the readiness of the British Government to cooperate with them in deposing Ráo Bharmaljí, and conferring the Government of Kutch on whomever they might consider to be the legitimate successor.'[2] Early in the following year a British force entered Kutch; and the camp was soon joined by the principal Járejá feudatories. Bhúj was stormed, and the Ráo captured on the 25th March; Captain McMurdo then consulted the Járejás regarding a successor to the *gadí*, and their choice fell on Bharmaljí's infant son, who accordingly was installed in the sovereignty of Kutch, under the title of Ráo Desaljí, April 9th 1819.

To provide for the interval of the new Ráo's minority a Regency had to be appointed; and, although the

[1] Page 95 of Major Shortt's Blue Book. Sir John Malcolm's Minute, para. 21.

[2] From Government of India, to Government of Bombay, 28th November 1818. Page 16 of Major Shortt's Blue Book.

British Government would have preferred to abstain from any direct share in the administration, it so far yielded to the earnest desire of the Bháyád as to consent that the British Resident, Captain McMurdo, should also be the head of the Regency.

One of the first acts of the Regency was to pacify Wághar. Many of the landholders in this tract had fled from their estates on the approach of the British force in 1816, and had ever since been in a state of outlawry, living by plunder. These now signed an engagement, of which the preamble may be reproduced here :—

> 'The Darbár, as a punishment for our bad conduct, had deprived us of our villages and Girás; at present, however, the Honourable Company's army having accomplished a reform in the affairs of the Darbár, the English Government has graciously interfered and restored to us our Girás, &c. We do, therefore, engage that henceforth none of us shall be guilty of improper or troublesome conduct, and we engage to abide by the following Articles.'

Of these 'following Articles' some are worth notice. For instance, Article VII. :—'We will perform the Ráo's service with fidelity. We will accompany the Darbár troops when they are acting, and act in concert.' And Article IX. :—'We have given a distinct deed to the Darbár, under the guarantee of the Sarkár, for the payment for ever of an annual jamábandí (rental). The specific jamábandí mentioned in it we shall yearly pay.' Article X. :—'Should we have a necessity for money, and wish to sell our villages, we engage to acquaint the Sarkár beforehand.' And the document winds up :— 'In the above manner we engage to behave justly, peaceably, and honestly, and not to act improperly or infringe on our engagements.'

The next matter for which Captain McMurdo had to

provide was the settlement of the future relations of the British and Kutch Governments. The instrument by which this was effected is known as the Treaty of 1819, and continues up to the present time the most important of all our engagements with Kutch. That the Treaty should be characterised by a special regard for the interests of the Bháyád is only what might have been expected, as well from the general policy of the time, which, under Captain McMurdo's direction, swayed strongly in their favour, as from the particular circumstance that their open co-operation in our recent proceedings deserved some kind of recognition at our hands. But even with allowance fully made on this account, the position secured to the territorial vassals under the new constitution of Kutch can hardly be regarded otherwise than as a singular divergence from the ordinary feudal system of Rájwárá.

Thus the deposition of Bharmaljí, ordered in Article II., is made to rest, not upon his proved incapacity to govern, but upon 'the desire of the Járejá Bháyád,' which the Honourable Company accepts. In the next Article the Company acknowledges Desaljí as Ráo of Kutch, not by right of birth, but by unanimous election of the Járejá Chiefs. In Article IV., it is the Járejá Bháyád which, as being at the time the sole depositary of power, 'determines, with the Honourable Company's advice, that a Regency shall be formed.' When, under the VIth Article, the Company agrees to leave a British force in Kutch, this concession is made 'at the desire of Ráo Srí Desaljí and the Járejá Bháyád;' and for the payment of the force, funds are guaranteed by the same 'Ráo Srí Desaljí and the Járejá Bháyád,' as though the normal Government of Kutch were not a despotism, but a limited monarchy with the Bháyád as a second estate. Again, in Article

XIV., which provides for the British Government obtaining military aid from the Kutch Darbár upon requisition, a special clause is added to the effect that this arrangement 'is not to be understood as imposing any duties on the Járejá Bháyád contrary to their established customs.'

But the most important Articles of the Treaty are the Xth, XVIth, and XVIIIth, which I proceed to give at length—

'ARTICLE X.

'The Hon'ble Company engages to exercise no authority over the domestic concerns of the Ráo, or those of any of the Járejá Chieftains of the country; that the Ráo, his heirs and successors, shall be absolute masters of their territory, and that the civil and criminal jurisdiction of the British Government shall not be introduced therein.'

'ARTICLE XVI.

'The British Government, with the approbation of that of Kutch, engages to guarantee by separate deeds the Járejá Chiefs of the Bháyád, and generally all Rájput Chiefs in Kutch and Wághar, in full enjoyment of their possessions; and further to extend the same protection to Mehtá Lakshmí Dás Wal-labhjí who, for the welfare of the Kutch Darbár, has acted in concert with the Járejás, and with great zeal and sincerity.'

'ARTICLE XVIII.

'Previously to the execution of the deed of guarantee in favour of the Járejá Bháyád, according to the tenor of the XVIth Article, a written engagement shall be entered into by them to abstain from the practice of infanticide; and specifying that, in case any of them do practise it, the guilty person shall submit to a punishment of any kind that may be determined by the Hon'ble Company's Government and the Kutch Darbár.'

With regard to Article X., above quoted, I may here mention that I do not agree with Major Shortt in his interpretation of the clause—'The Ráo and his heirs shall be absolute masters of their territory.' In para. 43 of that Officer's Report No. 22, dated 27th February 1867, he cites the Gujaráti version of the Treaty, to show that the word 'their' should be 'their own,' *i.e.*, the Ráo's Khálsá domain as opposed to the feudal estates of the vassals, and hence he derives an argument for the latter being exempt from the authority of the Darbár. Having read the Gujaráti, I quite agree that the word 'their' should be 'their own,' but the whole tenor of the Article convinces me that the distinction intended by the framers of the Treaty was not that of the Khálsá domain as opposed to the estates of the Bháyád, but that of the Kutch country as opposed to the British Empire. No argument for or against the independence of the Bháyád can be drawn from a clause which clearly has no reference to the internal distribution of power, and merely guarantees the Province at large from subjection to external domination.

Captain McMurdo's own view of the XVIth Article may be gathered from his letters quoted at pages 17 and 18 of Major Shortt's Blue Book.[1]

> 'In guaranteeing,' he says, 'the privileges and possessions of the Girásiás, we take most effectual means to secure the peace of the Province, to acquire the confidence and respect of all classes, and to introduce that degree of influence and control without which the State must again fall into anarchy and disorder.'

And again :—

> 'We[2] must continue to support our guarantee to them (the Bháyád) of their privileges. It was to secure this guarantee that the Járejás have come forward with so much, and such unexpected, and such unusual candour and sincerity. It was for this great benefit that they made common cause with us, and now

[1] Letter to Bombay Government, dated 20th May 1819, para. 27.
[2] Letter to Bombay Government, dated 10th July 1819, para. 5.

join without reserve in every public measure which we consider requisite for the strict preservation of terms of alliance and friendship.'

Captain McMurdo, it will be observed, speaks of the guarantee of 'privileges' as well as 'possessions;' and of course there can be no higher authority as to the *intentions* with which he framed the Treaty than his own language. But it is not the less worthy of note that the actual wording of the XVIth Article of the Treaty in its English version contemplates a guarantee for 'possessions' only and is silent as to 'privileges.' Also it may be mentioned that the general rule, which makes the English version of Indian Treaties the only authoritative one, has been specially declared applicable[1] to this particular engagement.

Another point which may be noticed in illustration of Captain McMurdo's policy on this occasion is, his reply to the Bombay Government's very reasonable enquiry whether some stipulation could not be introduced into the Treaty for commuting the feudal service due from the Járejá Chiefs towards the Ráo's Darbár into a pecuniary contribution. On his mentioning the project to the Chiefs[2] :—

'The utmost jealousy (he says), was evinced; as it struck at once at the roots of the independence of the Bháyád, which we were actually at the same moment guaranteeing, the proposal gave general alarm. I did not persist when I found the impression to be so serious, as I feel assured that, from the moment our interference in Kutch becomes obnoxious to this body of men, from that moment may be dated the ruin of the Province, and of a system of society and manners which alone can render Kutch useful to us in any point of view.'

[1] In 1843. See Major Shortt's Report No. 492, dated 9th November 1864, para. 22. Page 3 of his Blue Book.

[2] Page 17 of Major Shortt's Blue Book. Letter from Captain McMurdo to the Bombay Government, dated 20th May 1819, para. 24.

Evidently Captain McMurdo was possessed with a strong partiality towards the Bháyád, and the result of these feelings as brought to bear on the composition of the Treaty was, as has been well said by Captain Raikes,[1] that the utmost advantages of British interference were secured to the Járejá Chiefs, while 'the burthens inseparable therefrom were heaped on His Highness the Ráo, then a minor of two or three years of age.'

It has been already explained that the English is the authoritative version of the Treaty of 1819. The Treaty, however, does not itself contain the guarantee given to the feudatory Chiefs; it merely stipulates that guarantees in the form of 'separate deeds,' shall at some subsequent time be issued to those concerned. For the specific terms, therefore, of the guarantee, reference must be made to the 'separate deeds.' These documents are in Gujaráti. They are all in the same form, and, as a specimen, one issued to the Chief of Báláchor is exhibited as the last entry in the last page of Major Shortt's Blue Book. The following is as literal a translation of that paper as the crude structure of the Gujaráti dialect allows me to make:—

'Járejá Arjunjí, of Bálάchor, to wit:—Whereas, in the XVIIIth Article of the Treaty between the Company's Government and the Ráo's Darbár, it has been agreed that female children are not to be killed, and whereas you have accordingly executed a writing, pledging yourself to abstain from this practice: you are hereby granted the guarantee of the Government that your landed possessions, as they now are, shall so be continued to you from generation to generation, in perpetuity, according to established custom. Wherefore continue to fulfil your service to the Ráo's Darbár.'

[1] Page 51 of Blue Book.—Para. 12 of Captain Raikes' Report.

How many such deeds were issued, it is impossible now to ascertain. Major Shortt[1] imagines that as many as 215 must have been prepared for issue, but that the number actually issued was comparatively insignificant. He explains this discrepancy by the statement that the feudatories all relied upon the 'generally accepted interpretation of the sixteenth Article of the Treaty,' and therefore regarded the actual possession of their specific guarantee as a matter of indifference. It appears that the Gujaráti version of the Article referred to differs from the English version in the following particular; the latter engages to guarantee 'the Járejá Chiefs of the Bháyád, and generally *all Rájput Chiefs in Kutch and Wághar*, in full enjoyment of their possessions,' whereas the former engages to guarantee 'the Járejá Chiefs of the Bháyád and generally *all Girásiás, &c.*, in full enjoyment of their possessions '*according to the ancient custom*.' Out of the Gujaráti reading of the Article, the belief became prevalent that our guarantee would cover the possessions and privileges not merely of all Rájput Chiefs, but of all Girásiás at large, including even some Múl-Girásiás.[2] This belief, inasmuch as the Gujaráti version of the Treaty is not the authoritative one, had of course an erroneous foundation; but under its influence there were very few Chiefs who applied to the Resident for their guarantee.

It is stated in paragraph 6 of the Bombay[3] Govern-

[1] Page 3 of the Blue Book. Memorandum No. 492, dated 9th November 1864, para. 25.

[2] In the wilder times before British intervention, it was not uncommon for the weaker landowners to write over their girás to whomsoever they thought best able to protect them, reserving a fixed portion for themselves: these, where they have retained only a minor share of the village lands and taxes, without one in its government, are termed *Múl Girásiás*. 'Múl' means 'original.' [See *post*, 277 and 336.]

[3] Page 42 of the Blue Book.

ment's letter No. 3,242A, dated 14th August 1857, that 'during Captain McMurdo's administration from 1819 until his death, the rights of the Járejás and Chiefs in general were strictly respected.' This statement, as indeed the bulk of the letter, is taken from a Minute[1] by the Hon'ble Mr. Lumsden, who, having at one time been Resident in Kutch, was an authority on all matters connected with the Province. But as far as I can make out, the interval between the execution of the Treaty of 1819, and the close of Captain McMurdo's administration must have been very short. For, on the 1st October 1820 there was another Resident in Captain McMurdo's place, Mr. James Williams; and the letter,[2] bearing that date, which Mr. Williams addressed to the Bombay Government, is worth reading. Speaking of the Járejá Chieftains, he says :—

'Their towns are poor and villages thinly scattered, and I cannot conceive that such a race of men could ever have been formidable, or that it was at all necessary to consult their interests, so much as appears to have been done in the late Treaty. If we review the events in Kutch of late years, we do not find any remarkable instances of the devotion of the Járejás to the interests of their sovereign, the Ráo. We, on the contrary, find that they either assisted or tamely permitted Fathi Muhammad to possess himself of Bhúj and the person of their prince, and other usurpers of Mándaví, Múndrá, Lakpat, and other places.'

And, with reference to the deeds of guarantee, he remarks—

'I regret the multiplicity of guarantees which our Government are bound by Treaty to grant, as, even when the Ráo attains his majority, he cannot in any sense of the word be said to be independent. We shall constantly be obliged to interfere, either by his oppressing the Chiefs, whom we have guaranteed, or they taking advantage of that circumstance and opposing his just

[1] Pages 121-125 of the Blue Book. [2] Pages 77-79 of the Blue Book.

demands. I conceive that the Ráo hardly possesses one-third of the land in Kutch, the remaining two-thirds being divided among the Járejá Chieftains, the Waghelá and other Rájputs, and the religious establishments.'

Mr. Williams then sketches the characters of the principal Chiefs, and proceeds—

'Besides these chiefs, there are about 150 others, whom it would be tedious to enumerate. Nearly all have hereditary enmities against each other, and the intercourse is very little. They are very seldom acquainted with anything which passes beyond their own Districts, and of the country they are in general ignorant. It is only since the introduction of our influence in the Councils of Government, and the presence of our troops, they have discontinued plundering each other. However, outlaws and thieves abound in Kutch, chiefly Míánás; they are very daring and pay little respect to the Ráo's troops, and from the Chiefs no assistance is to be expected.'

In another letter,[1] dated April 14th 1821, the same officer pithily describes the standing difficulty between the Darbár and the Bháyád, as follows :—

'The Ráo will always be desirous of taking something from the Járejás, and they of withholding due obedience from him.'

In January 1821 the Hon'ble Mountstuart Elphinstone, Governor of Bombay, visited Kutch, and embodied the results of his personal inspection in a Minute[2] of considerable length. The following extract gives Mr. Elphinstone's view of our alliance with Kutch :—

'The use of a connection with Kutch to us is to curb the plunderers of Wághar, to check the Khosás' (robber tribes from the desert of Thar and Párkur), 'to keep Sind at a distance, and to afford an opening into that country in the event of our being engaged in a war with the Amírs. The most desirable situation of Kutch for us, is that it should be under a strong and independent Government. The first of these conditions was found to be unattainable, and the want of strength has led to the loss of independence. We are now too deeply engaged in the affairs of

[1] Page 19 of the Blue Book. [2] Pages 79–89 of the Blue Book.

Kutch ever to retreat, and the option reserved to us of withdrawing from the subsidiary alliance is rendered nugatory by our guarantee of the rights of the Ráo and of the Járejás. Of all our alliances, this is probably the most intimate and the most difficult to dissolve, since to free us from its obligations requires the consent not of one Prince, but of 200 nobles.'

Of the Ráo's position toward the Járejás, Mr. Elphinstone said—

'The Ráo's ordinary jurisdiction is confined to his own demesne, each Járejá Chief exercising unlimited authority within his own lands. The Ráo can call on the Járejás to serve him in war, but must furnish them with pay at a fixed rate, while they are with his army. He is the guardian of the public peace, and, as such, chastises all robbers and other general enemies. It would seem that he ought likewise to repress private war, and to decide all disputes between Chiefs; but this prerogative, though constantly exerted, is not admitted without disputes. Each Chief has a similar body of kinsmen, who possess shares of the original appanage of the family, and stand in the same relation of nominal dependence to him that he bears to the Ráo. These kinsmen form what is called the Bháyád, or brotherhood of the Chiefs, and the Chiefs themselves compose the Bháyád of the Ráo.'

Proceeding to further details of the condition of the Chiefs, Mr. Elphinstone observed—

'The last revolution was effected at the request of the Járejás, and the last Treaty affords them a guarantee of their possessions. It might therefore be expected that they would be content, and accordingly I have not been able to learn that any dissatisfaction exists among them.' . . . 'Some of them are reduced to poverty by the numerous sub-divisions of their estates, every younger brother being entitled to a share equal to one-third, and often to one-half of that of the elder, but on the whole, the number of estates that have descended to single heirs induces a suspicion that in Kutch infanticide is not confined to females.'

And in regard to the policy to be pursued by the Regency towards the Járejás, he laid down the following directions:—

'It is necessary that they' (the Járejás) 'should be treated with attention and civility, and that care should be taken not to encroach on their privileges. The vigilance of the Resident should guard against the negligence, partiality, or corruption which may be evinced by the Regency in deciding on the quarrels of the Chiefs. His authority should repress all attempts on their part to renew the practice of plunder or of private war, and his moderation should guard against the temptation of adding to the Ráo's possessions by forfeitures even in cases where the resistance of a Chief should have required the employment of military force.' . . 'Great care should be taken to avoid any appearance of arrogance in our treatment of the Járejá Chiefs; but I do not think there is any necessity for referring political questions to the decision of their body, to the extent which a superficial view of the correspondence of the Residency would lead us to think usual. It is natural to suppose that the former Ráos would consult the principal Járejás before they entered on any measure that required the cordial co-operation of the Bháyád, and, in the absence of an efficient sovereign, it is still more necessary that the Regency should learn the sentiments of that body, but it does not appear to be usual, or to be expected, or to be practicable, that all should be assembled to give their votes even on the most important questions. The Resident should continue to consult the greatest Chiefs, separately or together, as he thinks best suited to the occasion, and may extend or confine the number, according to the importance of the question; but I should think fifty or sixty the greatest number that need ever be consulted.'

Mr. Williams was succeeded in the Office of Resident by Mr. Norris, in whose time (May 1822) a fresh Treaty was concluded with Kutch. This engagement, however, has no bearing on the matters now at issue: it merely provides that the Parganá of Anjár, ceded to the British Government by Article X. of the Treaty of 1816, should be restored to the Kutch Darbár on payment of an annual compensation. In this way the British Government ceased to hold any portion of Kutch in direct sovereignty.

After Mr. Norris came Mr. Gardiner,[1] who made it

[1] Page 90 of Blue Book.—Para. 54 of Mr. Gardiner's letter to Bombay Government, No. 11, dated 23rd March 1823.

his aim to protect 'zealously and rigidly' the rights and privileges of the Járejás. In his turn Mr. Gardiner was succeeded, about the year 1827, by Major (afterwards Sir Henry) Pottinger, who appears to have retained the position through the fifteen following years.

Major Pottinger's incumbency forms an important portion of the present enquiry. The Regency continued until 1834, and during this interval Major Pottinger combined in his own person the two Offices of British Resident and President of the Regency. No doubt the people of Kutch were slow to distinguish the point at which his functions ceased in the one capacity and commenced in the other. It can easily therefore be understood that in his hands the Regency acquired a sway over the Chiefs, such as they would not have been equally ready to acknowledge, had it emanated merely from the Ráo's Darbár unsupported by any connection with British Authority. In the Minute by Mr. Lumsden, from which one quotation has been already given, it is said[1]:—

> 'With Sir Henry Pottinger and his able coadjutor, the Mehtá Lakshmí Dás, a centralising policy was steadily pursued; and while in the main the independence of the Járejás was respected, such rights as interfered with the prospect of preserving public order, or with the policy of a good and a strong Government, were firmly but quietly taken out of their hands. They could no longer put their rayats to death, nor could they venture openly to disobey the direct orders of the Regency acting for the Darbár.'

The tone in which Mr. Lumsden makes this statement appears to imply an opinion that Major Pottinger's policy, though springing from laudable motives, was not altogether constitutional; but it appears to me that, considering the extraordinary constitution which Captain

[1] Page 122 of Blue Book.

McMurdo's Treaty had erected, the course pursued by Major Pottinger is open to unqualified praise.

The Mehtá Lakshmí Dás, characterised by Mr. Lumsden as 'able,' was probably a Bráhman. What sort of coadjutors Major Pottinger had in the Járejá Members of the Regency may be seen from the following extract from a report[1] written in February 1828, by Captain Walter, Assistant Resident:—

'From the Járejá Chiefs who are members of the Regency no assistance has ever been derived. Considering the attainment of the commonest qualifications as beneath their dignity as Rájputs, they are as little adapted from their ignorance, as it is foreign to their habits, to interfere or advise in the affairs of the Ráo. On their own estates they evince the greatest ignorance of their own affairs; but during their customary residence at Bhúj, they appear to be solicitous of nothing else; and, without their own individual interests are concerned, neither an opinion nor judgment is ever expressed by them, excepting in cases where the ministers, wishing to give weight to their own proposals, bring the Járejás to assert their concurrence. The whole management and routine of the government will now devolve upon the Minister and the Resident. . . This is not, I am aware, the independent footing which was in the first instance designed for the Government of this country; but it has become, by the course of events, the only method by which it (the country) can become either a useful or respectable ally.'

In 1830 Sir John Malcolm, Governor of Bombay, proceeded in person to Kutch and held a conference with the Járejás assembled at Bhúj to the number of nearly one hundred. He told them plainly of the unexampled consideration with which they had been treated, and the bad return they had as yet made for such liberal usage.

'Your lands,' he said,[2] 'have been guaranteed to you and your descendants by the British Government without the stipulation of one kauri of pecuniary payment to it or to your prince,

[1] Page 20 of Blue Book. [2] Page 98 of Blue Book.

and without fixing any specific aid of troops in the event of invasion or of the public peace being disturbed. You have subsequently permitted small and despicable bands of plunderers to traverse the country and carry off booty from the principal towns of your prince. I have desired the Resident and the Minister to inform me of the name of any person that distinguished himself on the late incursion of the Míánás, but not a name has been brought to my notice; and I find that a large body of Rájput Chiefs, boasting the name of Járejás and of devoted allegiance to their ruler, considering themselves sheltered by our too generous guarantee from the just resentment of their prince, made not one effort to protect his towns from plunder, or his fields from devastation, apparently satisfied if they saved their own estates from similar evils; and, in some instances, it is strongly suspected that the exemption of these from attack was the price of a base, if not of a traitorous inactivity. This,' said Sir John, 'has passed, but let it be known in future that there is nothing in the Bhándárí, or guarantee obligation, which the British Government has given to the chiefs of Kutch, that exempts them from their allegiance, and the aid which, in virtue of that, they are bound to give to their prince on every occasion where his person or his property is at hazard. And any chief, who is hereafter supine, and who does not exert himself to the utmost to oppose and destroy his (the Ráo's) enemies or plunderers, will be dealt with as one who aids them, and shall, as the slightest punishment, be proclaimed to have forfeited all rights to British protection.

'The Resident,' Sir John added, 'has been instructed by me to communicate with all of you individually upon this subject, which is one of much importance for you fully to understand. He will explain to you the mode in which you can best fulfil obligations that belong to your condition, and which are not specified in any engagement or Treaty, because they are implied as duties that can neither be evaded nor neglected without the total dissolution of those ties by which a Government, like that of Kutch, can alone be maintained under its present form and administration.'

The text of this speech is taken from the very valuable Minute,[1] which Sir John Malcolm placed on

[1] Blue Book, pages 91 to 105.

record on his return from Kutch. The following extracts from the same paper are of even greater importance.

'My communications with the Járejás, and the line of conduct I prescribed to the Resident, were grounded upon the conviction that no motives but dread of the superior power of the British Government, and reliance upon its faith, could restrain them for a moment from those outrages which for generations have been habitual to this class of chiefs. These yield a respect bordering upon veneration, as far as outward show, to the family of their ruler, considering him the head of that aristocracy among whom Kutch has been long divided; but, with all their professions of allegiance, they have never hesitated, when it suited their personal interests or gratified their passions of revenge or ambition, to rebel against his authority, to plunder his lands, and at times to dethrone or murder the occupant of the masnad, placing, however, one of his family in his place. This conduct on their part has led their princes to similar acts of violence, when they have had absolute power, either through the aid of some of their dependent chiefs or foreign mercenaries. . . In dictating that Treaty with the Járejás, on which the present connection is founded, it is much to be regretted that we guaranteed their estates, and freed them from all specific duty or payment to their Prince, without imposing one obligation upon them in return, except that they should abandon the horrid practice of infanticide. This humane Article of the Treaty has, I fear, been much disregarded, and we possess no means of enforcing its strict fulfilment.—Secure in our protection, and freed by it from all supervision or responsibility in the management of their estates, the Járejá Chiefs have become indolent and indifferent to all matters that do not immediately affect their personal interest. Lost in the enjoyment of sensual pleasures, they neglect all improvement and endeavour to supply funds for such a course of life by every means of oppression and outrage they can venture upon without the hazard of their property. Not above one has exposed his estate to forfeiture, but that should be rigidly enforced whenever they join in rebellion or fail in their efforts to guard the country from foreign plunderers. They should, in such case, either be deprived of their estates or be subjected to heavy fines. Nazráná to their Prince, on succession or adoption, which they fully recognise, should be strictly enforced and fixed upon as high a scale as usage warranted. The Chiefs of Kutch have encroached upon their Ruler, till his revenue bears no just proportion to his condition as their head, and it should be a principle of our policy to take every fair advantage of events to increase his power to the diminution of that depraved, disobedient, and unmanageable class of petty Chiefs, whose existence in their actual state is at variance with all plans of improvement, and calculated to render unprofitable, if not to destroy, the alliance we have formed with this Principality.'

Sir John Malcolm's views, it will be observed, vary materially from those expressed by his predecessor, Mr. Elphinstone. When such high authorities differ it may appear presumptuous in me to offer an opinion either way; but my excuse must be that in Káthiáwar I have seen something, though not much, of the Járejás personally. Of the two, Sir John Malcolm, in my humble opinion, is far the better guide in this particular question. Mr. Elphinstone wrote at a time when the Treaty of 1819 had just been concluded, and when, besides the Officers whose political sentiments had inspired that Treaty, there were few, if any, who pretended to know anything about Kutch; naturally, therefore, he accepted the Treaty as it stood, and confined his attention to devising arrangements for the maintenance of the obligations expressed or implied within the four corners of that document. Sir John Malcolm, on the other hand, had the advantage of visiting Kutch after there had been a ten years' trial of the Treaty, and after a protracted Regency had given our Officers a closer insight into the working of Járejá institutions; further he had a personal familiarity, acquired in Central India, with Rájput Governments in what, as compared with Kutch, might be called their archetypal form. Hence, it is easy to understand why he should have taken a broader view of the constitution erected by us in Kutch than Mr. Elphinstone considered necessary. He looked beyond the text of the Treaty to the principles at its root, and finding those principles to be inconformable to a feudal organisation, he at once challenged them as unsound. I believe that the standard used by Sir John Malcolm in arriving at this judgment was the proper one. Except in the exaggeration with which inheritances are divided and sub-divided, and in the consequent aggravation of infanticide, Járejá institutions do not seem originally to have differed in any material respect from the ordinary Rájput type. The divergencies from that type which Kutch now has to show appear almost entirely traceable to British intervention as their cause. Land for service, and service for land comprised on either side the normal obligation of the Prince and of his Chiefs, as well in Kutch as in Rájasthán Proper; but by the Treaty of 1819 we guaranteed the Kutch Chiefs their lands without taking from them any compensatory security that the service due to the Ráo, or rather the pecuniary equivalent rendered necessary by our intervention, should be properly paid.

A new Treaty was executed with Kutch in 1832, but it is quite irrelevant to the present discussion. The discovery had been made that our pecuniary demands on Kutch were heavier than could be satisfied from the resources of so poor a State; so by the modification of former engagements on this head, a large remission was conceded.

The next Treaty, dated 5th July, 1834, is more to the purpose. By this time Ráo Desaljí had become old enough to assume the management of his country. Accordingly the first Article provided that the functions of the Regency should terminate, and that His Highness should 'be placed in charge of the Government of his country, *under the constitutional and established advice of his ministers and the members of the Járejá Bháyád.*'

The clause just quoted is a remarkable one, and I doubt if a parallel is to be found for it in any other Indian Treaty. It may be explained by reference to the peculiar circumstances of the time and the locality. The Ráo of Kutch was an inexperienced boy, powerless to demand respect for his prerogative, and without any choice but to accept whatever status the British Government might assign him. The British Government, for its part, desired to do only what was right; but Sir John Malcolm no longer guided its policy at Bombay, and his successor, the Earl of Clare, had fallen back on the old theory that Kutch was altogether an exceptional country, that it contained the germ of a limited monarchy, and that our obligations and our interests alike lay in the development of the limiting power.

As regards the ministers, the obligation placed on the Ráo to abide by their advice appears to me simply unmeaning. In countries where ministers hold their place by tenure other than that of the Prince's pleasure such as the suffrages of Parliament or people, it would have a very intelligible force; but in Kutch, where the Ráo has a right,[1] not to be gainsaid, of consulting his own fancy in the choice of ministers and changing them as often as he pleases, any attempt on the part of a minister, in virtue of the clause under notice, to force his

[1] As a matter of fact, there has, for many years, 'been no responsible Minister in Kutch.' See para. 45 of Major Shortt's Memo. dated 9th November, 1864, page 6 of Blue Book.

own political opinions on his master's acceptance would be futile; if persisted in, it could end only in his removal from office by the Ráo.

And, as regards the Bháyád, 'established and constitutional' seem, according to my judgment, the last words that should have been used to describe the position arbitrarily assigned to this class among the councillors of the Ráo. Such adjectives cannot be justified by reference to either our past experience in Kutch or the general custom of Rájputáná (a standard which the Rájputs of Gujarát decidedly affect), or to any special practice of the Járejá tribe. How unfitted even the best of the Kutch feudatories were for the duties of councillors, their conduct as members of the Regency had already proved; now and again, when their personal interests had been touched, they had waked up to undue activity, but otherwise they had taken no interest whatever in public affairs, and left everything to the disposal of the British Resident and the Bráhman Minister. Again, in Rájputáná—it is true that, in the fighting days of old, when the Prince had no other stay but the feudal contingents of his brotherhood, these martial vassals held and exercised the right of advising him in assembled Darbár on all questions involving issues of peace and war, questions of foreign policy especially; also that his Minister for War, charged with the political supervision of the fiefs (the *Pardhán*), has always been selected from this body; but still in the civil administration of the country none of the feudatory Chiefs have ever been admitted to a share. For this business there have always been one or more separate Ministers of a different caste, usually Bráhmans, and it is in consultation with them alone, irrespective of any aid from his Chiefs, that the Prince promulgates legislative enactments affecting the general rights and wants of the community. The Chiefs cling with pride to their right of a seat in the Darbár, and thus assembled, they still form nominally the Prince's Council of State; but their attendance, whatever it may once have been, is now little more than a matter of pomp and ceremony. So it is too with the Járejás themselves everywhere out of Kutch. The foremost Járejá Princes after the Ráo of Kutch are the Jám of Nawánagar and the Thákur of Murví in Káthiáwár; both spring from the same stock as the Ráo, the Thákur representing an elder branch of the family, and the Jám being the descendant of a Prince who usurped the throne of Kutch, but was afterwards expelled from the Province by the legitimate Ruler in the sixteenth century. Both the Jám and the Thákur are, if my recollection serves me right, perfect autocrats within their respective States, at any rate so far as their Bháyád is concerned. On all these grounds I believe that the British Government's specific recognition by Treaty of the Kutch Bháyád's right to a voice in their Prince's Councils was an unnecessary innovation.

The clause, however, let its merits be as they may, at any rate affords some argument against those authorities who contend that the normal position of the feudatory Chiefs was one of complete independence of the Ráo's authority. If the Ráo was to exercise his power subject to check from the Bháyád, then that power must have extended beyond the limits of his own Khálsá domain. Otherwise he would have been worse off than his subjects; for they would have had a right to interfere in the management of his private estate, while they on their estates would have been independent of any person's control, and specially of his. Thus the interposition of the Bháyád's advice must imply the possession by the Ráo of a general power to supervise the affairs of all Kutch, such as would naturally be attributed to a Prince deriving his title not from any city or District but from the Province at large.

From the date of Ráo Desaljí's accession to power, under the terms of this Treaty, up to the year 1842, an interval of eight years, the records contain little that is of interest. About the close of this period Major Pottinger was succeeded by Mr. Malet. On the 1st June 1842, Mr. Lumsden, as President of a Commission appointed to enquire into the relations of the Thákur of Murví towards the Ráo of Kutch in respect of the Parganá of Adui, submitted his report[1] on the subject, proving that Adui, though within the geographical limits of Kutch, was held by the Thákur, not as an estate derived by 'Bháyád' grant from the Ráo, but as an original and integral portion of an independent sovereignty, the bulk of which lay round Murví in Káthiáwár on the other side of the Gulf of Kutch. In this report Mr. Lumsden took up and discussed the several items comprising the Ráo's prerogative over his Bháyád, with a view to ascertain whether any such rights had ever been exercised by the Ráo in Adui. Mr. Lumsden's statements on this head are intended to be of general application, but, as might be expected, they are not altogether free from interfusion with the particular case of Adui. On the whole it may be deduced that he recognised the possession by the Ráo of the following rights over the Bháyád :—

I.—The right to summon the Bháyád for the perform-

[1] Pages 105 to 113 of the Blue Book.

ance of military service, subject to the condition of subsisting them and their troops.

II.—The right to settle appeals from the Bháyád in their disputes with each other.

III.—The right to recover stolen property, or its value, from those members of the Bháyád into whose towns it had been traced.

IV.—The sovereignty of the Kutch waters (a term which includes the enjoyment of the customs and other duties at all ports).

V.—The right to collect certain trifling dues from particular villages belonging to Járejá Chiefs.

VI.—The right, in cases of disobedience, to enforce the Darbár's legitimate orders by the imposition of Mohsuls,[1] or by the coercion of a military force.

Other points which Mr. Lumsden represented as being claimed by the Ráo were (VII.) the right to levy a subscription from the Bháyád for public works; (VIII.) the right to place police posts on all necessary occasions in Járejá towns, and (IX.) the power of saddling the estates of Járejá Chiefs with the perpetual payment of certain religious grants. Of these Mr. Lumsden disallowed the first, and considered the second doubtful; with regard to

[1] The word 'Mohsul' (meaning, I believe, 'sent') is peculiar to Gujarát, but the practice it represents is a common one in Rájputáná under the name 'Rozíná.' The following passage is extracted from Tod's 'Rájasthán,' vol. i., p. 146—'It often becomes necessary to see justice enforced on a Chief or his dependant, but it begets eternal disputes and disobedience. When delay in these matters, or to the general commands of the Prince, is evinced, an officer, or herald, is deputed with a party of four, ten, or twenty horse or foot, to the fief of the Chief at whose residence they are to take up their abode; and carrying, under the seal, a warrant to furnish them with specified daily (*rozíná*) rations, they live at free quarters till he is quickened into compliance with the commands of the Prince. This is the only accelerator of the slow movements of a Rájput Chieftain in these days, whether for his appearance at Court or for the performance of an act of justice. It is often carried to a harassing excess and causes much complaint.'

the third, he admitted that some rare instances of religious grants having been imposed on the Bháyád were discoverable in the early history of the Province. Beyond the nine items above enumerated, 'no other authority,' he wrote, 'was formerly exercised or is now claimed as an heir-loom by the Darbár.' Finally he considered that the right of the Bháyád to 'exclusive civil and criminal jurisdiction within their own towns and territories' was incontestable.

Mr. Lumsden's views, as summarised in the preceding paragraph, are of some importance, for he shortly afterwards succeeded Mr. Malet as Political Agent in Kutch, and thus obtained an opportunity for practically enforcing them. Writing from Bhúj in June 1843, he remarked on 'the social system of the Kutch Girásiás' as follows:—

> 'It recognises a partition of jurisdiction as well as of land; but as this is incompatible with an efficient government, and, indeed, would speedily lead to anarchy, we find it modified by circumstances, and an uncertain scale of independence accompanying the possession of landed property. The representatives of all the great families throughout Kutch are called the *Tilats*. These, in their turn, have shared girás with their younger brethren, and the latter again among their heirs. This minute sub-division of property and rights has led to the following results: we find everywhere numerous petty proprietors who live in perfect independence, exercising in their own persons the civil and political authority which is elsewhere vested in the Chief. In many cases younger branches, who have either equalled or surpassed the elder in wealth and influence, have come to be regarded, by prescription, as the representatives of distinct houses; while in others, by a sort of family compact, they acknowledge and support their *tilats*.' [See *post*, 336.]

Above, I have submitted an opinion that Article I. of the Treaty of 1834, in so far as it subjected the Ráo to the advice of his Bháyád, was inequitably prejudicial to the Ráo's prerogative. I now have to show that in the year 1849 Ráo Desaljí, after fifteen years' experience of power, sent in to the Political Agent (at this time Colonel Roberts) a formal protest against the clause in question, and demanded that the Treaty containing it should be authoritatively modified. The Ráo based his argument upon general principles, and expressly declared that, as he was on good terms with his Bháyád, his motion was not caused by the pressure of any special circumstances. The general government of the Province 'has always,'[1] he said, 'been carried on by the Ráo's own authority: so in this Article it should be plainly written that, wherever the Government guarantee exists, there the Ráo Sáhib, or his descendants, should act with the advice of his brethren; and, for the remainder, that it be in accordance with the ancient usages of the Province.' This requisition appears to me to have been a reasonable one. The Bombay Government, however, under the signature of Mr. Malet, now become Chief Secretary,[2] refused to alter the Article, on the ground that it concerned the interests of others besides the Ráo and the British Government.

After Colonel Roberts, the next Political Agent in Kutch was Mr. Ogilvie, whose views, so far as they can be gathered from the following[3] extract, appear to have been sound:—

'His Highness the Ráo finds it so difficult to satisfy the Chiefs of Wághar that he prefers that disputes among them should be investigated by the Political Agent. As the object of the guarantees to the Chiefs is, I apprehend, limited to protection from oppression, I have discountenanced the interpretation they wish to give them, of independence of their Sovereign, and have endeavoured to strengthen his Highness's authority by

[1] Page 23 of Blue Book. [2] Page 23 of Blue Book.
[3] Report dated 5th January 1850—page 35 of Blue Book.

encouraging references to him and by conducting all enquiries in concert with him.'

Mr. Ogilvie was succeeded about 1852, by Colonel Le Grand Jacob, an officer of considerable ability, whose previous training had been in Káthiáwár. At that time and up to the arrival of Major Keatinge, the present Agent, there was a school of Political Officers in Káthiáwár, whose distinctive feature was the extravagant length to which they carried the principle of protecting the subject from his Sovereign. Colonel Jacob cannot, I believe, have served so long as he did in Káthiáwár, without imbibing some at least of the prejudices of this school.

It was during Colonel Jacob's tenure of office that his Assistant, Captain Raikes, compiled the Memoir on the Kutch State contained in the printed volume of Selections from the Bombay Government's Records. The date of the Memoir is November 1854. Captain Raikes' description of the judicial system observed in Kutch will be found at pages 74-75 of the volume, and may here be quoted :—

'A considerable portion of the western part of Kutch appertains to the chief members of his Highness's Bháyád, whose possessions in that District far exceed the khálsá possessions. These Chiefs are virtually independent of the Darbár ; they pay nothing to their Sovereign, except some customary presents on the marriage of the heir apparent, or on some such occasion. Within their own estate they take cognisance of disputes, thefts, &c., and except in serious cases, such as murder, and the like, which come before the Darbár, no interference is exercised in their jurisdiction. The peculiar circumstances under which the Treaty of 1819 was entered into, will account for the easy terms on which the Chiefs of Kutch were allowed to benefit by our interference, while the Darbár had, and has still, to bear all the expenses resulting from the arrangements then and subsequently made. The Chiefs of the Arbrasar' (the Western Districts) 'then declared that the only claim the reigning Prince had on them was for service with their respective quotas of troops on any great emergency. This principle appears to have been admitted at the time, and thenceforward to have formed the basis of our relations with them, in addition to which they enjoy our guarantee for the security of their possessions, which has a tendency to make them feel more independent of the Darbár than previously. The Chiefs of Wághar or the *eastern* portion of Kutch (the greater part of the centre being khálsá) are differently situated. It was for their punishment that we first entered Kutch; after which, for a considerable period, they were treated as public enemies, and subsequently, on their estates being restored to them under certain restrictions, they bound themselves, amongst other things, to pay a certain sum per plough annually to the Darbár; in addition to which, the necessity of exercising a more direct control over Wághar, and the arrangements consequent thereon for the cognisance of all criminal cases, naturally led to more direct interference in the affairs of the different Chiefs than was requisite in the Arbrasar. The affairs of Wághar, however, have been more under the Agency than is the case with other parts of the Principality, the duties thereof devolving chiefly on the Assistant, under whom also is the police of the District. The above remarks were requisite to show the various degrees of subordination to the head of the State in which the different Chiefs are situated. All murders and serious criminal offences are supposed to be reported to the Darbár. In Wághar they would primarily be taken notice of by the police, and then handed over to the Darbár authorities; in the Arbrasar, by the Chief on whose state they occur; or by the Darbár officers, if in the khálsá possessions, other than those situated in Wághar, which are subject to the regular police system. Civil disputes in the Arbrasar are generally disposed of by arbitration, or by the Chief; and only in the event of some great outrage being committed and an appeal being made, would the Darbár interfere. In the khálsá possessions, such cases are generally disposed of by arbitration, and in Wághar also, though often in the latter District, the assistance of Government and the Darbár is called into requisition before an adjustment can be effected. It will thus be seen that comparatively few cases, either civil or criminal, come before the Darbár authorities in Bhúj, except such as arise at the capital, or one of the neighbouring large towns of Mándaví, Múndrá, &c.'

Colonel Jacob, during the last six months of 1856, which were also the last of his service in Kutch, sent in a series of reports[1] to the Bombay Government upon various disputes that had arisen between the Ráo and certain members of the Bháyád. Four general principles were at stake in the decision of these particular cases, viz., (1) whether or not the British Government, in vindication of the guarantee granted to the feudatories, was under any obligation to check the Ráo's systematic acquisition of claims, by purchase and mortgage, upon their lands; (2) whether the Ráo had the right of promulgating laws applicable to the Province at large without the consent of his Bháyád; (3) whether the Ráo was entitled to issue Mohsuls on the vassals of his Bháyád; and (4) what was the extent to which the Bháyád could enforce the power of advice reserved to them by the first Article of the Treaty of 1834. On all these points Colonel Jacob entertained opinions strongly adverse to the pretensions of the Ráo. In one letter[2] he even spoke of the Ráo as occupying towards the Járejá Chiefs the position 'in many respects' of a 'rival Zamíndár.'

Lord Elphinstone was at this period Governor of Bombay, and his Councillors were the same Messrs. Lumsden and Malet who, as successive Political Agents in Kutch, have already been mentioned in this Note. Even, therefore, if there were no certain information forthcoming on the point, it might reasonably be presumed that Lord Elphinstone, in disposing of the difficult questions submitted by Colonel Jacob, should have

[1] Two of these Reports are given in the Blue Book, viz. :—No. 113, dated 26th July 1856, at pages 39 to 41, and No. 188, dated 15th December 1856 (with enclosures), at pages 114 to 118.

[2] Para. 27 of No. 113, dated 26th July 1856, page 41 of Blue Book.

availed himself largely of the special local knowledge possessed by his colleagues. But in the Blue Book which the Bombay Government has now sent up to the Government of India, the arcana of the Bombay Secretariat in regard to this correspondence are laid bare; the whole Office-file of Draft Resolutions by the Secretary and Minutes by the several Members of Government is given at length, so that the share which each writer had in the orders finally issued by the Bombay Government, can be distinctly traced. In this way it is clear that the final orders, as contained in Mr. Secretary Anderson's letter[1] No. 3,242A, dated 14th August 1857, owe their inspiration to Mr. Lumsden.

The letter opens with a sketch of the relations between the Ráo of Kutch and his feudatories at the time when the Treaty of 1819 was executed: but, as this sketch is merely a summary of the conclusions at which Mr. Lumsden had arrived, sixteen years previously, in the course of his enquiry into the Adui dispute, and as those conclusions have been already given above, there appears to be no necessity for their further quotation. Perhaps, however, I may be permitted to remark that throughout Mr. Lumsden's views there appears to be insufficient allowance made for the circumstances of the times anterior to British connection with Kutch. First, in Kutch, as in Rájputáná and in every other country during the feudal ages, when might both at home and abroad was equivalent with right, the Prince's main desideratum was the military service of his vassals; this secured, he willingly conceded to them such

[1] This letter will be found at pages 41 to 45 of the Blue Book. By a method of arrangement calculated to confuse, the Minutes, &c., out of which it was evolved are separated from it by much other matter; they occupy pages 121 to 132.

a trifle as independence of action on their own estates; but, could he have foreseen that the days would come when, under the shadow of the British peace, military service should wane into an unmeaning formula, and his relations with the permanent power raise the consolidation of his jurisdiction into a great necessity, the arrangements he would have desired to make for the future would hardly have been the same as those that had sufficed for the past. In the second place there never was a State in which the power of the Sovereign had fallen to so low an ebb as Kutch just before our appearance; but for British intervention the dynasty would probably have altogether disappeared, and its place have been taken by some usurper of a calibre calculated to restore the central authority to its normal supremacy.

The letter proceeded to charge the Ráo with pursuing, cautiously but incessantly, a still more centralising policy than had been initiated by the Regency under Colonel Pottinger. He 'has lost no opportunity,' it is said, 'of aggrandising himself, and of increasing his own powers, while he lowered the powers of the Járejás.'

The specific issues raised by Colonel Jacob were decided in the following manner. Firstly, with regard to the Ráo's acquisition of claims on the estates of the guaranteed Chiefs, it was ruled that such claims could give him no right to encroach on the 'prerogative' of the Járejá Bháyád, nor to appropriate their lands without their express consent; further, that if he endeavoured to enforce any such pretension, the British Government would interfere and vindicate its guarantee. Secondly, with respect to legislation, it was decided that, as the Ráo, before the Treaties of 1816 and 1819, had not had power to legislate for any except his own subjects, he was not entitled now to transgress that bound and to legislate for the 'subjects' of the Bháyád, except with the consent of the Bháyád; it was necessary that he should be reminded that 'Section 16 of the Treaty of 1819 secures to the Chiefs, by the term "full enjoyment of their possessions," the enjoyment also of those privileges which such possessions conferred.' Thirdly, as to issuing Mohsuls on the rayats of the Chiefs, the practice was declared contrary to the ancient constitution and customs of Kutch, and could not be permitted by the British Government in case of an appeal being received from any Chief. Lastly, the right of advice secured to the Darbár by the Treaty of 1834, was defined as rendering their consent necessary to any law intended to have force throughout the whole of Kutch, but as not binding the Ráo to their views in matters which concerned his own prerogative.

The first of these decisions, placing restrictions on the Ráo's power of acquiring land from the guaranteed Girásiás, approximates to a reversal of orders issued by the Court of Directors. So far back as in 1843 Mr. Lumsden, while Political Agent in Kutch, had [1] invited the interference of the Bombay Government to prevent the Ráo obtaining lands by purchase and mortgage; and in May 1848 the Bombay Government had issued an absolute interdict on the practice. In 1849, however, the Court of Directors had [2] caused the interdict to be withdrawn by instructions to the following effect:—

'We do not, as at present informed, agree in your opinion that it is desirable to discourage the sale by Járejás of their

[1] Page 31 of Blue Book. Letter from Mr. Lumsden to Bombay Government, No. 363, dated 14th July 1843.

[2] Page 114 of Blue Book. Extract para. 34 from Court's Despatch, No. 17, dated 18th July 1849. See also, on same page, letter from Bombay Government to the Political Agent, No. 4021, dated 25th September 1849.

possessions to the Ráo. Lieutenant-Colonel Roberts states that there is nothing contrary to custom in the sale of such estates; and, as the Járejás are almost all greatly in debt, there seems no reason against their liberating themselves from it by restoring the lands to the authority from which they are held.'

It is open, therefore, to doubt whether the renewal of the interdict (for the decision virtually amounts to that) was within the competence of the Bombay Government to order.

Another of these decisions, that relating to the imposition of Mohsuls on sub-vassals, the Bombay Government was compelled to modify a few months after its issue, in deference to the strong representations of Colonel Jacob's successor, Colonel Trevelyan. The new Political Agent had, I believe, previously seen political service under the Central India Agency; and this circumstance would account for his taking a broader view of the Ráo's relations towards the British Government and the Bháyád than he might have favoured if his experience, like that of some of his predecessors, had been confined to Kutch and the neighbouring territory of Káthiáwár. On the 27th June 1858 Colonel Trevelyan[1] forwarded to the Bombay Government a Memorandum prepared by his Assistant, Captain Raikes, in which it was satisfactorily proved that the right of the Ráo to impose Mohsuls on his feudatory chiefs and their vassals was one which had long been exercised and but recently called in question. Colonel Trevelyan gave his opinion that the exercise of this right in no way infringed the British Government's guarantee to the feudatories, but on the contrary was essential to the maintenance of the Ráo's supremacy.

[1] Blue Book, pages 46 to 52. Letter from Political Agent, No. 58.

'Although,'[1] he added, 'the possession of their estates, security from oppression, and peaceable enjoyment of their rights were guaranteed to the Chiefs, it could never have been intended (in my humble opinion) that they should be exempted from the legitimate authority of their Sovereign.' With this vindication, however, of the Ráo's general title to impose a Mohsul on any person in all Kutch, Colonel Trevelyan coupled a suggestion that Mohsuls on vassals of guaranteed Chiefs should be imposed through the Chief, and that, in cases to which the Ráo might himself be a party, reference should in the first instance be made to the Agency. The compromise thus proposed was[2] accepted by the Government of Bombay and approved[3] by the Secretary of State. But when in May 1859 it was communicated to the Ráo, His Highness stood on his right as recognised by the Bombay Government, and refused to have that right circumscribed by any conditions. What Colonel Trevelyan may have thought of the Ráo's rejection of the arrangement, the papers received from Bombay do not show. He appears to have left Kutch without taking any further action in the matter. He even omitted to inform the Bombay Government of the objections entertained by the Ráo, notwithstanding that the Ráo had sent him a formal note[4] on the subject, specially requesting that it might be transmitted to the Government. The question, therefore, has remained open up to the present time.

Colonel Trevelyan's inaction, which at first sight ap

[1] Para. 5.

[2] Page 52 of Blue Book. Bombay Government to Political Agent, No. 157, dated 15th January 1859.

[3] Page 53 of Blue Book. Despatch from Secretary of State to Bombay Government, No. 29, dated 14th October 1859.

[4] This note, dated 27th May 1859, will be found translated at page 62 of the Blue Book.

pears so strange, is probably attributable to the circumstance that Ráo Desaljí, shortly after the presentation of his note of remonstrance, fell ill, and so, for the second time during his reign, the Government was undertaken by a Regency.

The following year (1860) Rao Desaljí died; the Regency ceased, and Desaljí's son, Prágmaljí, the present Ráo of Kutch, assumed the management of the country. Ráo Prágmaljí 'is young and not easy of access to those outside his palace walls, as his father was, and he is, though exceedingly well disposed, of an indolent turn of mind, and has an antipathy to business. He is much guided in his opinions of matters connected with the government of the country by a few of his Kárbháris' (ministers), 'by whom everything is done.'[1]

It is at this point in the narrative of the Ráo's relations with his Bháyád that the present Political Agent, Major Shortt, comes upon the scene. Major Shortt, like Captain McMurdo and Colonel Jacob, had received his political training in Káthiáwár, and he brought with him from that Province a lively sympathy for Girásiás appearing in any way oppressed by their Darbár.

Almost simultaneously with Major Shortt's arrival at Bhúj—whether before or after is not clear—a change took place in the administration of Wághar, which Major Shortt apparently views with some regret. This District at the time of our first connection with Kutch had been found in so disordered a state that the British Agent had been obliged to assume a direct share in its government. Thus, the police of Wághar, as stated above, had fallen under the sole control of the Agency; and further a

[1] Page 55 of Blue Book.

native representative of the British Government had been stationed in Wághar, through whom the poorer and more distant Girásiás had been wont to forward their complaints to the Agent. These arrangements continued until some date between 1860 and 1863, when the control of the Police was transferred to the Darbár, and the office of Native Agent was abolished. The change, of course, threw into the hands of the Ráo a greater power over the feudatories in that part of Kutch than he had before possessed, and made him, according to Major Shortt, covetous of yet more.

The first representation which Major Shortt addressed to the Bombay Government on the subject of the Ráo's attitude towards the guaranteed landholders of Kutch[1] is dated 24th February, 1863. In it he reported that the policy, which the late Ruler had started, of supplanting the Bháyád's jurisdiction over their own vassals, and of ousting Girásiás out of their estates by pecuniary accommodation, was still more conspicuous in the young Ráo, and that the Darbár had been much encouraged in this course by the spectacle of the great change which had recently come over the spirit of our administration in Káthiáwár. In that kindred country the Chiefs and Girásiás held a guarantee very similar to the one enjoyed by the same classes in Kutch; and up to the time of Major Keatinge's appointment to the Káthiáwár Agency, there had been no limit to the interference we had exercised in their behalf; but one of the first of Major Keatinge's reforms had been to reduce our interference to a minimum and to restore the Native Sovereign to the exercise of his legitimate authority over his own subjects. The course

[1] Page 54 of Blue Book, letter No. 21.

of events in Káthiáwár was eagerly watched by the Kutch Darbár; and the Ráo was sanguine that what had at last been conceded to the Native Rulers of Káthiáwár could no longer be withheld from himself.

Major Shortt submitted a more detailed report[1] on the same subject on the 26th of the following month. He quoted Mr. Lumsden's views as to the original independence of the feudatories, and the encroachments upon this status which commenced under Colonel Pottinger's Regency and were afterwards followed up by Ráo Desaljí. He explained how the questions regarding the Darbár's right to mohsul guaranteed Chiefs in cases in which it was itself interested, and to mohsul direct the vassals of such Chiefs, remained unsettled, as they had been left by Colonel Trevelyan. He exhibited his doubts as to the extent of the interference which the Darbár could legitimately exercise between the Zamíndárs and their[2] vassals; and he cited three instances in which the interference appeared to him pernicious. Then, to illustrate the indignation excited among the feudatory Chiefs by the Darbár's proceedings, he forwarded translations of two petitions of complaint which he had recently received from members of that body. Finally he stated that he had 'endeavoured, quietly, but firmly, to oppose these encroachments;' that his efforts had not been successful, and that, therefore, he desired to have a definite expression of the views of the Government upon the crisis.

'Should it,' he said, 'appear advisable to his Excellency the Governor in Council still further to withdraw interference, and

[1] Pages 56 to 66 of Blue Book, letter to Government, No. 30, dated 26th March, 1863, with enclosure.

[2] Major Shortt, following the custom of his predecessors, invariably speaks of the sub-vassals as 'subjects' of their respective Chiefs. This appellation seems to me a begging of the question at issue.

to concede to the Darbár the extent of its claim in regard to mohsulling the Chiefs and their subjects, some more defined rule as to the extent to which Darbár interference is justifiable in the internal management of their estates, might, I think, with advantage be laid down. But if his Excellency does not consider that, consistently with our engagements to the Zamíndárs, the power claimed in his Highness's[1] *Yád* can be conceded, I venture, with much deference, to suggest, as the only other course open, that his Highness the Ráo be invited to show some more detailed proof of what he claims as his hereditary exercise of this right than what is contained in Captain Raikes'[2] report on the subject.'

After a delay of nearly eight months, the Bombay Government disposed of Major Shortt's letter by the following Resolution,[3] dated 5th November, 1863:—

'The Political Agent's report shows very clearly how unsatisfactory is the present relation of His Highness the Ráo and the Chiefs of Kutch. The action of the Darbár in imposing Mohsuls on all sorts of pretences on the Chiefs and on the subjects of Chiefs must, at no distant period, drive the Chiefs into rebellion, and that result is probably only postponed because of disputes and divisions among the Chiefs themselves. The Hon'ble the Governor in Council altogether doubts the propriety of permitting the Darbár to mohsul the Chiefs except on some very emergent occasions, and then, in his opinion, the Mohsul should be imposed through the Political Agent. The Hon'ble the Governor in Council then thinks that His Highness the Ráo, as suggested by the Political Agent, should be called on to adduce further proof of his right to impose such Mohsuls. And if he succeeds in showing that he really does possess the right, the Political Agent should then submit his opinion as to the restrictions under which this right should be exercised.'

[1] This *Yád* is the note mentioned on p. 286 as having been presented by Ráo Desaljí to Colonel Trevelyan in May 1859. There is a translation of it at page 62 of the Blue Book.

[2] This report is the memorandum mentioned on p. 285 as having been forwarded by Colonel Trevelyan to the Government, as an enclosure of his letter, No. 58, dated 27th June 1858. The memorandum will be found at pages 47 to 51 of the Blue Book.

[3] Page 66 Blue Book.

I would venture here respectfully to submit that the opinion recorded in the above Resolution was incorrect, and the issue raised informal. In the first place to assert that the Ráo could not mohsul his vassals except on emergent occasions, and then only through the Political Agent, was tantamount to a denial of his supremacy and a recognition of separate sovereignty in them; whereas Major Shortt never questioned the possession by the Ráo of a certain authority over his vassals, and only entertained doubts as to the limits within which that authority legitimately lay. It was the latter point, and that alone, which constituted the real difficulty. As for the Ráo's right to enforce by Mohsuls such authority as he legitimately exercised over his vassals, that has never been questioned; for, under all circumstances, the right of visiting disobedience by penalties must be conceded co-extensively with the recognition of authority, and, in the particular case of Gujarát, there is no getting a Rájput to do anything without a Mohsul.[1] Secondly, Captain Raikes' Memorandum had been accepted in 1859 both by Lord Elphinstone's Government and by the Secretary of State as full and complete proof of the Ráo's right to mohsul both his vassals and his sub-vassals. In the absence, therefore, of any evidence to throw doubt on the accuracy of Captain Raikes' statements, Sir B. Frere's Government was hardly competent to re-open a point

[1] When I first went to Káthiáwár a fellow assistant told me that the system of administration was very simple, all comprised in the following formula:—'One *Hukm*, two *Táklds*, three *Muddats*, then a *Mohsul*.' This I found in fact to be the case. I issued an order, and no notice being taken of it, I issued first one and then another reminder; next I had to give a period of grace within which compliance must be made, and this period, on various pretexts, was extended to a longer, and again a yet longer date. At last a Mohsul issued, and then for the first time the man bestirred himself to obey. Altogether it took about a year, and sometimes twice that time, to get a decision enforced.

already settled. In a formal aspect, the only point remaining unsettled was whether, in vindication of our guarantee, any limitations should be imposed on the Ráo's general right, and, if so, what the limitations should be.

On the[1] 10th January 1865, Major Shortt, with reference to his former reports and to the Resolution of the Bombay Government, forwarded a Memorandum[2] No. 492, dated 9th November 1864, intended to place clearly before the Government the whole subject of the Ráo's relations towards his feudatories, as touching on the British guarantee. The first 31 paragraphs of this Memorandum contain a sketch of the past history of Kutch; paragraphs 32 to the end are more important and deserve careful perusal. Major Shortt represented (paragraph 32) that the result of the British connection with Kutch had been to increase immensely the power of the Darbár over the Bháyád and the country generally.

> 'The very fact,' he wrote, 'of the compact to abstain from female infanticide necessarily carried with it the power of punishing infractions, and this has been invariably delegated to the Darbár. This naturally led to the Darbár's taking cognisance of criminal cases involving the power of life and death. Subsequently cases of suicide were investigated by the Darbár Officers, and accidental death reported to it.'

Within the limits thus indicated, the consolidation of the Darbár's jurisdiction appeared to Major Short an unmixed benefit; for the matters arising for cognizance seldom affected the interests of the Darbár, and therefore offered no temptation to a warped judgment, But the Darbár had not paused within these limits; it had pro-

[1] Letter to Bombay Government, No. 1, printed on the preliminary and unnumbered page of the Blue Book.

[2] Pages 1 to 7 of Blue Book.

ceeded to exercise and to allow its ignorant and corrupt farmers of the revenue to exercise a 'daily increasing and desultory kind of interference' in 'the internal affairs of the Bháyád and the Zamíndárs,' such as had caused discontent and alarm among that body. Major Shortt, therefore, specifically put before the Government the question how far the independent jurisdiction of the Chiefs on their own estates was guaranteed by our engagements, and what support the Chiefs ought to receive towards its maintenance. He stated the complaints of the Chiefs to be as follows :—

'A.—That Mohsuls are sent on them not only by the Darbár, but by its subordinate officers.

'B.—That Mohsuls are sent on their subjects without previous reference to them, not only by the Darbár, but by its subordinate officers.

'C.—That fines are imposed on them.

'D.—That fines are imposed on their subjects by the Darbár and its officers, and the fines appropriated by the Darbár.

'E.—That a new tax, called *Taklifan* is levied by the Darbár on cases to which they are parties, the tax having been formerly only levied from the Darbár's own subjects.

'F.—That since the Police in Wághar has been put under the sole superintendence of the Darbár, now nearly five years, they have interfered in petty cases in which both plaintiff and defendant have been subjects of the same Zamíndár.

'G.— That the Darbár buys girás (landed property), or its reversion on mortgage deeds, in their villages, from parties who are not, by the custom of the country, competent to alienate it permanently.'

All these questions, Major Shortt pointed out, had more or less occupied the attention of previous Political Agents, but they had been met by successive authorities in a spirit so vacillating and inconsistent that the Darbár, in the long run, had been able to work its will, without any effectual check from the British Government. Major Shortt prayed that our policy might now be revised in accordance with a definite design. He suggested the necessity for 'a more exact and limited definition of the particular Chiefs or Estates to which the sixteenth Article of the Treaty of 1819 is to be applied;' and he asked for instructions 'in regard to estates guaranteed at the date of the Treaty, but which have since broken up, or in which the Darbár may have since acquired a direct interest.' Lastly, with reference to the 'constitutional' advisers assigned to the Ráo by the Treaty of 1834, Major Shortt entered on the present aspect of the Bháyád in that capacity. The Council of the Bháyád, though still preserved in name, had sunk into a nonentity; but, as containing the germ of a valuable political institution, it ought, in Major Shortt's opinion, to be revised and strengthened. Properly organised, it might, he believed, be constituted a Court 'to take cognizance of all matters connected with its own order, in other words, of all cases involving the interests of the Chiefs or their subjects.'

On receipt of this Memorandum the Bombay Government appears to have returned it to Major Shortt, requesting him to add to it a statement of the specific measures he would recommend in order to remove the evils he had brought to notice. Accordingly, on the 1st March 1865, by a Memorandum No. 15, Major Shortt wrote thirty-one paras.,[1] numbered 53 to 83, in continuation of his former Memorandum. In this new Memo-

[1] The *original* form of these additional paragraphs will be found at page 69 of the Blue Book, but the original form is *not* the one to be consulted. Major Shortt cancelled it, and submitted a *revised* form by letter to the Bombay Government No. 9 dated 31st January 1867. The revised form, which alone should be consulted, is not in the Blue Book, but printed separately, with the letter just mentioned.

randum Major Shortt laid down as premises that the normal position of the feudatories within the limits of their own estates was one of complete independence; that by the deeds of guarantee issued to them in 1819 we were bound to preserve that independence; and that up to the present time we had failed in our obligation, and rather from the absence of any policy than the pursuit of a contrary policy, had allowed their independence to be in many ways infringed by the Darbár. He further explained that, under the operation of 'the custom, all but universal in Kutch, of the sub-division of inheritance entailing sub-division of authority,' the majority of the guaranteed landholders had undergone since 1819 such a disintegration of financial means and administrative power as to be no longer fitted for the exercise of a completely independent jurisdiction, and that, in all these cases, therefore, a modified form of independence was the utmost we could now hope to secure for the holder of our guarantee. Major Shortt then specified his practical recommendations. These are not so lucidly stated as they might be; but I gather that his initial step would be to define the limits of the Ráo's legitimate jurisdiction over the guaranteed Zamíndárs generally. As to the nature of these limits Major Shortt held that every feudatory had a right to exercise internal *civil* jurisdiction on his own estate, except in cases wherein the shareholders might themselves be the disputants, and the custom of the country, passing over the *Tílat*, or head of the family, might point to the Ráo as the referee; but that the *criminal* jurisdiction, which the Ráo had acquired in matters of life and death over the vassals of his Chiefs, should continue in the Ráo's hands, although eventually even this might be transferred to the Council of the Bháyád, if that body could be erected into a judicial tribunal fit to discharge such functions. Next Major Shortt would make out an authoritative list of the Zamíndárs meriting to be recognised as holders of our guarantee. This list he would divide into two classes, viz., Zamíndárs competent to exercise independent powers on their own estates, and those, who, from sub-division of the fief or other causes, could not be considered competent. The first and smaller class would be admitted to the full enjoyment of the comparative autonomy recognised by Major Shortt as the general right of the feudatories; but for the second and far larger class, special arrangements would have to be devised. To meet the case of the latter, Major Shortt proposed that twelve men should be selected from the Bháyád (apparently by the Political Agent) on account of their being known to possess the confidence of their order, and constituted a Court sitting permanently at Bhúj for the adjudication of all those matters which, as occurring on the estate of one of the weaker landholders, might be beyond the Ráo's right, and beyond his vassals power, to dispose of. The Court would be under the presidency of the Ráo or any Chief named by him, and five members would constitute a quorum. Having thus stated his views, Major Shortt solicited a renewal of attention to the questions, on which he had dwelt in former reports, as to the Ráo being permitted to purchase land in the estates of guaranteed Chiefs from one or more of the shareholders, without the consent of the whole, and as to the right of the Darbár to mohsul such Chiefs. Finally, his Report wound up with a brief notice,[1] explanatory of the Ráo's new tax called *Taklifan*, to which the Bháyád objected.

[1] This notice will be found at page 133 of the Blue Book. The tax appears equivalent to the costs payable to the Court in Civil suits.

The Bombay Government was now in full possession of Major Shortt's views. His Reports were still under consideration, when, on the 25th August, 1866, the Ráo addressed to Sir B. Frere a protest[1] against Major Shortt's proceedings, describing them as subversive of the prerogative which by hereditary right and by the British Government's recognition was properly vested in the sovereigns of Kutch. The Ráo's communication, being a translation, apparently, from Gujaráti, is a prolix affair, straggling through five separate Sections, and with twenty-seven exhibits attached. Sections I. and II. refer to the question of the Ráo's right to mohsul guaranteed Zamíndárs and their vassals. The Ráo asserted that this question had been unnecessarily originated by Colonel Jacob, and after lying in abeyance for several years, was now as unnecessarily revived by Major Shortt, 'There are not,' he said, 'separate Tálukás in Kutch, but the whole is one, and that under our control. Consequently the civil and criminal jurisdiction, and the sovereign power in the country, belong to us alone. If then to serve Mohsuls be not in our power, how could we carry on the administration?' He maintained that the Darbár reserved to itself the criminal jurisdiction throughout Kutch, at any rate in all serious matters; and he specified the crimes of murder, suicide, abortion, affray with lethal weapons, infanticide, satí, 'samádh,' gambling, torture, slavery, and the violation of any general law already enacted, or to be hereafter enacted by his authority. Besides these, theft and robbery in the particular District of Wághar were cognisable by the Darbár. Civil suits, on the contrary, when occurring on the estates of the Bháyád, were, he admitted, generally

[1] Separately printed, not in the Blue Book.

settled by local pancháyats; but even in these cases an appeal lay to the Darbár. On the whole, the Ráo could not admit any limitation upon his power of mohsulling either vassal or sub-vassal; but he was nevertheless willing that in important suits decided by the Darbár there should be a right of appeal to the Political Agent. Section III. is devoted principally to an exhibition of the practical difficulties besetting any such limitation of the Darbár's interference in the Bháyád's domestic concerns as the injunctions from time to time issued by Major Shortt had endeavoured to establish. Section IV. is intended to refute Mr. Lumsden's opinions regarding the relations of the Darbár and the Bháyád; it also recapitulates the Ráo's old claim (long since negatived) to jurisdiction over the Thákur of Murví's Parganá of Adui in Wághar. And Section V. dwells on the British Treaties with Kutch, and British guarantee to the feudatories. With regard to the guarantee, the Ráo quoted the text of the guarantee-deeds to show that the sole thing specifically guaranteed to the feudatories was '*girás-wás*,' that is, landed possessions, and that, consequently, the intention of the arrangement was simply to secure to these persons the quiet enjoyment of the produce of their lands, and not by any means to assure to them the exercise of a civil and criminal jurisdiction incompatible with their sovereign's supremacy. Further, the Ráo commented on the circumstances of the time when the Treaty of 1819 was framed. 'My grandfather,' he said, 'was a prisoner; my father a minor, only two-and-a-half years old; and the Zamíndárs took advantage of these circumstances, benefited themselves, and put the State to loss.' He then proceeded to point out that whereas the entire tribute payable to the British Government had to be provided from the Crown revenues, and the whole cost of the country's civil and military administration had also to be defrayed from the same source, the pecuniary contribution leviable by the Darbár from the feudatories was in Wághar insignificant, and in the rest of Kutch *nil.* As for the military service, which nominally was still claimable from the feudatories, it had become a fiction of the past, productive of no benefit to the Darbár, and entailing no cost or trouble of any kind on the Chiefs. The Ráo concluded with a prayer that the Government, if indisposed to grant him that increase of authority over his Bháyád which the neighbouring Princes in Káthiáwár had recently obtained, would at any rate be pleased not to reduce his powers below the standard at which they actually stood.

The Ráo's memorial was added by the Bombay Government to the file of Major Shortt's Reports; and, on the 10th October last, the Political Secretary, Mr. Gonne, drew up a Note on the whole. The Note has been sent up by the Bombay Government, and is worth the perusal of the Governor-General in Council. Mr. Gonne gave it as his opinion 'that Major Shortt had over-rated the extent of the guarantee granted to the Chiefs by the Treaty of 1819; and that it was not at all clear that Government had guaranteed to them their independence, in such a sense that it might not be interfered with in the cause of good government.' Practically Mr. Gonne suggested that the Chiefs should be classified according to their ability to govern, as had already been done in Káthiáwár; and that after each Chief had been assigned his proper jurisdiction, all remaining power should centre in the Ráo.

At length, on the 10th of December, 1866, the

Bombay Government took definite action on the papers, by sending the Ráo's Memorial and Mr. Gonne's Note to Major Shortt for consideration and report, and by submitting the case generally for the orders of the Government of India and the Secretary of State.

Very shortly afterwards the Government of India received a telegram from Bombay, requesting that the disposal of the case might be postponed, pending the submission of a further Report from the Political Agent in Kutch. The further papers thus promised were received at the Foreign Office on the 3rd April, as enclosures of the Bombay Government's letter No. 83, dated 28th March. They included a communication from Major Shortt No. 22, dated 27th February last, offering observations on the Ráo's Memorial and Mr. Gonne's Note. With regard to the Memorial, Major Shortt remarked that the Ráo's possession of a certain criminal jurisdiction over the estates of the feudatories had its origin, not in the original organisation of the State, but in comparatively recent arrangements arising out of the Darbár's connection with the British Government; also that the Ráo, though pretending to have the right to legislate by his own individual authority for the Province at large, held really no such right, and could not issue any general enactment except in consultation with the Bháyád. In respect to Mr. Gonne's Note, Major Shortt contended that the correct interpretation of the guarantee was the one given by Mr. Lumsden, assuring the landholders a continuance not merely of possession of their lands, but of possession in accordance with the acknowledged custom of the country. Moreover, Major Shortt rejected Mr. Gonne's suggestion for a classification of the Chiefs as a measure beyond the scope of our authority, and adhered in preference to his own plan for the organisation of a judicial tribunal from among the members of the Bháyád.

It will thus be seen that there are two letters from Bombay which the Government of India now has to acknowledge and answer, viz., No. 283, dated 10th December 1866, and No. 83, dated 28th March. Besides these, however, there are two others, which may here be noticed, viz., No. 30, dated 26th January, proposing that the Political Agent in Kutch may be granted a European Assistant, and No. 164, dated 12th June, intimating that the sooner the relations of the Ráo and his Bháyád can be settled, the better it will be for the Province.

But of all the four letters awaiting the orders of the Government of India, the one of earliest date, No. 283 of the 10th December, is the most important, inasmuch as it states the course which the Bombay Government desires to take for the disposal of the main question. The proposal is, that 'a special Officer of weight and standing' should be deputed to Kutch 'for the purpose of drawing up and submitting to' (the Bombay) 'Government the draft of an adjudication on all disputed points connected with existing treaties and engagements. This draft would not, of course, be acted upon until it had been submitted to the Government of India.' The points, therefore, which the Governor-General in Council is invited to consider are, whether such a Special Commissioner shall be appointed, and if so, what general instructions shall be issued to guide him in the general treatment of the pending questions.

I think the Bombay Government's proposal not merely judicious, but the only one that offers any prospect of this important business obtaining a satisfactory settlement. Affairs in Kutch have fallen so altogether out of gear that something more is needed than a bare decision on the several issues raised by the Political Agent. A new constitution has to be created for Kutch, and this cannot be done except by some person on the spot, prepared to meet promptly every detail of the many difficulties which must attend measures of innovation and of compromise. There is the Political Agent, it is true, already on the spot; but, even if Major Shortt were less evidently biassed in favour of the feudatory Chiefs, an experienced Officer, having no previous connection with Kutch, would probably take a more comprehensive view of the position, and also carry more weight with both parties in the dispute than the local functionary, whoever he might be, could command. Any constitution which the Governor-General in Council may impose on Kutch will certainly be administered by Major Shortt with all the zealous loyalty towards Government and all the sympathetic patience and gentleness towards the natives for which he is conspicuous; but the framing of the constitution should, I submit, be left to other hands. As to the pay of the Commissioner, he might receive, if already in office elsewhere, Rs. 500 deputation in addition to the salary of his substantive appointment; or, if unemployed, a consolidated salary of Rs. 2,000. It may be presumed that the appointment would not last more than two or three months. To this Commissioner might also be left the duty of reporting on the question, whether it is necessary for the Political Agent to have an European Assistant; for the amount of work falling on the Agency will for the future largely depend on the extent of the interference which, under the new constitution, the Political Agent will be authorised to exercise in the internal affairs of the Kutch State.

A wide discretion may safely be left to the Commissioner in choosing the particular form of practical arrangements best calculated to please the parties concerned, and to work well in the long run. But it will be necessary, and the Bombay Government expects, that the Commissioner before entering on his labours, should hold from the Government of India an outline of the general principles by which he is to be guided. For this purpose it now becomes my duty to recapitulate the several points which appear to require special notice from the Governor-General in Council.

In the *first* place, I do not think the Commissioner need at all be hampered in his designs by the consideration to which Major Shortt more than once refers, that 'we[1] cannot now assume administrative and executive powers to introduce what may appear to us to be beneficial to' the Ráo or the Bháyád. Major Shortt probably bases this statement on Article X. of the Treaty of 1819, in which 'the Hon'ble Company engages to exercise no authority over the domestic concerns of the Ráo, or of those of any of the Járejá Chieftains of the country.' But what is to be done when both the Ráo and the Bháyád entreat the British Government to arbitrate between them? Clearly the restriction on British interference at once falls into abeyance, and the paramount power proceeds legitimately to deliver whatever kind of arbitrament it may consider just and expedient. Indeed, even though no appeal for aid had been received from either party, it would still have been our duty to interfere; for the machinery of the Kutch Government, which has now come to a dead-lock, is entirely the work of our own hands,

[1] Paragraphs 48 to 50 of Major Shortt's Report, No. 22, dated 27th February 1867.

and we are bound to cobble up our failure in the best way we can.

Secondly, there is much truth in the Ráo's complaint, that our existing treaties with Kutch, owing to the peculiar circumstances under which they were framed, are conceived in a spirit unduly favourable to the Vassal Chiefs. It is an anomaly that, in engagements professedly executed between two sovereign powers, any mention whatever should be found of the domestic status proper to the subjects of one of the high contracting parties; but the advantages secured to the Kutch Bháyád by the Treaty of 1819 were absolutely unjust. The British Government undertook the protection of all Kutch from foreign foes, thereby benefiting none more than the feudatory Chiefs, for not only are half the revenues of the country in their possession, but, further, the arrangement operated in practice as a remission of their military service, yet the entire cost of our intervention was saddled on the infant Ráo, and not a kauri of contribution, except the trifling amercement inflicted on the turbulent District of Wághar, was secured to him from his Chiefs. Similarly we guaranteed the Chiefs immunity from that aggression on their landed possessions, by which, in the lawless times of a real feudal system, the Darbár had from time to time been wont to recoup the losses consequent on the custom of providing a separate appanage for every cadet of the royal house; yet, in doing so, we took no thought of getting for the Darbár any compensatory concession from the Chiefs; we merely required the Chiefs to abstain from the practice of one very horrible crime. With regard to the Treaty of 1834, I have above endeavoured to show that the exaltation of the Bháyád to a place in the legislative councils of their Prince, however desirable in itself, or however 'constitutional' it may now have come to be regarded, was at the time a limitation of the Ráo's prerogative for which it is difficult to find a precedent in the annals of Rájasthán. These are matters which the Commissioner would do well, perhaps, to bear in mind.

Thirdly, it is a general rule which has been declared specially applicable to Kutch that our treaties should be interpreted by the English version, reference to the native version only being permissible to elucidate the meaning of terms left doubtful in the English text. Therefore, although it is permissible to discuss the scope of the guarantee given to the feudatory Chiefs on the text of the Gujaráti deed in which it is embodied, the Treaty of 1819, engaging that the guarantee shall be given, cannot be so handled; and the reference which, in dealing with the tenth Article of that Treaty, Major Shortt desires to have made to the Gujaráti version can only be admitted under protest. Major Shortt has shown that in the clause securing to the Ráo and his heirs absolute mastery over their territory, the word 'their' is by the Gujaráti version rendered 'their own.' But the inference which the Bháyád draw from this circumstance, that the mastery of the Ráo was to be confined to the Royal demesne, and not to include the estates of the Vassal Chiefs, cannot for a moment be sustained. Whether the word 'their' be retained or 'their own' substituted for it, the clear meaning of the clause remains precisely the same, viz., that the successive Ráos of Kutch are to continue 'absolute masters of their' (or their own) 'territory' *of Kutch*, 'and that the civil and criminal jurisdiction of the British Government shall not be introduced therein.' The object in view was to exclude the British Government's jurisdiction from the whole principality; certainly not to define by implication the extent of the Ráo's domestic authority. With reference to the latter subject, the clause had best be left unquoted, but if it is to be quoted at all, the only force it can have is wholly adverse to the pretensions of the Ráo; for, as Mr. Gonne remarks, it 'seems expressly to ignore the jurisdictions exercised by the Bháyád, and to imply their subordination in that respect to the Ráo.'

Fourthly, with regard to the number and description of persons to whom the guarantee was intended to be applicable, Major Shortt is, for the reason given in the preceding paragraph, debarred from quoting the Gujaráti version of the sixteenth Article, in order to extend the application of the guarantee to 'all Girásiás generally.' If, on this point, any reference to the sixteenth Article appears desirable, the reference must be made to the English version, which confines the arrangement to 'the Járejá Chiefs of the Bháyád and generally all Rájput Chiefs in Kutch and Wághar.' But after all, the sixteenth Article is less to the point than the eighteenth, which makes the grant of the guarantee contingent on the execution of a written engagement for the renunciation of infanticide. So far, therefore, as the question can be decided by arguments taken from within the four corners of the Treaty, the guarantee can have applied only to those Rájput Chiefs who actually executed the conditional engagement and to none others. I think, myself, however, that under the peculiar circumstances stated by Major Shortt (p. 261), the equitable course would be to turn aside from the text of the Treaty, and to look solely to the interpretation which public opinion in Kutch and the practical action of the Political Agent has hitherto placed on the scope of the guarantee. This principle would obviously be very favourable to the feudatory landholders, but it seems to me the fairest that can be adopted.

Fifthly, the same must be said in respect to the object that was guaranteed. Judged by the text of the guarantee deed, this was simply the continuance to the Chiefs of their 'landed possessions from generation to generation in perpetuity, according to established custom.' There is little in such a phrase to imply that with the landed possessions went privileges also, including the enormous privilege of independent jurisdiction. Yet from the date of the issue of the guarantee down to the present time, the practical rendering of the words 'according to established custom' has always been that the supposed holders of the guarantee were entitled to be supported by us in the maintenance of a certain form of independence on their own estates; and it is too late now to enquire whether this was the interpretation that ought to have been adopted. We must take it, and make the best we can of it.

Sixthly, as regards the extent of the modified independence properly allowable to the Chiefs, I think the Commissioner might reasonably be warned that, as the remarks made by Mr. Lumsden in 1841 on the status of the Kutch feudatories as a body occur in a report, the final object of which was the settlement of the very exceptional relations subsisting between the Ráo of Kutch and the Thákur of Murví, and are much mixed up with the main topic, there possibly may be some foundation for the Ráo's complaint, 'that the conclusions arrived at by Mr. Lumsden's Commission with regard to the position of the Thákur of Murví in Adui have been wrongly applied to the position of all the other Chiefs in Kutch.' Perhaps, also, the Governor-General in Council might not object to the communication to the Commissioner of the remarks which I have ventured to make on previous pages, on the bent of Mr. Lumsden's general views as embodied in the orders of the Bombay Government, No. 3,242 A., dated 14th August, 1857.

Seventhly, I would expressly guard the Commissioner from giving the Ráo the slightest pretext for re-opening the old quarrel with Murví about Adui. It has been finally settled long ago, and has no bearing whatever on the present dispute.

Eighthly, the attention of the Bombay Government might well be invited to the following remarks by the Court of Directors quoted in Sir John Malcolm's Minute[1] on Kutch:—

> 'It is always an advantage to know what we want, and to have a distinct object in view. If the object of a Government be always the same, the changes produced by time will ultimately afford the means of obtaining it; but neither success nor credit is to be found in the following languidly, or without plan, decision, or pertinacity, any object, however desirable may be its possession.'

What then is it that the Government of India wants? The answer, I would submit, is to be found in para. 39 of the same Minute, where Sir John says:—

> 'It should be a principle of our policy to take every fair advantage of events to increase the Rao's power to the diminution of that depraved, disobedient, and unmanageable class of Chiefs whose existence in their actual state is at variance with all plans of improvement, and calculated to render unprofitable, if not to destroy, the alliance we have formed with this Principality.'

If these views were sound in 1830, how much greater is the necessity for their being borne in mind at the present time, when the Chiefships, which thirty-seven years ago

[1] Page 92 of Blue Book.

may have been compact and strong, are broken up among a dozen different proprietors, none of them sufficiently powerful to maintain order on their estates, and all determined that the responsibility shall not be undertaken by anyone else. Of course a strong Government is not necessarily a good one, but, on the other hand, a weak Government is invariably a bad one, and in India a very bad one. Our only hope of introducing any moral and material improvements into a Native State is by the exercise of influence on the central authority; and we ought not to hand over half the Province of Kutch to a daily increasing anarchy under petty and still pettier Zamíndárs, if anything can be done to prevent it. Our clear object, therefore, is to strengthen the hands of the Ráo over all Kutch as much as we in any way can, consistently with the redemption of our pledge to the Zamíndárs.

Ninthly, it might tend towards an avoidance of misconception, and consequently of erroneous action, if the designation of 'subjects,' which Major Shortt and several of his predecessors have used to denote the relation of the rayats on guaranteed estates towards their immediate masters, were discontinued. As imputing rights of sovereignty to a body of men, who never have had, and never even have claimed such rights, it is clearly a misnomer. The lords of the guaranteed estates are the vassals of the Ráo, and they in their turn have *vassals*, not 'subjects,' who stand in the position of *sub-vassals* to the Ráo. The adoption of the correct appellation would in no degree weaken the dependence of the sub-vassal on his immediate superior: for it is an axiom of the feudal system that the sub-vassal's first duty is to his Chief, and that, except as an appellant from his Chief's injustice, he can enter into no direct communication with his Sovereign.

Tenthly, I come to the several points specified (p. 293) as needing, in Major Shortt's opinion, an immediate settlement.

A.—I think it would be as well, provided no serious hindrance to business were the result, if the Darbár kept in its own hands, and never confided to any of its District Officers,[1] the right of issuing Mohsuls on guaranteed estates. The practical working of such a rule might be considered by the Commissioner.

B.—I think that the Ráo, so long as his Mohsuls are issued merely for the enforcement of an order which it was within his competency to make, has an indisputable right to mohsul both his vassals and (even directly) his sub-vassals; and that it would be equally unjust and inexpedient in us to impose any modifications on that right. It might, perhaps, appear more in conformity with the spirit of feudal institutions, if Mohsuls on the sub-vassals were only issued through the intermediate lords; but where the original form of the constitution has already been so far broken through that the serving, under some circumstances, of direct orders on sub-vassals has acquired a recognised legality, I do not see how the process, by which alone an enforcement of such orders is to be obtained, can any longer be regarded as illegitimate.

C. and D.—As with Mohsuls, so with fines. I do not think that the local Thánádárs or Farmers of the revenue should be allowed to fine any person off the Khálsá domain. But any vassal or sub-vassal disobeying an order which the Darbár was entitled to issue, would

[1] At pages 21 and 22 of the Blue Book will be found several orders from Colonel Pottinger, as head of the Regency, interdicting the issue of Mohsuls by District Officers of the Darbár on villages of guaranteed Zamíndárs. These orders, however, do not touch on the right of the Darbár itself to do what its Officers were forbidden to attempt.

properly be liable to be fined by the Darbár, and all such fines would fairly be appropriated by the Darbár as an ordinary item of State revenue.

E.—'Taklifan' is described by Major Shortt as the fees payable by parties in civil suits towards the maintenance of the Ráo's Courts of Justice. I think the Ráo is fully entitled to exact such fees from all persons taking advantage of his tribunals, and that it can make no difference whether the litigants belong to his Khálsá domain or to the guaranteed estates. In saying this, I of course presume that the Ráo's judges only take up cases which lie within their cognisance; if they act otherwise, they act wrongly, but their misconduct cannot affect the general principle that people who go to law are bound to pay for the luxury.

F.—The Commissioner will have to investigate the complaint of the Bháyád that in Wághar the Ráo has taken advantage of his recent assumption of the Police administration of this tract to interfere in petty cases, in which both plaintiff and defendant have been vassals of the same Zamíndár. It is obviously desirable that trivial civil suits of this description should be settled locally by the common lord of both parties, without any interference from either the Ráo or his officers. At the same time the Commissioner may perhaps find on inquiry that there exists among the Zamíndárs of Wághar an inclination to dispute the exercise by the Darbár of functions which are but the continuance of a system instituted by ourselves, and to which no one thought of taking exception, so long as the Police remained in our hands. In evidence of this feeling may be cited the complaint against the standing arrangements for the suppression of cattle-stealing, detailed in paragraphs[1] 25 to 29 of Major Shortt's Report, No. 30, dated 26th March 1863. And, while on the subject of Wághar, I may observe that, however culpable may have been the conduct of the Darbár in keeping alive the dissensions between the Wághelá Chief[2] of Pulanswá and his vassals, I do not understand how it can have become necessary for the Political Agent year by year himself to collect the jamábandí payable by this Chief to the Darbár under Article 9 of the Engagement dated 15th April, 1819;—unless, indeed, the authority of the Chief may have been so much impaired by Darbár intrigues that he became unable to realise from his rayats the rent enjoyable by himself—a circumstance which the Political Agent has omitted to mention.

G.—I think the Darbár should certainly *not* be allowed to buy landed property, or its reversion on mortgage deeds, in guaranteed villages, from persons who, by the custom of the country, are not competent to alienate it personally. The primary object of our guarantee is to secure to the Chiefs, as against the Darbár, the continued possession of their landed revenues; and whatever changes may have been brought about, or may be impending in respect to their territorial jurisdiction, no such alteration has occurred, or may be expected to occur, in the political requirements of Kutch as would justify us in departing from our obligation to prevent the aggrandisement of the Khálsá domain by pickings from the estates of the feudatories. The nature of the Darbár's proceedings in this respect is well illustrated in the following extract from paragraph 16[3] of Colonel Jacob's Annual Report for 1865:—

[1] Pages 58–59 of the Blue Book.

[2] Page 59 of Blue Book. Paragraph 23 of Major Shortt's letter, No. 30, dated 26th March 1863.

[3] Page 35 of Blue Book.

'A Chief will not scruple to pledge his land to a Baniá of his village or District on favourable terms to the lender, because he fears nothing from him, and has the power of again freeing himself on easy terms, the land being in his possession or under his influence: it is not the interest of the other to drive a hard bargain with him, or even to demand all he may have stipulated for. But the transaction becomes totally changed when the ruler of the country steps into the money-lender's shoes; for he has the power of exacting the "pound of flesh" or whatever may be in the bond, by Mohsuls and confiscations, and does so accordingly.'

Moreover, Mr. Lumsden asserts, and my recollections of the Káthiáwár Járejás confirm his statement, that the practice is especially forbidden by the Mulk-i-Sarishtá, or custom of the country.[1]

'Immemorial usage,' says Mr. Lumsden, 'permits the Bháyád to sell or to mortgage their property, without restriction, *except to the Darbár*. This exception originated in a jealous sense of independence. The seignorial rights which were alienated to inferiors or to equals might be recovered and the jurisdiction of the *tilat* might be maintained; but where the Darbár became the proprietor, the Chiefs could neither expect to preserve their authority or to resume suspended rights.'

And Major Shortt has shown[2] that the transaction is in itself unjust, as superseding the claims to inheritance vested in third parties; for although the Ráo, as theoretically the original fountain of every landed estate, has the ultimate reversion of all, yet the several other shareholders have an intermediate and prior claim which he is not justified in ignoring. For these reasons then, notwithstanding that the orders of the Court of Directors in

[1] Page 31 of Blue Book.—Para. 15 of letter to Bombay Government, No. 363, dated 14th July 1843.

[2] Para. 79 of his Memo. (printed separately, not in the Blue Book), No. 15, dated 1st March 1865.

1849 are of a contrary purport, I think that the Ráo ought not to be allowed to acquire lands by sale or mortgage from any guaranteed Zamíndár, except with the clear and willing consent of all the other members of the proprietary body, and of all persons generally, who stand between him and the reversion of the property.

Lastly, I reach the sketch which Major Shortt has submitted of a new constitution for the Kutch State (*ante*, 295–6).

In defining the several rights which collectively constitute the Ráo's prerogative, the Khálsá domain may, I think, be at once eliminated from discussion. In his own villages the Ráo is absolute, and the Council of the Bháyád can have no voice in their administration. It is the extent of the sovereign's authority over the guaranteed estates which is the only difficulty. On this point I suggest that whatever power, executive or judicial, the Ráo may at the present time exercise should be confirmed to him, without reference to the circumstances under which it was acquired. Such a course would, after all, be merely conceding to the Ráo what, as regards the meaning and the application of the guarantee, has already been proposed for concession to his Chiefs, viz., a recognition of the form into which vague and floating elements have been crystallised by time. In judicial business of a civil character it might be necessary for the Commissioner to introduce some safeguards against a miscarriage of justice in cases wherein the Ráo's personal interests should be concerned; but, subject to a drawback on this account, the Ráo's authority, as it now stands, might be made the basis on which to fit whatever superstructure a regard for the guaranteed privileges of the Bháyád should lead the Commissioner to conceive.

The Commissioner's next step would be, as Major Shortt suggests, to make out an authoritative list of all the Zamíndárs, who for the future shall be recognised as holders of the British guarantee. The Commissioner might be guided in this task by the liberal principle indicated at p. 306, *i.e.* he might admit to the guarantee all persons whom the general estimationof the country has hitherto regarded as entitled to its benefit. Every estate not included in the Commissioner's list would, for purposes of jurisdiction, fall into the same category with the Khálsá domain. The Chiefs entered in the list would need, as Major Shortt points out, to be divided into two classes, according to their ascertained competency, or incompetency, to discharge judicial functions on their own estates.

As regards the first-class, the course to be adopted seems clear. Each Chief might be invested by Sanad from the Ráo, with certain definite powers for the disposal of civil and criminal cases. In the latter class of business, the Ráo's present right to take cognisance of serious crimes would have to be preserved; and, in the former, appeal should lie to the Ráo, either in his individual capacity or sitting in judicial conclave with select members of the Bháyád, as the Commissioner might think preferable. The powers of a Sanad-holding Chief would be for his life only, and subject to resumption even within that interval, at any time when the Political Agent and the Darbár in concert might have proof of misconduct deserving such a penalty. On the death of a Sanad-holder it would be for the Political Agent, in communication with the Darbár, to determine whether powers should be continued by fresh Sanad to the successors, and, if so, what kind of powers.

There remains for consideration what should be done with the numerous class of Chiefs to whom no powers can be given. Major Shortt's plan to evolve out of the present effete Council of the Bháyád, a new body of men invested with judicial functions, and sitting under the presidency of the Ráo, for the disposal of all business arising on the estates of such Chiefs, will deserve very attentive consideration from the Commissioner. Any measure which Major Shortt's experience and moderation might recommend, would probably have the merit of being, on the whole, not distasteful to the parties concerned; and the present scheme as contemplating the utilisation of materials already to our hand, has an air of special facility about it. Moreover, the principle of the thing seems in itself good, for, as Major Shortt[1] justly observes, although the despotic form of government has hitherto sufficed for the wants of Native States, a day may be coming when the spread of intelligence and education among the masses shall necessitate the grant of a more liberal constitution; and we ought, therefore, not to lose the special opportunity now offered us in Kutch of forecasting the organisation of that State in conformity to the possible requirements of the future. Major Shortt does not specify the authority with whom the selection of the twelve Chiefs to constitute the new Court should rest; but I do not myself see any objection to the Political Agent's assuming this responsibility, and being guided in his choice by reference to the amount of confidence which the Bháyád at large may repose in the independence and sagacity of the respective candidates for office. Some such precaution is essential, for otherwise the Darbár would continue to

[1] Page 6 of Blue Book, paragraph 44 of Memorandum, No. 492, dated 9th November 1864.

nominate, as at present, creatures of its own, powerless to counteract the Ráo's schemings for despotic power; and in their hands the proposed arrangement would infallibly break down. Again, Major Shortt's plan for a re-organisation of the Council of the Bháyád looks solely to the provision of a judicial tribunal, whereas it appears to me that a legislative body, with clearly defined powers, requires also to be constructed from the same source. Major Shortt's theory is, that no legislative enactment, applicable to the whole Province, can be promulgated by the Ráo without the consent of the existing Council of the Bháyád, holding office under Article I. of the Treaty of 1834. But the powers of the existing Council have never been defined,[1] the Ráo, as a matter of fact, has legislated[2] without any reference to its wishes; and, for practical purposes, it is[3] but the shadow of a name. I would abolish the existing Council altogether, and form a new Legislative Council out of the same men who may have been already selected for the Judicial Court of the Bháyád. I have submitted (p. 273) a doubt whether the limitation ot the Ráo's legislative authority, created by the Treaty of 1834, was, at the time of the execution of that engagement, in consonance with the traditions of Rájput government; but, considering the long interval since that date during which the semblance of a House of Lords has been maintained in Kutch, I believe that the institution may rightly be utilised as a basis from which to form the legislative complement of the new constitution. As to

[1] Page 45 of Blue Book.—Para. 21 of Bombay Government's orders, No. 3,242A, dated 14th August 1857.

[2] Paras. 20–23 of Major Shortt's letter, No. 22, dated 27th February 1867 (not in Blue Book).

[3] Page 6 of Blue Book.—Paras. 46–47 of Major Shortt's Memo., No. 492, dated 9th November 1864.

the powers of the future Legislative Council, its consent should, in accordance with the present theory, be necessary to all enactments affecting the guaranteed estates; but measures applying only to the Khálsá domain should be expressly declared beyond its cognisance.

So far as the Commissioner is concerned, the paragraphs from p. 303 perhaps embrace all the heads on which he requires instructions from the Government of India. But there are three other matters, which, after his labours shall have concluded, the Bombay Government, acting through the Political Agent, might see to with advantage.

Firstly.—Infanticide: there is no doubt that the practice has received a severe check from our exertions, but it as certainly still exists. I think that, considering our guarantee rests upon the condition of an abandonment of infanticide, it will be equally just and politic if every case in which an infraction of the condition may be proved, should be visited by an immediate and formal withdrawal of our guarantee from the guilty Zamíndár, who would thenceforward be left to fight his own battles with the Darbár, as he best might.

Secondly.—Major Shortt complains[1] that there is no written Code of the common law of the country. I would suggest that, as soon as the termination of the Commission allows him leisure, he should endeavour to summon a meeting of the best jurists of Kutch, including, of course, spokesmen from the Darbár and from the Bháyád, and get them to agree to a set of Rules, embodying the main principles of the *Mulk-i-Sarishtá*; such Rules at first would necessarily be crude and imperfect, but by periodical repetitions of the assembly,

[1] Page 5 of Blue Book—Paragraphs 39 and 40 of Memorandum, No. 49?, dated 9th November 1864.

something like a generally acknowledged Code would, in the end, be obtained, and would assuredly be most useful.

Thirdly.—Major Shortt reports the native officials of Kutch as universally corrupt. They must be very bad indeed if Major Shortt, with his Káthiáwár experience, singles them out for special reprobation; and advantage, might, therefore, be taken of any concessions which the new arrangements should secure for the Ráo to call His Highness's serious attention to the necessity which exists for a reform in the *matériel* of his administration.

It has been stated (p. 300) that the Government of Bombay, at the same time that it referred this weighty case for the orders of the Government of India, transmitted the papers to England for the information of the Secretary of State. I imagine that, under the urgent necessity which exists for a settlement of the case, the Government of India is at liberty, even though the creation of a new temporary appointment is involved, to sanction the deputation of a Commissioner and to instruct him regarding the general policy to be followed without any previous reference to Sir Stafford Northcote. The orders of the Governor-General in Council, however, after issue to the local Government, should be reported without delay to the India Office.

KATHIAWAR AND THE WAGHARS.[1]

KÁTHIÁWÁR (Kattiwar) is the peninsula of Gujarát; bounded on the South by the Indian Ocean, on the East by the Gulf of Cambay, and on the West by the Gulf of Kutch. Northwards towards the military station of Disá, and the large territory known as Rájputáná, it is in great measure cut off from the mainland by a couple of those peculiar compounds of salt marsh and desert locally known as *Răns*; these stretch in on either hand from the apex of each of the gulfs, leaving a space of barely seventy miles open to invasion. And isolated as is even its present position, Káthiáwár in the olden time was, no doubt, wholly an island. It is about 150 miles long by about the same distance broad, and contains an area of 22,000 square miles. The chief physical features of the Province are the Bardá Hills in the west, with their southern continuations, the Alich range and the Osham; the lofty and holy mount of Girnár overshadowing the ancient fortress of Junágarh; and lastly a remarkable

[1] From the *Calcutta Review*, December, 1860. This was one of Mr. Wyllie's earliest essays; but I insert it as Mr. Wyllie served in Káthiáwár, and contributed some new knowledge on that Province.—W. W. H.

ART. VIII.—1. *Rás Málá, or Hindu Annals of the Province of Gujarát, in Western India.* By ALEXANDER KINLOCH FORBES, *of the Honourable East India Company's Civil Service.* 1856.

2. *Travels in Western India, embracing a Visit to the sacred Mounts of the Jains, and the most celebrated Shrines of Hindu faith between Rájputáná and the Indus, with an account of the ancient city of Agarwálá*, by the late LIEUTENANT COLONEL JAMES TOD, Author of "Annals of Rájasthán." 1839.

3. *Selections from Bombay Government Records*, No. 37. 1856.

tract in the South, stretching 50 miles East and West by 30 North and South, known as the Gir, and consisting of a succession of ridges and hills which towards the South reach to a considerable elevation, covered with the densest forest trees and jungle, full of almost inaccessible fastnesses which for ages have afforded shelter to robbers, outlaws, and a sect of wild fanatics (Aghorís) long reputed to be cannibals.

We waive those legendary times when the Black Race whose supposed descendants are to be found in the still half-savage Bhils and Kols, roamed their forest without one prophetic fear of the coming foe from Arya. Nor shall there be any pause over the pastoral myth of Krishna, either as he Apollo-like tends his sheep and romps with rustic Daphnes, or as he subsequently emerges into the Hero-King and God of Gujarát, longer than may suffice to mark the confirmation hence accruing to the natural supposition that the Bráhmanic races should have found a home and settled in Gujarát, many a long year before any outer ripple of their wave of emigration had spread onwards into the valley of the Ganges. Similarly the wonders of the Girnár inscriptions must be noticed only for the proof they give that in the third century before our era Gujarát was portion of an empire seated in Central India and stretching as far East as Cattack.

It is fortunate that almost the whole authentic history of Káthiáwár is bound up with two or three sites, which to this day have a name wherein the past still echoes, and which exhibit distinct remains for the pilgrim who gazes on them to re-people with the shades of those men of yore who there fought, loved, sorrowed, and rejoiced even as men do now.

Of such sites the most memorable is a spot just outside the walls of the Gohel Thákur's town of Waleh, some twenty miles North-Westwards of the flourishing port of Gogo. Before the traveller lies a thicket of ancient Pilu trees, round which eddies a stream known to our guide as the Ghilá, or Mad River, and at our feet long tufted grass, only half concealing masses of old brick work or occasional fragments of granite over which it is not easy to avoid stumbling. Yet this is all that now remains of Wallabhípur, a capital which during the seventh century of our era boasted the most brilliant Court in India. To see and admire it came from China the Buddhist priest, Hiouen Thsang, and from Arabia the no less famous geographer El Edrisi. Cyclopean walls and a deep moat embraced within their circuit of thirty miles, a city wherein rose the fair proportions of a hundred ornate palaces, with cool depths of waters in many a spacious reservoir. The call to prayer issued from the spires of 360 temples. This splendid seat of empire—whether its subversion be due to Scythians, as Colonel Tod would have it, to Indo-Bactrians according to another authority, or to Persians under Nashirwan the Great, as Mountstuart Elphinstone believes—fell before an irruption of barbarians from the North at a date which conjecturally may be given as A.D. 770. How sudden and complete was the overthrow may be judged from the fact that the remnant of inhabitants which escaped death or captivity fled away to found new cities in Málwa without making an effort to rebuild their ancient homes; and that a still current legend ascribes the event to the operation of a miracle resembling that which overwhelmed Sodom and the cities of the Plain. From Wallabhí the sceptre of Gujarát departed to Anhilwárá Pattan, a city near the modern cantonments of Disá, which, founded by Wan Ráj the Forest King in 746, passed from the Chaurá dynasty to the Solankhís in 925, and from the Solankhís to the Waghelás in 1172; the Waghelás in their turn being crushed and Anhilwárá as a seat of Hindu power destroyed by Alah-ud-dín, the Emperor of Dehli, in 1294.

Another historical site is the city of Dev Pattan. At our entrance we are met by a grave handsome Arab, who holds the surrounding District in hereditary lieutenancy from the Nawáb of Junágarh: he wheels his horse by our side, and courteously points out each object of interest on either side of the narrow streets. The whole plan of the city is of the early Hindu period; so are the mutilated images and architectural ornaments which ever and anon protrude from the masonry of mosque or private house into which they have been wrought in most cases inappropriately enough. Outside the Western walls of the city, and as yet invisible, we know that there is the river Haran which, winding down from the wild Gir, is broadened near its mouth by the confluence of two smaller streams, and thus affords to the Hindu pilgrim a Trivení, or holy meeting of three waters, where foliage-shadowed steps lead down from Krishna's shrines to a bathing-place of peculiar efficacy. Still pressing onwards through the cool shadow of the streets we emerge at length on a comparatively open space towards the sea, littered with rubbish and dustheaps. Huge blocks of stone lie around, and fragments of once polished slabs mingle with the flowered capitals of fallen pillars, the maimed trunks of what have of old been carven Caryatides, or the shattered half of the well-known emblem of Siva, the mysterious Linga. In the midst, black with the age of centuries, rises a structure of great solidity though (as compared with other celebrated shrines of religion) of inconsiderable dimensions. The bell-shaped spire is wanting, and the central dome, massive as it appears, is obviously the work of more recent and less careful architecture than that which fashioned the jasper lintel of the entrance door, encrusted the outer walls with innumerable niched figures of shapely design, and made the coarse sandstone droop in fringes delicate as lace work. There is a cow calving in the holiest penetralia, and on the inmost wall, the exterior base of which is within a few feet of the sea, a solitary splash of red paint attests at once the cow-herd's rude piety, and the completeness of the degradation to which Mahá Kál's great oracle has fallen. For this before us is the far-famed Temple of Somnáth.

'It was about the time when Canute the Great was employing himself in decorating the old minster at Winchester with such magnificence as confounded the minds of strangers at the sight of the gold and silver and the splendour of the jewels, that another sovereign, as successful a soldier and as enthusiastic a lover of architectural display, undertook in the far East an enterprise in which he sought to perpetuate his name by the destruction of an idolatrous shrine, perhaps more splendid than that Christian temple which the politic Western Sovereign was engaged in founding. . . . . Mahmúd left Ghazní on his expedition aginst Somnáth in September A.D. 1024: his numerous army was accompanied by crowds of volunteers the flower of the youth of Turkistán.'

Ajmír and Anhilwárá fell before him; but 'it was 'against the Gods, and not the Kings of the Hindus, that Mahmúd made war;' and he hastened on without a pause to Somnáth. And, whatever may be the present state of the Temple, 'to behold it as it met the eye of the army of Islám, we must recall its lofty spire rising far above the blue horizon of its ocean back-ground, the tawny banner of Siva fluttering from its summit, the porticoes and pyramid-like dome, the courts and columned aisles that surrounded them, and the numerous subordinate shrines which, as satellites, heightened the splendour of this chosen dwelling of the Lord of the Moon.' Rapid as had been Mahmúd's approach, he found an army ready to oppose him. His herald proclaimed defiance, the green ensign of the Prophet was unfurled, and the assault delivered. For two days his best efforts were vain, and the most devoted of the stormers, as fast as they scaled the walls, were beaten back by the valour of the Rájputs. On the third day, when victory seemed still more decidedly turning in favour of the besieged and their relieving army, Mahmúd himself led a furious charge that saved the day. Five thousand Hindus lay dead at his feet and the city of Dev Pattan was his own. When the victorious Sultán

'entered the shrine of Someswar, he beheld a superb edifice of hewn stone, its lofty roof supported by pillars curiously carved and set with precious stones. In the adytum, to which no external light penetrated, and which was illuminated only by a lamp suspended from the centre by a golden chain, appeared the symbol of Someswar—a stone cylinder which rose nine feet in height above the floor of the temple and penetrated six feet in depth below it. Two fragments of this object of idolatrous worship were at the King's order broken off, that one might be thrown at the threshold of the public Mosque, and the other at the Court-gate of his own palace at Ghazní. Other fragments were reserved to grace the holy cities of Mecca and Medina. While Mahmúd was thus employed, a crowd of Bráhmans, petitioning his attendants, offered an enormous ransom if the King would desist from further mutilation. Mahmúd hesitated, and his courtiers hastened to offer the advice which they knew would be acceptable; but after a moment's pause the Sultán exclaimed that he would be known by posterity not as the 'idol-seller,' but as *the destroyer*. The work of spoliation then continued, and was rewarded by the discovery, in the vaults below the adytum, of untold treasures.'

From the fall of Somnáth to the destruction of Anhilwárá by a still fiercer storm of Islámism nearly three centuries afterwards, the story of Gujarát presents nothing but a melancholy sameness of intestine strife; Rájput contending fratricidally with Rájput, and nowhere anything like union against the common foe. The Muhammadans had consequently little difficulty in conquering the country after a fashion. Conquer it thoroughly they never did; and Káthiáwár which, according to their own authors, fermented with a chronic insurrection, at no time became to the Sultáns of Ahmadábád that compact portion of a subject empire, which it had been to the dynasties of Wallabhí and Anhilwárá. It profits little to look into the successive struggles made now by the paramount power to confirm its ascendency, now by turbulent tributaries to re-assert their independence; efforts in which neither side gained any material advantage, and which leave the general plot of the drama advanced scarcely a step towards final development. The Musalman in his turn bowed and fell before the Marhattá; but before the appearance of the latter comes an episode which—no less for the interest attaching to the first exhibition of the Christian cross in Káthiáwár than for the heroism of a people to whom, perhaps because of old they pressed us closely as rivals, and now seem to have fallen almost beneath our notice, we, the present lords of India seem inclined to mete scant justice—deserves equally prominent mention with the stories of Wallabhí and Somnáth.

Two marches South-eastward from the last-named place, we come to our camping ground on a narrow neck of land, across which, from the sea on one hand to the mud of a salt creek on the other, stretches a row of iron cannon evidently marking a once disputed boundary. This line as it passes over a sandy attempt at a road in the middle of its course is additionally marked by two glaring white pillars, bearing inscriptions, which, as far as we can gather from their Latin-like Portuguese, inform us that we are passing from the limits of the Junágarh territory to those, as defined by an Anglo-Portuguese Commission in 1859, of the Colony of Diu. Presently a small stone erection on the beach to our left attracts notice, and it is with that strange thrill of alien pity and unreasonable interest which it is impossible to suppress at the sight of a fellow-countryman's solitary grave in a far foreign land, that we decipher the quaint old *Hic jacet* of an English sea-captain who died and was buried here just one century ago. As we approach the town of Goglá, we are challenged by the cry of a sentry on guard at the gate, and out tumble his comrades, a batch of neatly dressed little fellows in dark greenish blue, who carry arms to our English excellencies, in mute surprise at the unaccustomed advent of a white face. The Havildár sends off a message in haste to warn the Governor of coming visitors, and himself escorts us through the streets of the village till we come out upon the brink of the little creek, on the opposite shore of which we hail the yellow houses and dark rock-built fort of Diu. The latter juts out into the sea from the eastern extremity of the island, and from its topmost citadel floats the tower-charged blue-and-white of Portugal. Five minutes suffice to transport us past the little Páni Kothá, or Water Fort, rising from a rock in mid-channel to command the entrance of the port; and as our boat touches the shore, again comes the shriek of a sentry, and we pass under the gates of Diu with the same military honours which we had hoped to have endured once for all at Goglá. Here the Town Major joins us and carries us off to pay our respects to the Governor. The latter is a dark, stout little man of polite manners and energetic character, whose medals show that, as a Major of Dragoons, he has seen active service in Europe; he receives us at the top of his outer stairs, and leads us to a long apartment rather bare of furniture with a dais and gubernatorial chair at one end over which hangs a coloured print of the young King of Portugal. His excellency seats us beside him on a red sofa of Spartan hardness, and unless we have taken the precaution to bring an interpreter with us, jerky civilities are exchanged through the medium of a not slipperless Baniá equally versed in our own Gujaráti and our host's Portuguese. The view facing us through the open windows is charming; it looks northward across the sail-specked harbour to our tents on the white sand-hills opposite; near them at intervals may be marked those curious double-headed palm trees peculiar to the Southern coast of Káthiáwár, and, further beyond, the swelling outlines of the Nandevilí and other hills of the Gir hanging like a cloud in the horizon. We sip the Governor's 'tinto,' and take our leave with a view to visiting the sights of the place. Pigs, churches, stone-quarries, Negroes, Sombrero straw hats, and brilliant-patterned pantaloons figure largely among first impressions of Diu. The pigs run untended about the streets, and, as we know by our previous experience at Damaun, share with the omnipresent pariah the duties and privileges of the public scavenger. Churches, churches everywhere—the majority in various stages of dilapidation, one turned into an hospital, and two or three still occupied for devotional purposes: of these last the largest is dedicated to St. Paul, a name which the natives of the island, many of them professing a convenient polytheistic form of Christianity, have converted into Shrí Pál. It is a large stone building with a façade, which, but for its coat of yellow wash, would have been handsome, and an interior where the majestic effect of vaulted height is marred by most tawdry ornamentation.

Attached, and in fact forming part of the same pile, is a convent, where welcome relief from the outer glare and heat may be found in the shadow of arched cloisters, pierced by windows, whose semi-transparent shells, supplying the place of glass, shed a religious light which harmonises delightfully with the murmur of a fountain among the cool dark foliage of the little arboretum in the centre. Here paces a spare elderly man in slippers and a gaudy cotton dressing-gown, to whom we are introduced as the Bará Padre of the place, and he offers us a cigarito with a *bonhommie* quite captivating. On again venturing outside we are more than ever struck with the appearance of the stone quarries: all Diu is honeycombed with them, and by the side of every edifice of any size one sees the hole in the rock out of which its materials have been hewn. Some of these quarries are of considerable depth and extent, families have settled at the bottom, and thus little settlements of Troglodytes have been created, nestling under tall old trees, the tops of which scarcely soar to the mouth of the pit. The frequent occurrence of African faces suggests the enquiry where they come from, and the response teaches us that what little commerce the decaying colony can still boast is chiefly with the Portuguese possessions in the Mozambique. Until the present system of passes for Málwa opium was introduced, a smuggling traffic in the precious drug diverted a good deal of money to Diu: but that source dried up, the place no longer paid its expenses, and although the present Governor has struck out a new channel for receipts by the establishment of a regular fishery, it is doubtful if even this ingenious device can avail in a financial point of view to justify the retention by the Portuguese of this their ancient footing in the country. The fort is at present garrisoned by about 200 men and the guns it mounts are very old pieces of ordinance; but the position has certainly strong natural advantages for fortification. Near the harbour wall, and between the fort and the town, stands a tall pillar commemorative of a Sultán slain in battle. And it is for the sake of the old days when this event occurred that we have given to Diu so prominent a place in our sketch of Káthiáwár.

It was in 1537 that Nunho-da Cunha, who had five years previously made an unsuccessful attempt on Diu, gained his object by the promise of aid to Sultán Bahádur of Gujarát, then engaged in war with the Dehli Emperor, Humáyun. Bahádur, when the war ended, wished to retract his gift, and became involved in desultory hostilities with his former allies. It was then agreed that these differences should be settled by a personal interview with the Captain of the Feringhis. The parties had scarcely met each other on Diu beach, before mutual suspicions of treachery led to a scuffle at the boats, in which the Indian Monarch and the European Commander were both slain. When we hear that in this encounter, the Portuguese bullets having run short,[1] one soldier tore a tooth out of his mouth and fired that instead, and that another ran with a barrel of powder and a lighted torch into the midst of the Muslim bands, and then blew him-

[1] Taylor and Mackenna's *Ancient and Modern India.*

self and forty of the foe to pieces, we feel that the pillar before which we stand is scarcely needed to give assurance that victory remained with the handful of adventurers from the West. Subsequently the Grand Seigneur, as Defender of the Faith of Islam, despatched from Suez 70 galleys, carrying 7,000 Turkish soldiers, and a perfectly equipped train of artillery, under the command of the Governor of Cairo, to co-operate with 20,000 troops of Gujarát in exterminating the 600 Káfirs who held Diu for the house of Avis.

The first siege is memorable for the bravery of the defendants. Donna Isabella de Vega assembled the women, told them that their husbands and brothers were all wanted for active operations against the enemy, and then herself led them out to work with mattock and spade at the ever-crumbling parapets. Ann Fernandez passed from post to post even while the assault ran hottest, cheering and encouraging the soldiers, and, when her son was slain, carried his body out of the press of battle, and then returned to the *mêlée*, where she remained till the repulse of the stormers allowed her to depart and weep over his burial. The last grand effort of the besiegers failed. On the 5th November 1538 the garrison, or rather forty men, the sole remnant of 600, haggard and war-worn, but still unconquered, stood on the seaward ramparts of their battered fort, and watched the white sails that bore away from them for ever Sulaimán the Cairene, baffled and discomfited.

Seven years slipped away and then Diu, this time defended only by 210 men, sustained a second siege in the course of which to the usual horrors of war were added the miseries of famine.

But at last there came rescue from Goa with Juan de Castro; and he not only relieved Diu, but attacked the enemy in their fortified trenches and routed them. He then carried the war inland, and so humbled the Kings of Gujarát and the Dakhín that they were fain to accept peace on any terms. De Castro's fame has been immortalised in the verse of Camoens. He too it was, who when in want of a loan to complete the fortifications of Diu, cut off his beard and enclosed it in a letter to Goa; the only security which his knightly patriotism had to offer, and one accepted by his countrymen with enthusiasm.

But we must hasten away from the brave little island of Diu, which from that time to this has remained the unmolested property of the Portuguese. The Muhammadans, whose yoke, as we have already noticed, had ever sat lightly on the half-conquered Rájputs of Káthiáwár were compelled in their turn to submit to the Marhattás, and in the wake of the Marhattás came the mightier Sovereignty of England. In April 1755 the Peshwá and Gaikwár took possession of Ahmadábád, and proceeded to divide the revenues of Gujarát between them. Forty-five years afterwards the Peshwá granted his share in farm to the Baroda Government, and in this way the collective claim for tribute of both the Marhattá Princes against Káthiáwár fell to the Gaikwár to collect. The business was performed in a mode eminently characteristic of the people, with whom, according to Grant Duff, 'to collect revenue and to make war were synonymous.' Bodies of three or four thousand predatory horse, unencumbered with camp equipage or artillery, would be let loose upon the country, usually about harvest time, and as they 'approached the territory of the Chief from whom the tribute was demanded, it was his duty if he meditated no opposition to despatch an accredited agent to the boundary line, furnished with the means of affording security for his compliance with all reasonable demands.' But it was a point of honour with the Rájputs to resist as long as possible the levy of any tribute whatever; and the Marhattás, for their part, ill-brooked any delay in yielding to their requisitions. What usually ensued therefore was that

> 'the Pindárís were thrown out on all sides and the march of the army was thenceforth marked by every species of plunder and desolation; the ripe crops were swept from the fields, the villages were wantonly fired and destroyed, nothing was allowed to remain but the bare walls of the houses, and it frequently happened that every acre of his lands was left bare, and every hamlet in his territory reduced to a heap of smouldering ruins before the Rájput Chieftain condescended to the payment of the tribute demanded.'

Such was what the Marhattás called their Mulkgiri, or circuit of the country. Apparently not quite aware of what it was to which we were pledging ourselves, we had become bound by treaty to give military assistance to our Baroda ally in these expeditions. But in Colonel Alexander Walker the British Government of the day had a representative at the Gaikwár's Court, on whose tact and judgment they could thoroughly rely. By his intervention an arrangement was concluded which, while it not only more than redeemed our promises, at the same time satisfied the scruples of Christian conscience and European civilisation, and legitimately expanded the sphere of our growing influence. The Gaikwár welcomed the idea of realising his dues without the trouble, uncertainty, and expense of an armament specially despatched year after year; and the various States of Káthiáwár, as soon as they had got rid of the notion that we intended a Mulkgiri expedition on our own account, were not behindhand in expressing their satisfaction with any system that would rid them of the recurring Marhattá scourge. Given these feelings on either side, the problem was soon solved. The Gaikwár consented to forego his Mulkgiri, and the Peninsular Chiefs, in lieu of all demands whatever that the Marhattá Suzerain might have against them, were severally rated at a certain fixed sum to be paid annually, not to the Gaikwár, but to a British Agent, who in his turn was to account for the sums so received to the Gaikwár. This triple bargain was ratified in the year Samvat 1864 (A.D. 1808), and to this day, under the familiar title of the settlement of sixty-four, remains the most important landmark in the modern history of the Province. It is the foundation-stone on which the structure of British administration has since been raised.

Our first appearance then in Káthiáwár was in the character of arbitrators between a native ally and his unruly tributaries. But when we vanquished and deposed the Peshwá of Puná in 1817, we suceeded to his share in the tribute, and thus became entitled to assume on our own account a commanding position towards the swarm of vassals, whom both Mughul and Marhattá had found it impossible to keep in permanent subjection. And now, practically, Her Majesty is sole Suzerain of Káthiáwár. At present (1860) the gross revenues of the country may be estimated at rather less than half a million sterling: out of which about 100,000*l.* are paid as annual tribute to the British Government and the Gaikwár, in the proportion say of two-thirds to the former and one-third to the latter. The population is about 1½ million (1860).[1]

[1] Population is now (1874) over 2½ millions. For a brief account of the present condition of Káthiáwár, see my note at end of this essay.—W. W. H.

Put simply, the duty of a Political Agent in Káthiáwár is twofold, to collect the tribute and to keep the peace. For insuring the first of these objects he is entitled so far to interfere in the internal management of every Táluká as to see that its owner does not endanger the realisation of the Government demand against him. To secure the second he, under certain limitations, administers Civil and Criminal Justice. A position, it will be seen, not adequately expressed by the title, Political Agent; for the word Political has in India come to signify Diplomatic; and tributaries neither are nor have the right to be treated with that formal delicacy of suggestion characteristic of an embassy accredited from one august ally to another. The name Káthiáwár too is a perpetual stumbling-block, inasmuch as Káthiáwár is not only not the proper name of the Peninsula, but it is the name of something else, namely, of one of the ten divisions into which the Peninsula is divided. The word Soreth is open to a similar objection. Some such designation, therefore, as Warden of Southern Rájasthán would better denote both the country and the nature of the duties carried on by the British officer posted there.

Nevertheless payment of a tribute does not deprive the tributary of his independence. Even under our sway each Tálukdár is supposed to possess exclusive jurisdiction within his own Táluká. Several of the smaller fry have little practical ability to enforce the execution of justice, and under these circumstances the right of taking cognisance of injuries lapses naturally to the paramount Power. But the majority are quite capable of dealing with most of the contingencies calling for interposition; and three or four of the more important actually retain the power of life and death within their own hands. As a general rule a subject can look for justice only to his own Tálukdár; his grievance, if lying against a fellow-subject, must be redressed by the common lord of both; if against the subject of another jurisdiction, it must be first taken up by his own Chief, and only through him can it be prosecuted, the plaint in that case holding good not as against the particular defendant, but against the state to which such defendant may belong. Downright oppression or denial of justice by a Tálukdár is prevented by the operation of the old rule of Rájput hospitality, which the Agency never allows to fall into abeyance;—the rayat can migrate into the lands of another Tálukdár, who is then bound not only to give him shelter, but to espouse his quarrel against the oppressor and to see it fought out in the British Courts. This provision, seconding the natural worldly wisdom of a landlord, who knows that his rent roll varies in proportion to the number of his cultivators, brings it about that the Tálukdárs do not generally indulge in those practices of tyranny and extortion towards their tenantry which, we are too much given to believe, so markedly distinguish the Native Revenue system from our own. There is but one class of men in the Province admitted to the right of direct litigation with their own Chiefs. These are the Girasiá and Mul-Girasiás, as they are called, who being either originally portioned cadets of the ruling tribe, or the less respectable descendants of some cateran who in the old time established his black-mail upon a village or District, have become possessed of certain proprietary rights in the land, which they defend with all the proverbial tenacity of the Rájput.

In 1860 there were 224 Tálukdárs of sizes; each basing his right to the title upon the fact of the estate which he represents having been entered in the Domesday Book of Colonel Walker's settlement as paying its quota of tribute by a separate and direct transaction with the British Agent. The following are the principal men :—

H.H. the Nawáb of Junágarh...	Chiefs of the first rank.
„ the Jám of Nawánagar ...	
„ the Rawal of Bháwnagar	
TheRáná of Purbandar	Of the second grade.
The Ráj of Drángdrá	
The Thákur of Murví	

Junágarh is the premier state of the Province. The city lies at the entrance of a valley, and at its north-eastern angle the dark bastions of the old Rájput Acropolis, the Uparkot of Rá Khengar, still frown over 'the streak of gold,' the river Soná Rekhá ; whilst high above city and citadel towers the temple-crowned mount of Nimináth, the royal Girnár. Many a time did the old Churasamá princes, who held their Court here as Ráos of Soreth, and whose memory is still cherished in the country, do battle with the Muhammadan invader. After a gallant resistance the last of the Ráos was starved into submission and forcibly converted to the faith of the Prophet by Mahmúd Begará in 1468. A century afterwards when Akbar overran Gujarát, the place was still further Islamised, and became occupied by a garrison subordinate to the Subah of Ahmadábád. Finally amid the general anarchy which proceeded the subversion of the Mughuls, Sher Khán Bábí, a soldier of fortune, usurped the royalties of Junágarh : and it is his descendant who still is seated on the *gadí.* The present Nawáb, after a good deal of hard usage in his earlier years, was still in his nonage when his brother, Hámid Khán, died, a youth of great promise. A Pancháyat of administration was appointed, with special injunctions from the Court of Directors that not less attention should be paid towards the preparation of the young Chieftain for the position he was destined to fill in after life, than to the nursing of the Táluká's revenues in the interval. The result, however, has been—chiefly no doubt attributable to the crass nature on which the Regency were expected to work, but also in some measure, we suspect, owing to crafty views of future ascendency over an incompetent master—that while great general prosperity was attained for the estate, its owner grew up in the Zanáná ignorant, enervated, and almost fatuous. The intrigues of a disreputable old slave-woman, who had been the indulgent nurse of his boyhood, led to the unjustifiable repudiation of his consort, a Princess of the house of Rhádanpur, and to a degrading alliance with the slave-woman's niece. Soon the Darbár became rent by two factions; one behind the *Pardá* aiming at an acknowledgment from the Bombay Government of the legitimacy of a son by the last-mentioned connection; which, once obtained, would be the sure forerunner of the Nawáb's sudden demise; and another supporting the Díwán, or chief minister, who strong in the Agency's approval of his general administration, attempted to seat himself permanently as Mayor of the Palace over this *Roi Fainéant.* About two years before this article was written, the Chief Minister was dismissed from his office. But he still intrigued for the recovery of power, and thus with a weak ministry *de facto* struggling against a powerful opposition, a fresh element of confusion is added (1860).

It is a relief to turn from Junágarh to Nawánagár. The Jám is the head of the Káthiáwár branch of the great clan of Járejá Rájputs, which surged into the country from Sind about the middle of the fifteenth century; and another stem of which is represented by the Ráo of Kutch.

Personally, though ignorant of the English language, and possessed of a high spirit of independence that chafes under a yoke stricter than his fathers ever knew, the Jám has more of the essentials of an English gentleman about him than any Hindu it has yet been our lot to meet. European society is not particularly courted at Nawánagar, but no sáhib, great or small, official or independent, has ever visited its well-ordered Darbár without carrying away a real feeling of hearty regard for the active little Prince, whose punctilious courtesy, frank and easy assumption of perfect equality, readiness to join in the chase, and liberal hospitality render social intercourse with him an unaffected pleasure. The Táluká is well managed and its large compactness is the chief reason why the Hallár District gives but little trouble to the officer in charge.

But the best administered Táluká and possibly the wealthiest belongs to the Ráwal of Bháwnagar. Descended from a dashing sea-rover, Mokherájí, who in the fourteenth century had his eyrie in the isle of Pirim at the mouth of the Gulf of Cambay, and whose shade is to this day propitiated by the passing mariner, the Ráwal is the head of the Gohel Rájputs, a race driven in from Márwár by the Ráthors A.D. 1200.

Himself boasting neither abilities nor attainments, he has the fortune to command the services of the most enlightened and upright Chief Minister in the Province, and the good sense not to quarrel with him (1860). Commerce has been the traditional policy of the State for a considerable period, and on this common field of enterprise

Bháwnagar has been brought into close and frequent contact with our own traders of Bombay and Surat; the natural consequence being that Bháwnagar has become honourably identified among Káthiáwár feudatories with the cause of progress and civilisation. Part of the Ráwal's territories, ever since one of his ancestors put to death some unhappy wretch who, in a season of famine, had ventured on the sacrilege of killing a cow for its beef, has been placed by Government under the sway of English laws. And for purposes of jurisdiction it was originally incorporated into the Zilá of Ahmadábád.[1]

We now come to Chiefs of the second class. Foremost is the Ráná of Purbandar, representing the Jetwás, one of the four ancient races still extant in the Peninsula. The Ráná professes to trace his origin back to a patriarch got by Hanumán, the Monkey-God, out of a female alligator. His genealogy is asserted in the family title of Puncheriá, or long tailed, and the household bard in Colonel Tod's time 'stoutly contended for a superfluity of down in Prince Sontán, only four generations ago.' In the days of Ghaznívide invasion all the West and part of the North of Káthiáwár belonged to the Jetwá Rájputs, but the forays of Jhálá and Járejá have now narrowed their possessions to a small tract called Bardá, south of the shaggy range of hills of the same name. The Ráná of to-day is a man of plain business habits, whose Bráhmanic simplicity of attire strikes an eye accustomed to the blaze of jewels usually presented by his fellow chiefs. Formerly there was a British detachment stationed at Purbandar,

[1] This was written in 1860. On the death of the Bháwnagar Chief, his successor being a minor, the territory passed under a regency, with a Bombay civilian and the old native councillor as joint Ministers. Under their rule it continues the most prosperous and best governed State in Káthiáwár.—W.W.H.

its expenses being defrayed by a cess on the Ráná's port dues; but the troops have now been withdrawn, and nothing but the Christian cemetery raising its crosses by the blue waters of the bay, is left to tell of what has been.

The Jhálás, sprung probably from an offshoot of Anhilwárá, on the extinction of which dynasty they obtained large territorial aggrandisement, own the Ráj of Halwad-Drángdrá as their Chief.

The Thákur of Múrví is a Járejá, and deserves notice from the fact of his ancestor in Colonel Walker's time having been the first of the tribe who consented to abandon the fell custom of infanticide. The present incumbent of the *gadí* possesses better abilities than has fallen to the lot of most of his peers, and retains the management of his Táluká considerably in his own hands. He keeps in tight check the landed proprietors under him, and from this circumstance has incurred the not wholly deserved odium of a grasping and oppressive policy. Having possessions in Kutch, he has been for long involved in various disputes with the Ráo of that State, and some recent decisions of the Bombay Government in these cases have given him much dissatisfaction.

It now remains to notice generally the ten divisions of the Peninsula. These are:—

Five Southern.	Soreth, Babriáwár, Und-Surweyá, Gohelwár, and Káthiáwár Proper.
Five Northern.	Jhááwár, Machu-Kánta, Hállár, Bardá, and Okhámandal.

Soreth contains the Girnár Hill and Junagarh city, the port of Virawal-Pattan and Somnáth Temple—all discussed above. If we except the Shaikh of Mángrol on the coast as too insignificant to glance at, the only other Táluká is Bantwá, a Musalmán township held by a junior branch of the Bábís of Junágarh. The two principal shareholders, Sir Baland Khán and Kamal-ud-dín Khán carry on a chronic feud, which in March 1859 was further embittered by a fight between their retainers of unusual ferocity; fifteen men killed and fifty wounded. A sham reconciliation was then got up with the object of tricking Government into a commutation of the penalties to which they had become liable; and finally they put the crown to their misdeeds by treasonably harbouring the rebel Wághars.

In *Babriáwár*, a small and poor District lying between the Gir forests and the sea, and held by Babriás and Ahirs with land-tenures of singular complication, the only town of note is Jafarábád, or more correctly Muzaffarábád, a fortified port said to have been colonised by the Turks, and now belonging to the Habshi Chief of Zanjirá near Bombay, who deputes the management of his distant estate to a violet-bearded Faujdár of indubitably African physiognomy In connection with this District may be mentioned the sulphureted hot springs of Tul-sisám in the heart of the pestilent Gir. Superstition has ascribed the phenomenon to Divine agency, so by the side of it is reared a diamond-eyed image of Krishna, tended by a small colony of monks.

Und Surweyá is no bigger than Babriáwár, and even more insignificant.

Gohelwár, at the mouth of the Cambay Gulf, is occupied by the Ráwal of Bháwnagar, and his Bháyád or brother-kindred. Noticeable Thákurs are those of Walleh, Láthí, and Palitáná. The town of Walleh has been already remarked as standing near the ruins of the once splendid Wallabhípur. Láthí gave a daughter in marriage to one of the low-born Gaikwárs, a condescension repaid by that monarch agreeing to accept the yearly Nazaráná of a horse in lieu of his former demands for tribute. But emphatically the glory of Gohelwár is the hill of Satrunjai (*Satrunjaya*) at Palitáná, dedicated to Adináth, the first of the twenty-four hierophants of the Jains. The beauties of this ancient haunt of Indian Buddhism are described by Mr. Forbes as follows :—

'There is hardly a city in India, through its length and breadth, from the river of Sind to the sacred Ganges, from Himálaya's diadem of ice-peaks, to the throne of his Virgin daughter, Rudra's destined bride, that has not supplied at one time or other contributions of wealth to the edifices which crown the hill of Palitáná ; street after street, and square after square, extend these shrines of the Jain faith, with their stately enclosures, half-palace, half fortress, raised in marble magnificence upon the lonely and majestic mountain, and like the mansions of another world, far removed in upper air from the ordinary tread of mortals. In the dark recesses of each temple one image or more of Adináth or Ajit, or of some other of the Tírthankars, is seated, whose alabaster features, wearing an expression of listless repose, are rendered dimly visible by the faint light shed from silver lamps ; incense perfumes the air, and barefooted, with noiseless tread upon the polished floor, the female votaries, glittering in scarlet and gold, move round and round in circles, chanting forth their monotonous, but not unmelodious hymns. Satrunjai indeed might fitly represent one of the hills of Eastern romance, the inhabitants of which have been instantaneously changed into marble, but which fairy hands are ever employed upon, burning perfumes, and keeping all clean and brilliant, while fairy voices haunt the air with voluptuous praises of the Devas.'

And in plain truth we believe that no fabric of man's workmanship in India, not excepting even the Táj, is more calculated to arouse wonder, admiration, and lasting remembrance than the temple-city of Palitáná in its unique and mysterious perfection.

Káthiáwár Proper is a large inland District, and, as its name denotes, the country of those redoubted freebooters who, by the awe they inspired into the Marhattás, have unwittingly given their name to the whole Peninsula. They immigrated into the country in the eighth century, A.D., and from their stature, facial linaments, and blue eyes have been by some authorities supposed to be of Scythian origin. Their religion is a loose form of Hinduism grafted upon an ancient veneration for the Sun ; the list of witnesses appended to any of their documents still leads off with 'Srí Súrjyani Shákh,' the testimony of the holy Sun. Unlike the Rájputs who enjoy a modified form of primogeniture, the sons of a Káthí inherit by equal partition ; and the minute subdivision of estates with no recognised heads of houses effected by the operation of this custom, added to an innate turbulence in their blood, renders the Káthís the most troublesome tribe of all that the agency has to deal with. What they were in former times when they could act up to the good old maxim—'Thou shalt want ere I want,' may be gathered from the following specimen embalmed for us by Colonel Tod :—

'Jessá, or, with the more respectful postfix, Jessáji, was a fair specimen of his race. After sitting at his ease, for some time, indulging, like a true Káthí, in the most unrestrained freedom of speech, I turned the conversation to his past life, by asking whether he had not carried the honourable profession of arms to some distance beyond his own sequestered abode. A mere 'trifle' replied the moss-trooper with the greatest *nonchalance*, 'never further than Bháwnagar, Pattan, and Jháláwár.' If the reader will consult the map he will find that Jessáji's three points form a triangle, embracing the most remote quarters of the Peninsula, East, South, and West ; and that a trifle beyond in either direction, both the horse and his rider must have gone into the sea. On pushing him a little further, by observing that these were very confined limits, and enquiring if he had never tried the

Northern or continental portion, with the same simplicity of manner and tone, he replied in his metaphorical diction, 'Why I have driven my lance into the gate of Ahmadábád.' I wanted no more; Jessájí, the Suzerain of Deolá, and of one dozen subjects, his township covering about as much soil as a good-sized mansion, had, single-handed, insulted the capital of Gujarát.'

Of the Northern Districts, *Jháláwár* is a large and fertile tract, rich in wheat and cotton, lying towards Cambay and Ahmadábád. The Jhálá Chiefs ranking next after the Ráj of Drángdrá are the Ráj of Wánkánir and the Thákur of Wadwan. In these parts there is a capital device for providing in every robbery either for the detection of the robber or compensation to the party robbed. The village within the limits of which any such occurrence may have happened becomes *ipso facto* bound either to produce the thief, make good the value of the property, or point out some other village whereto their own primary liability may be justly transferred. The last alternative is effected by tracking the footsteps of the robbers from the scene of their depredation into the limits of a neighbouring community, who again in their turn are at liberty, if they can, similarly to pass the responsibility on to a third village, the third to a fourth, and so on, until either the fugitive offenders are run down or their steps are no longer traceable. And where the track ceases there the final liability rests. Large sums are not unfrequently at stake on questions arising out of this system, and, although the dexterity of the Jháláwár Pagis is such that, we suspect, even one of Cooper's impossible Red Indians might learn a hint or two from them, the doubtful proofs upon which an estate is mulcted sometimes in penalties out of proportion to its means, makes these 'Waltar' (compensation) cases among the most unsatisfactory which the officer in charge of the Northern Districts has to adjudicate. Still, in an unsettled country, the system is too valuable to allow of its being weakened by the admission of exceptional cases of impunity. And certainly great precautions are taken to exclude some obvious abuses to which its provisions are liable, by requiring every Pagi to pass a practical examination in his profession before being admitted to practice, and by largely cutting down or occasionally altogether disallowing the claim for compensation in cases where there may appear to have been want of proper precaution against loss.

Machu Kánta, or the banks of the River Machu, constitute a wedge-shaped District on the Răn of Kutch, the greater part of which is ruled by the Thákur of Múrví. The other Tálukdár is the Thákur of Máliá, a Chief of singularly limited authority. For the real masters of Máliá are the Míánás, who may be characterised as the most lawless race on the face of the earth. To the local Rájá they own no kind of allegiance, but under their own Chauattiás, or Heads of tribes, form a special 'imperium in imperio' of their own. The basis on which we deal with them is a formal agreement between the Agent on the one side and the Chauattiás on the other, by which in consideration of certain annual stipends the Chauattiás have agreed to consider every outrage committed within a certain circle round Máliá as necessarily the work of some Míáná or other, and at once without more ado to produce the culprit or make fit reparation for the offence. The Míánás do not confine their doings, however, to Máliá and its neighbourhood: numbers of them take service as Sepoys, and every boundary fight shows a Míáná or two among the killed and wounded. Mr. Forbes hits their character exactly in the following anecdote :—

'One day while an Arab soldier of the Gaikwár's was at his prayers, a Míáná passed by and asked him whom he was afraid of that he bent his head that way. The Arab replied with some indignation that he feared no one but Allah. "Oh, then," said the Míáná, "come along with me to Máliá; we don't fear even Allah there.'"

Hállár on the gulf of Kutch belongs to the Jám of Nawánagar, and to the Cadets of his house seated at Gundál, Rájkot, and other places. The Gundál Darbár is in a most disreputable state just at present (1860). Rájkot derives its only importance from its central position having recommended it as the site for our own Civil and Military Head Quarters.[1] The usual strength of the force cantoned there is one regiment of N. I., one of regular cavalry, and a post of guns. It may be doubted whether a better base for military operations might not have been found somewhere on the cool south coast: a complete armament could then have been poured into the country at a moment's notice from Karáchí or Bombay.

Bardá belongs entirely to the Ráná of Purbandar.

Okhámandal is the last, and in point of value and extent, the least of all the Divisions. It is the extreme Western claw of the Peninsula, and as it has the sea on three sides of it and on the fourth a Răn about 17 miles long, stretching from the Gulf of Kutch southward to within a few hundred yards of the Indian Ocean, it is in fact a little Peninsula on its own account, isolated from the rest of the Province by the same physical features which serve to cut off Káthiáwár itself from the Continent

[1] Rájkot is now the seat of a public school for the young chieftains of the Province. It is admirably conducted under an English principal with assistant masters. The lads have taken kindly to athletic sports, and show much of the public school spirit and manliness which the institution was intended to develop.—W. W. H.

of India. The inhabitants of this sterile and jungly District, which does not contain altogether 50 villages or 13,000 inhabitants, are the notorious Wághars. Their only important places are Dwárká and Bait, the former on the West coast, occupying the site of one of the most ancient cities of the Aryan race, and possessing all that sanctity in the eyes of the Hindu which its mythic origin at the hands of Krishna should confer; the latter on a small island of the same name a few miles to the North, boasting shrines of scarcely inferior holiness; and both, until recent events, strongly fortified. The history of the Wághars is briefly this. Their buccaneering practices brought down on them a British invasion: we conquered the country in 1816, and finding it not worth retention made a merit of handing it over for a handsome consideration to the Gaikwár, who desired to clothe his humble origin in the prestige which lordship of their Holy Places would confer upon him in the estimation of the Hindus. He was inducted into his new possession in 1817, and thenceforward managed it through his deputies with a happy mixture of weakness and bad faith of which his turbulent subjects were not slow to take advantage. In 1820 it required a brilliant little campaign under Colonel Stanhope to put them down; and still their insurrection went smouldering on until in March 1858 it again broke into a flame. By the end of that year they seemed to have been once more effectually coerced, but the following June brought a fresh outbreak more serious than the last. The British Government had now lost all patience with a Prince on whom incessant exhortations to better his administration had so long idly fallen, and insisted on the Gaikwár's handing over Okhá to our own direct management. The rebels received timely notice of this change of masters, and had certain distinct terms of surrender offered them. These terms were dictated by the Resident of Baroda, and were perhaps needlessly severe; such as they were, however, the Wághars were allowed ample grace within which to consider them, and as they refused to acccpt them, were from that time to the termination of hostilities, rebels in arms no longer against the Gaikwár but against the Supreme Power of India. Troops by land and sea were thrown into Okhámandal early in October. We attacked Bait and were for the third time within little more than half-a-century (1803 and 1858 being the dates of the two preceding disasters) defeated from its walls with severe loss. The Wághars evacuated the place during the night: our forces entered next morning, and proceeded to *loot* (as they were entitled) and to blow up (as they were in prudence bound to do) the rich buildings, which, notwithstanding their sanctity as temples, had but the day before been fortifications manned by triumphant marksmen. The Wághars fled to Dwárká: we followed and besieged them there. One dark November night they made a sally, cut their way through the pickets of H.M.'s 28th foot, and escaped across the Răn into Káthiáwár with all their families and baggage. They took refuge in the Bardá Hills, and in a fort well supplied with water on the top of a precipitous and jungle-covered hill seemed at last to have reached a shelter from whence they might long defy our best efforts to dislodge them. However, their good fortune had now culminated. A fresh force from Karáchí was disembarked at Purbandár, and a week afterwards the dashing *élan* of Colonel Honner had stormed this inexpugnable position, taken 300 prisoners and broken the neck of the rebellion. The Wághars everywhere surrendered or were hunted down, and before the close of the hot weather of 1860 there remained not a dozen men still at large and unaccounted for. Civil authority personified in an Assistant to the Baroda Resident had been established in Okhá almost immediately after our capture of Dwárká in 1859, and the whole rainy season of the following year was a period of repose, during which it was hoped that the Wághars would settle down in their homes and learn to reconcile themselves to their English governor. But October last brought tidings of their again having risen, again having crossed the Răn, and committed greater mischief in Káthiáwár than they had ever dared to attempt during their previous incursion, by penetrating as far South as Korinár, and pillaging that city,—belonging to their old enemy the Gaikwár—with great ease and success. All that can be said about this last outbreak is that the Assistant Resident had an extremely difficult task before him when he undertook the pacification of Okhá, and that fortune has not smiled upon his efforts (1860).

From first to last it will be observed the Káthiáwár Agency have had nothing whatever to do with the Wághars.

And in making this statement we touch upon a sore in our administration of the country, which urgently calls for cautery. Besides Okhámandal there are two other estates, Amrelí in Káthiáwár Proper and Korinár in South, over which the Gaikwár has by force or fraud, or both, managed to acquire the directly dominant rights of a Tálukdár. Both have been subjected to the same misrule as Okhá, and though a less headstrong population, unaided by the advantages of isolated locality, have had neither the daring nor the ability to rise in organised rebellion like the Wághars, yet both Amrelí and Korinár simmer with an unceasing anarchy, fed not only by broils of an indigenous growth but by numbers of others imported into its congenial atmosphere from neighbouring Tálukás. The Gaikwár's Khás Mahals are the Alsatia of Káthiáwár. The Political Agent is powerless to meddle with them; only the Resident of Baroda, who never visits Káthiáwár and has necessarily but an imperfect knowledge of its condition, has any voice in their Government. It requires no conjuror to guess that they are fruitful sources of misunderstanding between the two offices; Rájkot for ever feeling peremptorily called on to interfere, and Baroda with equal justice resenting the intrusion. We have no hesitation in asserting that had Okhámandal been under the supervision of the local Agency these Wághar campaigns of the last three years, so damaging to our prestige, would never have occurred. When they did occur, the vehement protest of the military authorities against the anomaly of two political powers in the same country compelled Government to concentrate their representation in the single person of the Political Agent; and now again, when a cry is raised that the Nawáb, the Jám, and the Ráná give lukewarm or no aid in discovering the whereabouts of the fugitive rebels, does it not occur to those who have the ordering of these matters, that if the pacification of the Wághars and the control of those who decline the trouble of catching them were both equal objects of consideration to one and the same officer, Englishmen might be spared the shame and expense of a wild-goose chase after a handful of miserable barbarians? There can be no shadow of a doubt but that the officer, be he personally who he may, who is put in charge at Okhá, should bear the title and office of an Assistant not to the

Resident of Baroda but to the Political Agent at Káthiáwár. Amrelí and Korinár are as yet differently situated; their case stands in this wise. The Gaikwár, as an ally, has a right to demand that our representations on the subject of his estates and their management should be addressed to him through the sole channel of the Resident at his own Court; but this form of procedure has been found in its working to entail much bloodshed and unhappiness upon neighbouring states paying us tribute upon the condition of our protection. Is this, or is this not sufficient reason for our saying to the Gaikwár,—'Henceforward your deputies in Káthiáwár shall stand on the same footing and be amenable to the same control with all other Tálukdárs of the Peninsula'? (1860).

Yet another cause of quarrel with His Highness of Baroda. By treaty he is bound to keep up an efficient Contingent of Irregular Cavalry for service in Káthiáwár. And, as the founders of our rule foresaw, it is absolutely necessary for the peace of the country that there should be a body of light troops at the disposal of the Agency. To do the Gaikwár justice, he spends an enormous sum annually on the corps, but his disbursements are fruitlessly appropriated by courtiers in nominal command of squadrons, to whom it would be absurd to entrust any duty more important than that of carrying the letter-bag from camp to camp. All that we require is the fulfilment of a very plain engagement. If the Gaikwár cannot himself raise and maintain an efficient Contingent of Cavalry, let him hand us over the funds required for the proper redemption of his pledge and we will do it for him. There is already a body of Irregular Arab Infantry, attached to the Agency, which, though now fallen into decrepitude, was originally raised for exactly that kind of flying service against small bodies of outlaws, wherein regulars suffer much and effect little. These footmen, together with a troop of mounted police, called Mohasalí Sawárs, require thorough reorganisation: they might then be combined with an improved Gaikwár Contingent into a really useful force of Irregulars; and so without the cost of a rupee to the State, the Political Agent might be invested with a strength and prestige which he very materially needs, and which would be the surest safeguard against the occurrence of another 'little war' such as that of the Wághars. Disturbances in a country which, like the Oudh of a few years ago, bristles with forts and is rich in jungle fastnesses, while her population is habitually armed to the teeth and largely interspersed with mercenary desperadoes from Mekran, Arabia, Sind, and Beluchistán, are no trivial matters. Our Model Corps would be raised on somewhat the same principles as the Panjáb Guides; but the Commandant would be strictly confined to executive functions, never moving out his men without express order from the chief Political Authority,—so firmly would we guard from all chance of infraction the salutary rule of holding each Tálukdár responsible for the peace of his own dominions.

Another reform that we would advocate is connected with an abuse for which the local officers of the day are in no degree responsible. It is a traditional part of our policy in the country, having its probable origin, we are inclined to think, in the fact of an inefficient Contingent having left the Political Agent powerless to maintain the peace. We refer to a feeble method of dealing with disputes about land. In a Rájkot court the maxim seems to be that a land case can never be finally settled, and that the most unreasonably litigious Girasiá, whose shadowy claims may have been heard twenty times over, must still be received with some temporising expedient that may turn away his wrath. This system not only serves to retard the administration of justice in cases of genuine urgency, but, as giving scope for the admission and retention on the file of cases that never can come to any definite issue, leads to the Agent's camp being followed about, month after month, and year after year, by a posse of people for whom nothing ever can or ought to be done, but who still live on in hopes of interference some lucky day in their behalf. All this has its secret spring, we believe, in a dread of Báhirwatiá. 'This term,' writes Colonel Walker, 'is derived from *Báhir* outside, and *wát* a road. The offence consists in the Rájputs, or Girasiás, making their Rayats and dependents quit their native village, which is suffered to remain waste, and the Girasiá with his brethren then retires to some asylum, whence he may carry on his depredations with impunity. Being well acquainted with the country, and the redress of injuries being common cause with the members of every family, the Báhirwatiá has little to fear from those who are not in the immediate interest of his enemy, and he is in consequence enabled to commit very extensive mischief until he may be extirpated, or his principal forced to compromise the dispute.' In fact a Káthiáwár Báhirwatiá is just what an Oudh Dákáit was in the late king's time. Hitherto it has been usual to coax and wheedle the outlaw into surrender; and his crimes have been visited with slender punishment. Let us cite the first case that occurs to our memory. The date, we think, was in 1844, the Girasiá's name Visájí Unarjí; at any rate he was 'out' against the Thákur of Palitáná, and the Political Secretary for the time was Mr. J. P. Willoughby, now of the Home Council. Visájí was tried on several counts by a Criminal Court presided over by the Political Agent with three or four natives of rank as Assessors. For want of judicial proof he escaped a general conviction, but on the first count, embracing the three crimes of *murder, arson, and robbery*, he was unanimously found guilty. The Court sentenced him to a pecuniary fine, and detention until he furnished proper security. The Government of Bombay, in reviewing this decision, upheld the conviction but mitigated the fine, and directed that the prisoner should be at once released, adding that his conduct in the *existing state of Káthiáwár society called for a merely nominal punishment!*

Generally, indeed, we are disposed to think there has been too much leniency in Káthiáwár. Colonel Lang, the late admirable Warden of the Chiefs, on this head merely kept going a policy originated before his time. Moreover, in Colonel Lang's case, a clear intellect and warm sympathies devoted unreservedly for thirty years to the single study of furthering the happiness of his beloved Káthiáwár had justly invested him with an extraordinary personal influence which would have enabled him to work single-handed and successfully the craziest machine of state that ever was started. Yet the work must be done; and much of it, we fear, calls for the unpopular duties of a reformer, who shall abolish what has become effete, put new life into more useful principles that have been allowed to slumber, and at all points patiently, gradually, and surely brace up our rule to a state of stricter discipline. Especially do we deprecate the false benevolence of interfering with the domestic affairs of a Táluká to save it from pecuniary embarrassment. Spoiled children have rickety health; and a Chief, who after having imbibed the best education which we have been able to throw in his way, may once have discovered by experience that his prodigality will hurt no one but himself, and that if he takes to boundary-fights we shall infallibly make him smart for them, will be a far more valuable member of society than one whom we have for ever been trying to keep out of harm's way. At present Káthiáwár is a barbarism pure and simple, her people having just two virtues, patriarchal hospitality and comparative truthfulness. And the first lesson to be instilled into all ranks is the same which Lord Canning taught the Khâns of Peshâwar: 'You shall have justice, but your Suzerain will have peace.'

A word or two in conclusion may be acceptable regarding the two species of Káthiáwár denizens that have made the name of the country familiar to most people, viz., the lions and horses.

The famous old breed of horses that bore the Káthís on their forays—they, by the way, always affected mares for their singularly unfeminine quality of superior silence—and that mounted H.M.'s 17th Dragoons in such a style that two successive Colonels (one of them being the same Honourable Lincoln Stanhope who suppressed the Wághar revolt of 1820) testified to the Regiment being better mounted than any other cavalry corps in the service, is either extinct, we regret to say, or fast dying out. Now-a-days there is nothing to be found in the country with legs even decently strong-boned. The half-dozen Arab stations of the Government Remount Agency scattered through the country are too few to leaven the mass. A regular Stud Farm and a Race Meeting at Rájkot in which the Chiefs of the Province might be induced to take an interest would effect real good.

From accounts still to be read in back numbers of the

Indian Sporting Review it is clear that formerly lions were to be met with in many parts of Káthiáwár. Now, however, these animals are only to be found in the Gir jungles; and consequently the sport they afford, like tiger-shooting in the Oudh Tarái, offers itself at the risk of fever from malaria and unwholesome water. Colonel Le Grand Jacob, who shot numbers, maintains that it is a mistake to suppose the Gujarát lion has no mane, and imagines that the hair is thinned by perpetual entanglement with the thorns and underwood of the forest; but, on the other hand, a writer in the *Quarterly Review*, describing a specimen presented to the Zoological Gardens of London by the late Nawáb of Junágarh, compares it with a young African lion that boasted a fine mane, and says :—

'The full-grown animal from Gujarát is, on the contrary, comparatively maneless, and his tail takes a short curl upwards at the end. The caudal extremity of both is furnished with a rudimentary claw. This little appendage was supposed by the ancients to be instrumental in lashing the lion into fury, and Mr. Gordon Cumming informs us that the natives of South Africa believe it to be the residence of an evil spirit which never evacuates its post until death overtakes the beast and gives it notice to quit. The Gujarát or maneless lion is supposed to be the original of the heraldic beast we regard with such respect as a national emblem, but which foreigners maintain is nothing better than a leopard.'

There are no tigers in Káthiáwár: indeed they are seldom found anywhere, we believe, in the neighbourhood of lions. With this exception the sport all over Káthiáwár is first-rate. The fanatical Hindu and Jain inhabitants who consider virtue and religion to consist in the preservation of animal life, indeed who never stick at robbery to prevent the butchering of a sheep, and even some times not at murder to revenge the death of a cow, are the finest game preservers in the world. In many parts you may shoot black-buck from your tent-door, or pick off a *chinkara* with your revolver while driving on the public road. Nor is there any lack of hog to be hunted, or of hares and foxes to be coursed. In the cold weather *Kulam*, bustard, and wild-duck are capital eating; and in the rains it is always matter of emulation at Rájkot who shall shoot the first purple-crested florican. Quail and partridges abound all over the Province.

One last word as to the climate. The whole year round it is equable and temperate, and in the hot weather when everywhere else in India doors and windows are barred to exclude the furnace puffs of outer air, the coast of Káthiáwár is balmy with the wet breath of Ocean breezes. The whole Agency lives under canvas, and the tent of each Political Officer becomes a nucleus, round which in pic-nic fashion gather the tents of everybody who can manage to slip away from dust and duty at Rájkot, with sometimes a stray sportsman from even the more distant stations of Surat and Ahmadábád, to bathe, shoot, hunt, eat pomfret and oysters, and enjoy that perfection of *dolce far niente* which can be found only in the soft languid atmosphere of a summer sea.

NOTE BY THE EDITOR.

Since Mr. Wyllie wrote this essay, in 1860, much has been done to improve the administration of Káthiáwár. The difficulties proceeding from the mismanagement of the Gaikwár, and the inefficient state of his contingent, remain. But a British Commission appointed in 1873 to deal with the charges against him laid the foundation of a thorough reform (1874). In 1875 the Gaikwár was publicly tried and dethroned by the British authority, and a fitter man raised to the sovereignty of Baroda. The lions of Káthiáwár continue to decrease in number, and retreat deeper into the jungle fastnesses of the south-west. A marked improvement has taken place in the Káthiáwár horses. The Chiefs vie with each other in their studs; importing costly stallions and keeping up large establishments of selected brood mares. Mr. Wyllie's suggestion about race meetings at Rájkot is now an accomplished fact, and these gatherings, with the horse shows which the Government so liberally fosters in the Bombay Presidency, are doing much to again give bone and muscle to the once famous Káthiáwár breed. As regards the civil and criminal administration, regular tribunals have been gradually substituted for the *agrestis justitia* which Mr. Wyllie describes. I derive the following account of the present system from the Political Agent's Report for 1872–73. As at the time when Mr. Wyllie wrote, the Political Agent at Rájkot directs the whole administration of Káthiáwár, and represents the chief British authority in the Province, alike to the native Chiefs and to his own assistants.

The province of Káthiáwár has an area of more than 20,000 square miles and a population in 1874 of upwards of two and a third millions of souls. The ancient name of the whole peninsula was Sauráshthra. The British Government has perpetuated from the Marhattás the name of 'Káthiáwár,' a term applied by them to all Sauráshthra, from the Káthí race or tribe which gave most trouble to the invading forces. The Province is divided into four divisions called *Prántís*, viz., Jháláwar, Hállár,

Soreth, and Gohelwár. Each of these divisions contains one first-class State. That in JHÁLÁWÁR is Drángdrá, the chief state of the Jhálás, with the kindred Jhálá States of Wankánír, Wadwán, Limrí, Sáelá, and others. The first power in HÁLLÁR is His Highness the Jám of Nawánagar, the head of the Járejás in Káthiáwár ; along with the offshoots from Nawánagar, the Járejá principalities of Muroí Dhrol, Rájkot, and Gondul. The principal State in SORETH is Junágarh, a Muhammadan power, fully described by Mr. Wyllie at page 337. It is the Premier State of the whole Province. Within the south division, also, are the small principalities of Bántwá, held by the Junágarh family, and of Jafarábád, held by the descendants of the Mughul Admirals, the Sidís of Jinjirá. The Jetwa State of Purbandar has also, for convenience, been placed in the Soreth Pránt. In GOHELWÁR, the State of Bháwnagar has risen within the last century to be the leading power, and now ranks above the Gohel houses of Palitáná, Láthí, and Walleh.

Down the centre of the Province, from the heart of Jháláwar to some distance south of Junágarh, extend the estates of the Káthís, who appear to the present Political Agent to have come into Sauráshthra after the Jhalá, Járejá, Gohel, and Fetwá Rájputs, and to have obtained from them and the Nawáb of Junágarh, by the sword or diplomacy, the Tálukás they now hold. Further south the Gaikwár's territories march with the Káthí estates, and partly overlie them.

Below the ruling houses there are many petty Rájputs, landlords, and yeomen, representatives of old families now ruined or supplanted, or of the younger brothers of chiefs who have received their *gírás* or portion from the State. The discontent of this class caused by the insufficiency of their land to feed their increasing numbers, by the chronic agitation of old unsettled claims, and by new oppressions on the part of the superior Darbárs, still disturbs the Province. There are also several distinct sets of dangerous communities, the descendants of the mercenaries formerly kept up by ambitious chiefs, such as the Míánás under Máliá, and the Miyáns under Junágarh. The Kolís, Ahírs, and other aboriginal people who form the lowest grade of society, have an inborn taste for plunder, and require an efficient and a watchful police. The Mekránís are always ready to join a leading freebooter. The wild tribe of Wághars in the Gaikwár's old district of Okhá on the west coast, described by Mr. Wyllie at pages 348-50, and the marauders who descend on Jháláwar from the Răn (Runn) of Kutch and Jatwár, complete the list of predatory races in Káthiáwár.

The peace of the Province has become, however, merely a question of Police. Internal warfare and resistance to the supreme power have been put down under the British rule. Since 1807-8, the Chiefs have been bound to pay their tribute regularly, to respect each other's possessions, and to keep the highways safe within their own limits. But no definite measures were pressed on them for the due performance of the latter duty. And as with the repression of crime, so with the remedy of those civil wrongs which drive men to outlawry and murder. There was an infinite number of unsettled proprietary rights, and claims to jurisdiction, rank, and independence as between those who actually possessed and those who had formerly possessed political power. These conflicting titles, the British Agency when first established did not attempt to treat in such a way as to ensure finality. The Agent generally confined himself to mediation, and irreversible decrees were seldom issued. Mr. Kinloch Forbes, the Political Agent, found in 1860 that the country had pretty nearly stood still since 1808, and that nothing conclusive had been done with a mass of civil business of which a part ought to have been settled by diplomatic means, while the rest could have been dealt with under ordinary civil procedure.

With the exception of the Criminal Court of the Political Agent established in 1831 to aid the Darbárs in the trial of great crimes, the whole interference of the Political Agent with the internal justice of the State had, up to 1863, been exercised diplomatically. He never took action magisterially. The criminal jurisdiction of only the first and second class chiefs was defined. Since 1863, the country has undergone a great change. The jurisdiction of all the Chiefs was in that year classified and defined. The Chiefs of the first and second class have full judicial powers in both criminal and civil suits. The lesser Chiefs are arranged in grades, on a diminishing scale of jurisdiction. As a rule no appeal lies from the Chiefs. But on presumption of mal-administration, their proceedings may be called for and reviewed. The residuary jurisdiction is exercised by four Political Assistants, each resident in his own826 (or one of the four great divisions), who have the civil powers of Judges of British Districts, and the criminal powers of District Magistrates. They commit to the Sessions of the Political Agent's Court of Criminal Justice. Civil and criminal appeals lie from the Political Assistants to the Political Agent. Each Political Assistant in charge of a Pránt has a subordinate Assistant, who resides at the head-quarters of the Pránt and has civil and criminal powers up to a fixed limit. In each Pránt, moreover, subordinate native judges named Thánádárs exercise a lower grade of civil and criminal jurisdiction over the group of villages contiguous to their respective Thánás. These Thánádárs are under the Assistant Political Agents, and form the point of contact between the British Administration and the people. They also take charge of the management of small or disintegrated estates. And as a matter of fact, out of the 187 States into which Káthiáwár is now (1873) divided, 134 are administered under the Thánádárs. For, interspersed among the large States, are clusters of small properties so sub-divided that the owners no longer hold the place of chiefs with right of jurisdiction, and, indeed, are often glad to surrender it. The Thánádár conducts the civil and criminal business up to the limit of his powers, along with the general administration; but has not any responsibility for the police. It is clear that the area thus administered is destined to increase; for wherever a Gadí (State-Cushion) and the strict right of primogeniture are not maintained, and wherever the State is sub-divided anew among each successive generation, the chiefs must in time subside to the level of petty landlords. On the other hand, as the States that maintain a Gadí comprise 15,000 square miles out of the 20,000 forming the Province, the area which the Agency may be called on, from this reason, to administer, will not at any time exceed 5,000 square miles.

W. W. H.

INDEX.